Yesenia,

Continue to set your sights high
And always strive for perfection!

Matt 5:48

# STRIVING *for*
# PERFECTION

## DEVELOPING PROFESSIONAL BLACK OFFICERS

CURRY BROTHERS MARKETING
AND PUBLISHING GROUP

## GERALD D. CURRY, COLONEL (RETIRED)
## UNITED STATES AIR FORCE

iUniverse, Inc.
Bloomington

# STRIVING FOR PERFECTION
## DEVELOPING PROFESSIONAL BLACK OFFICERS

iUniverse books may be ordered through booksellers or by contacting:

iUniverse
1663 Liberty Drive
Bloomington, IN 47403
www.iuniverse.com
1-800-Authors (1-800-288-4677)

ISBN: 978-1-4759-8481-1 (sc)
ISBN: 978-1-4759-8479-8 (hc)
ISBN: 978-1-4759-8480-4 (e)
ISBN: 978-1-60402-709-9 First Edition

Library of Congress Control Number: 2013906354

Request for information should be addressed to:
Curry Brothers Marketing and Publishing Group
P.O. Box 247
Haymarket, Virginia
geralddcurry@yahoo.com

Printed in the United States of America.

iUniverse rev. date: 04/19/2013

# DEDICATION

This book is dedicated to the many men and women who freely and gallantly volunteer for military service and protect the American way of life. America's history is peppered with those men and women who were willing to make the ultimate sacrifice in preserving our freedom and sustaining America as the premier world power.

I am forever indebted to the memory of my first wife, Cheryl, and daughters, Cherie and Chantay, for grounding me during the first years of my career by ensuring that I focused on family. I think of each of you daily and sincerely appreciate the Lord for loaning you to me for the time that he allowed. To the memory of my father, Robert Sr., who provided the framework of success and excellence by teaching me the importance of spirituality and family, and always being there when needed. To my mother, Ella Ruth, the person who first gave me life, love, and happiness. My mother was a very kind soul who exhibited love each and every day of her life. To the memory of my brother Thomas, who was the one guy I could always lean on when no else was available or willing to assist. In the memory of my brother Kenneth, who died the year following the publishing this book. This project would never have been possible if it was not for Kenneth. He is the founder and creator of Curry Brothers Marketing and Publishing Group, and provided the initial editing, original cover design, marketing, and distribution for the first edition. To all of you, thank you for your love, support, dedication, and making me the man that I am.

# TABLE OF CONTENTS

# ACKNOWLEDGMENTS

Like most works of this magnitude, there are many people who were a part of this endeavor and made this possible. Throughout my career I have been fortunate enough to have always surrounded myself with positive, spiritual people who have constantly pointed out their humility and pride in being members of the United States Armed Forces. Many of these amazing leaders pulled me aside and vector me in the right direction when I was going down the wrong path, and I will be forever indebted to the people whom I have served.

My career success spans back to the founding of our great nation, and it is important to note that each of the people who came before me—black, Hispanic, Asian, white, and all other nationalities of people that have contributed to the building of this country—played an integral part in not only my success but yours as well. I choose to remember each of them by learning our history, and I invite you to do the same. The Lord made us in his image, created with the ability to think, learn, and distinguish between right and wrong. What I have learned over the years is that tapping into our legacy, calling up the important events of our past, and applying them to my betterment and improvement sustains me through tough times.

During the course of research for this book, I was assigned to the United States Air Force Academy as a cadet group commander, and I supervised over 1,100 cadets. Each of them came from diverse places and varied backgrounds from around the globe, and their motivation and talent excited me. Never have I been in an arena with so much creativity and ability than when I was working with these young people.

I worked every day to get these young people to value their opportunity and access to learning. Attending a military service academy is a privilege, not a right, and it needs to be cherished. I owe a hearty thank-you to the cadets, faculty, and staff who took pride in developing these young minds into professional warriors and, after years of grooming, will eventually become the leaders of our air force and nation.

My parents were simple people who stayed together through thick and thin regardless of the stress and hardships they faced. They taught my brothers and me the value of family and that, as long as God is first in your life, everything else is possible. My father was a minister in the Church of Christ, so we spent almost every waking hour in church or working in the church. These early years of service taught me that I was much more valuable than life's daily circumstances or situations. It exposed me to understanding that, with God on my side, nothing is impossible and as long as I continue to live by these principles I would find success in due time. Going to church was a very special time, because it provided me with the opportunities to learn public speaking, enhance my reading skills, and assist in organizing activities—all skills that I would later use as a military officer.

Church did more than offer me spiritual gifts and professional skills; it provided the values and standards that served to keep me grounded by anchoring me in a deep belief in God. During the many adverse situations that I would later encounter, it was the Lord that I called on to find sanity and support. There were few in my inner circle that understood the crisis that I had endured or could offer meaningful ideas on how properly to move ahead, so I turned to my faith. These hard times taught me that the Lord answers prayers and will not disappoint you, as long as you believe. For me, God has been the answer to finding the success in life, regardless of the circumstance. He is my deliverer!

Our people love the Lord and have always loved the Lord, and it is this faith that has sustained us throughout the generations. America has not been kind to black Americans and has called on our service only when it was convenient for the nation. Each time, African Americans eagerly answered the call and performed gallantly. Black Americans learned to rely on the Lord, because they surely could not harbor any faith within the American system to be treated fairly or receive equal treatment during the first four hundred years of this nation's existence. In spite of the many obstacles they faced, they continued to endure and empower their belief of a better tomorrow.

It has been only in the last few generations that African Americans have had the opportunity to gain a college education and enter positions that were once reserved only for whites. Finally, it is illegal to discriminate and withhold opportunities based on race, ethnicity, or religion. African Americans can seize and exploit every benefit and compensation made available to all men.

I thank God for the struggles our people have endured over the centuries, and I keep my promise to live up to the tenets and opportunities they have provided, which are so dutifully illustrated by their strength, courage, and steadfastness. Traditional American history would have the masses believe that the only successes blacks have collectively made have been because of the white people who we have served. Nothing could be further from the truth. This book attempts to illustrate the expansive canvas on which black contributions to American society took place. Most of these accomplishments and successes were out of necessity and sheer survival. The courage and commitment our ancestors displayed on a daily basis should be celebrated at every opportunity, and it is in this celebration that we find our blessing and receive the knowledge of how to press ahead in applying this wisdom to our current and future situations and circumstances.

This work could not have occurred if it were not for the many officers and senior noncommissioned officers that supported it with their sage advice. I owe a debt of gratitude to Chief Master Sergeant (Ret.) Robert Vasquez, who is my brother in Christ, mentor, and constant motivator. Bob is a motivational speaker and author himself, and he has used his talents in developing new officers at the United States Air Force Academy in the Leadership and Character Development Center. He is the one person in my life on whom I rely to learn how to apply timeless principles by closely monitoring your spiritual walk with the Lord in everything you do.

During the course of my research, I was able to gain invaluable insight from several senior leaders in our air force to whom I will always be indebted. I sincerely appreciate their excitement and willingness to discuss leadership, mentorship, diversity, and military readiness. Those senior officers are Lieutenant General Daniel Leaf, Major General Richard Spooner, Major General Roosevelt Mercer, Major General Johnny Weida, and Brigadier General Dana Born. To each of you, thank you for your service and dedication to making our nation better. I consider each of you a personal hero, friend, and mentor. Dr. Samuel Betances—gifted writer, diversity professional, and mentor—continues to train the brightest minds in this nation by teaching them the value of our past, present, and future. Dr. B, as I have so fondly grown to refer to him, opened my eyes to the adverse impact that can occur when diversity is not valued or incorporated into the fabric of an organization. He provided insight and encouragement in completing this work because of the need for truthfulness and honest strategies contained herein.

I truly would be remiss if I did not mention my family, who continued on as I labored, conducting hours of research, writing drafts, and sending out surveys. I sincerely appreciate their cooperation and sacrifice in allowing me to work undisturbed while life continued. I will forever be thankful to their support and critiques throughout this entire process. My daughters Candace, Chanel, and Aubria hold a very special place in my heart and always will. They are my motivation and give me reasons to live and constantly strive for perfection in my own life.

This book could not have been written if it were not for my brother Kenneth, who provided the literary guidance, editing, formatting, cover design, copyrighting instruction, encouragement, and unyielding support in the spirit of God. I love you and have learned from you since my arrival here on earth. For your support and nurturing, I must say thank you.

To Robert Jr., my oldest brother, I sincerely appreciate your candor, humor, oversight, and support in keeping me on target and ensuring our family remains together, as God intended. You have provided the love and support required to care for both Mom and Dad when no one else was around. Your efforts will live forever and will always be remembered. To my wife, Gloria, who provided steadfast love and support during the late hours and many interviews, rewrites, and putting up with my clutter of papers and books as I plowed through this endeavor. I love her with all my soul and realize that her support is truly another gift directly from God. God's grace continues to blanket me with undying love and forgiveness.

Thank you for taking the time to read this work. It is my hope that this book serves as a catalyst in boosting your career to the next level. I hope that you find this work easy to understand, and will be able to apply the principles, strategies, and suggestions offered by so many helpful to your career. If there is ever a question concerning this book, please do not hesitate in contacting me directly to receive clarification, by emailing me at GeraldDCurry@yahoo.com.

Happy reading!
Gerald D. Curry, Colonel (Ret.), USAF

Watch Out

Watch your thoughts, for they become words.
Watch your words, for they become actions.
Watch your actions, for they become habits.
Watch your habits, for they become character.
Watch your character, for it becomes your destiny.

—Anonymous
(Submitted by U.S. Air Force 2LT Ayana N. Floyd-James)

*If you're going to pass through the door, the way I've been raised, you have an obligation to see that someone else can pass through the door. Some of that comes by your example, some of it comes by facilitating passage through the door, some of it comes by standing alone and being unafraid that if you're the only one, then it's you. Don't look for someone else to make it happen—make it happen.*

—Lieutenant General Vincent K. Brooks, USA, 2003

# CHAPTER 1

## WHERE WE'VE BEEN

God is my strength and power, and He makes my way perfect.

—2 Samuel 22:23

No people come into possession of a culture without having paid a heavy price for it.

—James Baldwin

I am America. I am the part you won't recognize. But get used to me. Black, confident, cocky; my name, not yours; my religion, not yours; my goals, my own; get used to me.

—Muhammad Ali, 1975

A wise man once said, "If you don't know your history, you're bound to repeat it." Let's face it, knowing the origin of your people and their many accomplishments is vitally important, because it creates pride and defines culture within a people by serving as an example of what is possible. Most will agree that the history of African Americans is like no other ethnic group in America. We were the only people deliberately brought to this country for the sole purpose of servitude. You may be wondering, *What about the thousands of free people who lived in America as free citizens or indentured servants?* At the start of the Revolutionary War, it is reported that there were over five hundred thousand blacks living, earning a wage and owning land like their white neighbors. At the time of the American Revolution, many African Americans had been living alongside white colonizers for about one hundred years with little to no problems.

They took pride in their land and belongings, and they were just as committed to freeing themselves from British rule as their white neighbors. You might be wondering, *Then what happened?* I do not want this book to be just another lesson in history, but one that illustrates the leadership and tenacity blacks demonstrated throughout America's turbulent past. As a professional military officer, I highly recommend that you know your history! You need to understand that black history is American history, and you need to know the stories of Peter Salem and Crispus Attucks from the Revolutionary War, all the way through to our recent heroes from the Global War on Terrorism. You need to know about the blacks who fought in every war since the Revolutionary War, the 5,000 blacks who supported the Confederacy, and the 186,000 blacks who fought for the Union during the Civil War.

Blacks have fought in every major military conflict in which America has ever engaged. It is imperative that you take time out and learn the stories of the Buffalo Soldiers and Tuskegee Airmen. I don't remember learning of any of these details while in high school or during college undergraduate training. It took me coming on active duty and seeking out this knowledge on my own by holding conversations with other black officers and investing time in the library to fill this void.

As a child growing up in the 1960s and '70s, I watched war movies with my father, and even though I knew my grandfathers and father fought in World War II and Korea, respectively, we never saw blacks playing a significant part in war movies, so I knew that account was not accurate. My brothers and I would ask my father about what it was like being in the army and having the opportunity to live in foreign countries and fight in wars. I can clearly remember him talking about the exotic foods and the friends he made during this period of his life. All of these stories made a huge impression on me at an early age and created a deep desire to serve in the military.

What you need to remember about your history is that black

Americans have always answered the call to their nation's defense. Throughout the United States of America's history, the government turned its back on black Americans. But these brave people continued to gallantly serve because they had dreams and visions of a better future. We need to remember that formal education was not allowed for these blacks during the first two hundred years of their existence in this country. Blacks had a definitive purpose for serving in our military; they desired a better life. Any life was better than living in bondage or working for meager wages in unfair living conditions. The prevailing thought of the day was: *if you are going to die, then die for something*. Which would you prefer, dying as a slave or as a military man serving your country and being known for holding a recognizable and respectable profession?

## American Revolutionary War, 1775 – 1783

Let's take a quick look back and see how African Americans contributed to developing this country. Did you know that more blacks actually fought for the British Army and the American colonials? Blacks typically sided with whoever promised freedom for their service. The British actively recruited slaves and promised to reward them with their freedom at the conclusion of the Revolutionary War. History writes that blacks played an active role five years before the American Revolution began. On March 5, 1770, Crispus Attucks confronted a crowd of angry British soldiers while leading a group of colonists that were protesting the laws of England. The British soldiers, led by Private Hugh Montgomery of the British regulars, fired on the colonist, killing Attucks and four other white settlers. These five men were buried in the first integrated grave in the New World, which is located in Boston Commons, Massachusetts.

We all know that the Continental Army eventually won the war and defeated the British and that slavery continued. George Washington initially prevented blacks from serving in the Continental Army. It was not until the enormous problems with desertion prior to Valley Forge that General Washington decided to recant on this policy and allowed blacks entry into the army. During this period it is reported that over one hundred thousand slaves escaped to Indian lands in Canada and Florida. In 1776, Thomas Jefferson reported that he lost a large percentage of his slaves. In May 1775, one month after blacks had fought at Lexington and Concord, the Committee for Safety of the Massachusetts Legislature presented a legislative resolution that read:

> Resolved, that it is the opinion of this Committee, as the contest now between Great Britain and the Colonies respects the liberties and privileges of the latter, which the Colonies are determined to maintain, that the admission of any persons, as soldiers, into the army now raising, but only such as are freemen, will be inconsistent with the principles that are to be supported, and brought dishonor on the colony, and that no slaves be admitted into this army, upon any consideration whatever.

This position on blacks serving was not shared by the British, who suffered manpower and resource shortages. On November 7, 1775, John Murray, the earl of Dunmore, issued a proclamation:

> And I do hereby further declare all intended [sic] servants, Negroes and others (appertaining to Rebels) free, and that are able and willing to bear arms, they joining His Majesty's Troops, as soon as may be, for the more speedily reducing of the colony to a proper sence [sic] of their duty, to His Majesty's crown and dignity.

Shortly after the Dunmore proclamation, George Washington authorized recruiting of free Negroes "desirous of enlisting." Slave participation was still forbidden, and Washington reinforced this general order on February 21, 1776. Many blacks fought under Lord Dunmore's Ethiopian Regiment. During Valley Forge, General Washington's troop strength was dangerously low and he was forced to accept slaves. He continued to accept them until the end of the war. During this same period, half of the Colonial Army that drove the British from Louisiana was black.

At the end of the war, approximately five thousand black soldiers fought in major battles in the American Revolution, from Bunker Hill to Yorktown. In 1792, Congress passed an act restricting blacks from serving in the army, and all blacks were quickly dismissed from its ranks and returned to slavery. Some twenty thousand blacks that served with the British at the end of the war were transported to Sierra Leone, Canada, and the Caribbean. One little known fact is the eight hundred or more blacks who served in the British Ethiopian Regiment were comprised primarily of ex-slaves committed to serving the British Crown, and they fought gallantly in three major battles. Even though many blacks fought heroically during this war, America quickly forgot and turned her back on them, forcing them back into slavery.

This would be the first of many times that this episode would occur. In my opinion, America has a serious problem with selective amnesia when it comes to the rights and accomplishments of African Americans. Many of the more notable blacks who fought in this war were Salem Poor, who was cited for bravery at Bunker Hill; Jack Sisson, who fought in the raid on General Prescott's headquarters; James Armistead, who served as a spy for General Lafayette; Prince Whipple and Oliver Cromwell, who accompanied George Washington when he crossed the Delaware; Edward Hector, who fought bravely in the Battle of Brandywine in 1777; and James Robinson, a Maryland slave who fought at Yorktown. By 1778, each of General Washington's brigades had an average of forty-two black soldiers assigned.

## War of 1812 (1812 – 1815)

In 1798, the secretary of war wrote to the commander of the Marine Corps that "no Negro, mulatto or Indian is to be enlisted." Louisiana became a state in 1812, and its legislature authorized the governor to enroll free black landowners in the militia. In 1803, a group of free blacks who called themselves Free Men of Color were denied voluntary service in the territorial militia but were allowed to enlist as a battalion in 1812. This unit's commanding officers were white, but they were allowed three black lieutenants.

The War of 1812 was primarily a naval war, so in 1812 nothing prevented blacks from serving in the navy. Blacks were still barred from serving in the army during this period. Blacks comprised approximately 10 to 20 percent of sailors assigned to the Great Lakes region. Commodore Perry had hundreds of blacks serving with him during his victory on Lake Erie. Early during the war, the Navy petitioned Congress to recruit blacks within its ranks. Finally, in March 1813, Congress abolished this policy and allowed blacks into the armed forces. England and Spain refused to return slaves to their owners if they fought against the Americans. Many blacks fled to Florida to live among the Seminole Indians. These slaves did not realize their value, because the first Seminole War was started to recapture runaway slaves. The second Seminole War began because of white land encroachment.

White settlers wanted to move the Seminole Indians aside to make room for their expansion. The large number of blacks living among the Seminoles was one of the primary reasons Seminole extraction was pursued. Approximately, one-third of the Seminole Indians willing to fight were blacks living amongst the Seminole nation. Later, after the war, the Seminoles were forced to live in Indian territories, but blacks were returned to their original plantations if records could confirm, or they tried to escape to Mexico.

It is important to note that the largest number of black American troops was assembled for the defense of New Orleans in December 1814 and January 1815. When Andrew Jackson was gathering his forces for the imminent British invasion, General William C. C. Claiborne advised him that he could gather four hundred Free Men of Color. More than six hundred were recruited. Two battalions were formed under the command of Colonel Michael Fortier. The ranking black officer and the first commissioned African American in the US Armed Forces to reach field-grade status was Second Major Vincent Populas.

# Civil War 1861 – 1865

Many would agree that the Civil War was the most divisive war in American history for several reasons. The war was fought on American soil, pitted brother against brother, separated the Union, and put the morality of slavery on center stage of national politics. History gives credit to President Abraham Lincoln for abolishing slavery, but the little known fact is that President Lincoln originally had no intention of eliminating slavery. His primary focus was on preserving the Union at all costs. He knew that slavery was the most divisive issue facing the nation, and his emphasis was not making this an issue but keeping states from seceding from the Union.

On April 12, 1861, the Confederacy attacked Fort Sumter in Charleston, South Carolina, and the war was on. Soon after this attack, North Carolina, Tennessee, Arkansas, and Virginia cut their ties with the Union and joined the Confederacy. The Union wrestled with how to handle runaway slaves. As slave masters headed to war, thousands of slaves immediately ran away. During this period the Union had no policy on fugitive slaves. Consequently, unit commanders made their own decisions concerning fugitive slaves. Many decided to return the slaves to their owners, while some decided to use them for cooking, digging ditches, doing laundry, and doing other meager tasks. On August 6, 1861, the Fugitive Slave Law was passed and slaves were considered as "contraband of war." If the slaves were considered contraband, then they would be characterized as being legally free.

By 1862, President Lincoln realized that as long as blacks remained enslaved, the Confederacy would use them as free labor in support of the war effort. Blacks were not allowed to serve in the army, fighting for the Union. In an effort to level the playing field, the president started considering setting the slaves free via emancipation. At this point blacks were tasked to build fortifications, serve as nurses and blacksmiths, and work in hospitals, factories, and armories. Black free labor leveraged support in favor of the Confederacy.

Many European countries were prepared to enter the war in support of the Confederacy because President Lincoln still did not want to make the war about abolishing slavery. He also would not allow free blacks to fight in the war in support of the Union. According to European public opinion, if the president decided to free the slaves they would overwhelmingly side with the North.

On January 1, 1863, President Lincoln issued the Emancipation Proclamation that freed the slaves that lived within the states that rebelled, leaving approximately one million blacks still enslaved that resided in the North. Blacks, now free, ran immediately to join the Union forces and serve in its Army. For years blacks had worked in the Navy aboard ships, but now they had the option of serving in either the Army or the Navy. President Lincoln's war department did not expect the overwhelming numbers of blacks, both free and former slaves, to enlist in the army. In some places these numbers were so amazing that a separate colored unit had to be created.

The first colored unit to form was the 54th Massachusetts Colored Regiment commanded by a white officer, Colonel Robert Gould Shaw. By 1863, the war department created the Bureau of Colored Troops. Blacks endured not only segregation but discrimination, as well. Black soldiers were paid meager wages compared to their white military brethren. Blacks received $7 per month and a $3 clothing allowance, while whites received $13 per month and $3.50 for clothes. Finally, in 1864, the War Department gave equal wages for black soldiers. The army did not have a policy yet to commission black officers. Only a mere one hundred black officers served during the Civil War. By the war's end, more than 186,000 blacks served in the Union Army, 40,000 came from border slave states, 53,000 from free states, and an amazing 93,000 from Confederate states in the South, fleeing slavery. Twenty-four black soldiers were awarded the Congressional Medal of Honor, and a whopping 200,000 blacks served collectively in the US Armed Forces during this war. Over 38,000 blacks gave the ultimate sacrifice, fighting first for respect and then freedom.

On April 18, 1865, the Civil War ended, with over 620,000 Americans dying, and setting over four million blacks free. Many blacks remained in the South, yet millions migrated to the industrial North, attempting to create a better life than they had in the South. Some blacks traveled back to their plantations in an attempt to find relatives and loved ones. Some Southern whites resisted the change with all their might and continued to prey upon blacks with little interruptions or interference from anyone. The period for the next ten years would be termed "Reconstruction," because the country was in dire need of healing and rebuilding.

## The Spanish – American War (1898)

After the Civil War, the War Department kept four colored regiments: the 9th and 10th Cavalry and the 24th and 25th Infantry. These proud Americans would serve in Indian territory, clearing the way for the movement west. The Spanish–American War was primarily a naval war. As white troops exhausted supplies and the Spaniards were taking the best of the famous Rough Riders, the 9$^{th}$ and 10$^{th}$ Cavalry were summoned to come to the rescue. These brave fighting men left their horses behind and fought on foot supporting the Rough Riders. Amongst this famed unit was the future President of the United States, Theodore Roosevelt.

Twenty-two black Americans went down with the USS *Maine* when it was sunk in Havana Harbor in Cuba on the night of February 15, 1898. The declaration of war was issued on April 25 and approved on April 26. Congress authorized ten black regiments for this war. The 9th and 10th Cavalry and the 24th and 25th Infantry Regiments were in the war from the start. The 7th and 8th Regiments were organized as line units with full authorization, but only the 9th and 10th Regiments survived the various reductions and reorganizations for any length of time. The 9th and 10th Regiments were a horse cavalry; however, they did not see combat in this war on their horses. That was because they came to Cuba on one ship and their horses were put aboard another. They were pressed into combat before their animals arrived; therefore, they went into action and served as combat infantry troops.

## World War I (1917 – 1918)

The War Department continued to allow black soldiers within its rank in the army, but not in the marines, Coast Guard, or army air corps. Blacks have always served in the navy and continue to do so. During this period, blacks served primarily as messmen, cooks, and other laborers. Shortly after the start of the war, the War Department stopped accepting blacks because it reached its quota of blacks in the army. On January 1, 1918, the 369th (Harlem Hellfighters) arrived in France to support the French Army. This heroic unit would eventually be the recipient of eleven French unit citations and was recognized for being the first unit to reach the Rhine River in 1918. Before this period, when the 92nd Division originally arrived in France in 1917, the British were tasked with training. Later, when the 369th arrived in France, the British refused to train the black soldiers. General Pershing spoke in defense of the black soldiers to British General Haig: "These Negroes are American citizens. I cannot and will not discriminate against them." These black soldiers fought gallantly side by side with French soldiers on September 1918 during the Meuse-Argonne Offensive, where they gained the advantage against the Germans. Later, 171 black soldiers would be awarded the French Legion of Honor for their heroic acts.

There were 371,710 blacks serving in the army, 200,000 overseas, and 1,352 commissioned officers, all fighting courageously. Several regiments were decorated. Blacks could move about freely in France. Emmett J. Scott was appointed special assistant to the secretary of war. Henry Johnson and Needham Roberts were the first two Americans to receive the Croix de Guerre. Note that all troops were segregated.

## World War II (1941 – 1945)

The majority of blacks remained in Southern states, where they suffered the persecution of Jim Crow laws. These laws demanded they ride on the back of buses and trains, eat separately from whites, live in different neighborhoods, and be educated in segregated, poorly staffed, and poorly resourced schools. Northern black military men trained in the South often had problems adjusting to this harsh reality and quickly found themselves in trouble with the local law.

Black society as a whole wanted to use their involvement in the war as an opportunity to gain respect and equal justice at home. Black newspapers protested segregation and discrimination within the armed forces and did everything in their power to bring attention to this cause. In 1941, lawyer, activist, and labor leader A. Philip Randolph threatened a march on Washington, DC, by thousands of blacks as a way to protest job discrimination within the defense industry and the military. The march did not take place, but it did provide the foundation for what would later occur with Dr. Martin Luther King Jr. twenty-two years later.

To avoid this protest, President Roosevelt signed and issued Executive Order 8802, reaffirming the policy of full participation in the defense program by all persons, regardless of race, creed, color, or national origin. Blacks were later given the chance to fight in this war, and it gave birth to the Tuskegee Airmen, who would earn the unique honor of being the only bomber escort unit to never lose a bomber within their responsibility.

## Korean Conflict (1950 –1953)

Following World War II, from 1946 to 1948, the army practice of attaching rather than assigning black combat units to white "parent units" weakened the morale of African American troops and hampered their training because of the men's sense of importance and alienation. By 1950, the Army changed this policy by assigning black units as organic parts of white combat divisions. It also started assigning African American personnel "to fill vacant spaces in white units." Many army leaders still opposed the combination of black and white units into a larger single battalion. Such practices continued to elicit harsh criticism from black leaders throughout the United States.

On July 25, 1947, Congress passed the National Security Act, reorganizing the US military establishment. The new legislation created the Office of the Secretary of Defense (OSD), a separate Air Force, the Central Intelligence Agency, and the National Security Council. This legislation reorganized the War Department as the Department of the Army and made the Joint Chiefs of Staff a permanent agency.

By April 1948, there were only forty-one black officers in the regular Army, an increase from eight in June 1945. The Army began a major effort to recruit more African American officers. In compliance with

Circular 124, the Army was able to significantly improve these figures by June 30, 1948, when it reported a total of one thousand black commissioned officers, five warrant officers, and sixty-seven nurses serving with sixty-five thousand black enlisted men and women.

The Korean War was the first war to test the new integration policies of the armed forces. On October 15, 1948, President Harry S. Truman issued Executive Order 9981, ending segregation in the armed forces. Neither the Army nor the Navy planned to alter their existing racial policies. Their decisions were partly based on the mistaken assumption that Circular 124 and Circular Letter 48–46 were already in compliance with the president's order on equal treatment and opportunity. Despite evidence to the contrary, the US armed forces in this period did not consider segregation to be discriminatory. The Air Force took the lead by eliminating segregated units, and the Tuskegee experiment ended. The end of World War II ushered in the beginning of the Cold War and occupation forces in Germany and Austria.

On June 25, 1950, North Korean troops armed with Soviet-made weapons crossed the 38th parallel, invading South Korea and sparking the outbreak of the Korean War. In June 1950, at the start of the Korean War, only the 25th Infantry Regiment of the old demobilized 93rd Infantry Division was still identified as a black unit.

Eighth Army commanders in Korea began filling losses in their white units with individuals from a growing surplus of black replacements arriving in Japan. By 1951, 94 percent of all Negroes in the theater were serving in some forty-one newly and unofficially integrated units. Another 9.3 percent were in integrated but predominantly black units. The other 8.1 percent continued to serve in segregated units.

## The Vietnam War (1955 - 1975)

The Vietnam War witnessed the largest number of blacks serving in any war in American history. Blacks comprised 12.6 percent of soldiers serving in Vietnam. Back at home, blacks were only 2 percent of the total population between the years of 1965 and 1969. Blacks continued to serve in record numbers throughout this war, rather than face the humiliation and injustices created by the high tensions of the civil rights era.

African Americans continued to play a significant role in this war and even changed the complexion and culture of the entire armed forces. The strength of America has always been the diversity of its people. Through integrated military service, blacks were given new opportunities never presented before. The Air Force and Navy led President Harry Truman to order desegregation of the military in 1948, and they completed integration by 1950. It took the Army a little longer, and during the Korean conflict they finally reached the mark of full integration by October 1953. The Vietnam War was the first major war in which America would experience complete integration, where black officers would supervise white enlisted men. The Vietnam War would yield African American servicemen twenty medals of honor, and many officers would go on to earn the rank of general. Blacks were trained in specialized schools and given unique opportunities to receive professional military education, once only reserved for white officers. Blacks in record numbers continued to reenlist and volunteer to serve in hostile areas at a higher rate than whites.

Many African Americans would surmise that it was far better to serve in war than have to return home to the riots that were burning down our cities. Several larger cities experienced severe damage and civil unrest. Some larger cities—Detroit, Atlanta, Montgomery, Birmingham, Chicago, Los Angeles, and Miami—endured significant damage and destruction from riots. Black servicemen could not understand how they could serve in fighting in a war overseas for Vietnam's freedom while unrest and discrimination waited for them at home after the war.

While in uniform, blacks were not free from discrimination and unjust treatment. This war saw its share of militant uprisings from both whites and blacks. At Cam Ranh Bay Naval Base, white sailors dressed as the KKK, burned crosses, and raised Confederate flags. The Vietnam War became the most unpopular war in America's history. The United States was in such a state of confusion and unrest that it was very difficult for the American public to support a war overseas while domestic unrest overwhelmed the nation.

In 1973, President Richard Nixon brought the last troops home and ended the war with a cease-fire agreement. This war had taken its toll on America's spirit. The previous decade had seen the murder of President John Kennedy; his brother, Senator Robert Kennedy; Malcolm X; and Dr. Martin Luther King Jr. Major cities were in ruin, and the country suffered an enormous budget deficit. Domestic policy had been ignored during a large part of the war, and the civil rights bill signed on June 29, 1964, did not help in quelling the strife at home.

## Gulf Wars (1990 – 1991)

In August 1990, Saddam Hussein invaded Kuwait and took control of 24 percent of the world's oil supplies. It appeared that he would target Saudi Arabia next if his aggressive exploits were not halted. King Fahd of Saudi Arabia asked the United States for assistance, and we answered the call by setting a deadline of January 15, 1991, for all Iraqi forces to be out of Kuwait. Saddam ignored the deadline, and his actions triggered Operation Desert Shield. Desert Shield led to the buildup of US forces in the region that would eventually be called Desert Storm, an all-out attack to free Kuwait.

The size of the Iraqi Army in the Kuwait Theater of Operations was probably much smaller than what was originally claimed by the Pentagon. On the eve of the war, Iraq may have had as few as 300,000 soldiers, compared to 540,000 estimated by the Pentagon. Of the American servicemen and women who perished on the battlefield, 24 percent of the total killed in action were victims of friendly fire.

As a whole, the battles in the ground war showed that American military maneuverability clearly outclassed the plodding tactics of the Iraqis. They emphasized pitched engagements and linear movements, as they had been taught by their Soviet advisers. The largest tank battle of the war demonstrated the superiority of American tanks and fighting doctrine over that of the Soviets. On the final night of the war, within hours of the cease-fire, two US Air Force bombers dropped specially designed five-thousand-pound bombs on a command bunker fifteen miles northwest of Baghdad in a deliberate attempt to kill Saddam Hussein. The decision to seek United Nations involvement was part of a larger strategy of the Bush administration to bypass the constitutional authority of Congress to declare war.

## Global War on Terrorism (2001 – Present)

The Global War on Terrorism was started as a result of al-Qaeda's attacks against America on September 11, 2001. President George W. Bush increased America's homeland security and built a worldwide coalition that 1) began to destroy al-Qaeda's grip on Afghanistan by driving the Taliban from power, 2) disrupted al-Qaeda's global operations and terrorist financing networks, 3) destroyed al-Qaeda's terrorist training camps, 4) helped the innocent people of Afghanistan recover from the Taliban's reign of terror, and 5) helped the Afghans put aside long-standing differences and form a new interim government that represented all Afghans, including women. Many innocent people lost their lives as a result of attempting to save others during the 9/11 attacks. The world will never forget those brave heroes. More than three thousand people died or remain missing following the attacks. They came from more than eighty different nations, from many different races and religions.

Of the emergency responders, 343 firefighters and paramedics, 23 police officers, and 37 Port Authority police officers perished at the World Trade Center. Approximately 2,000 children lost a parent on September 11, including 146 children who lost a parent in the Pentagon attack. One business alone lost more than seven hundred employees, leaving at least fifty pregnant widows. President Bush was focused on building a worldwide coalition against terrorism. More than 80 countries suffered losses on September 11, and 136 countries have offered a diverse range of military assistance. The president's policy puts the world on notice that any nation that harbors terrorism will be regarded as a hostile regime.

Operation Enduring Freedom, the military phase, began October 7, 2001. Since then, coalition forces have liberated the Afghan people from the repressive and violent Taliban regime. As President Bush and Secretary of Defense Donald Rumsfeld have said, this is a different kind of war against a different kind of enemy. The enemy is not a nation; the enemy is terrorist networks that threaten the way of life of all peaceful people. The war against terrorism is the first war of the twenty-first century, and it requires a twenty-first-century military strategy. Secretary Rumsfeld worked with our coalition allies and the courageous men and women of the US military to craft a cutting-edge military strategy that minimizes civilian casualties, partners with local forces, and brings destruction to the oppressive Taliban who supported the al-Qaeda terrorist network.

## All Black U.S. Army Units from 1866 - 1950 Cavalry Units

- 9th US Cavalry organized on September 21, 1866, in Greenville, Louisiana
- 10th US Cavalry was organized on September 21, 1866, at Fort Leavenworth, Kansas
- Infantry regiments and units not part of the 92nd and 93rd Divisions
- Out of the 38th and 41st Infantry Regiments, which had been founded in 1866, 24th Infantry Regiment founded in 1869. After the Indian Wars, the 24th fought in Cuba, Philippines, Mexico, and finally Korea, as part of the 25th Division.
- Out of the 39th and 40th Infantry Regiments, which were organized in 1866, 25th Infantry Regiment formed in 1869.
- The Triple Nickel, the 555th Parachute Infantry Company, was the first black airborne unit. After training they were sent to operate as smoke jumpers, fighting forest fires caused by Japanese incendiary balloons at the end of the war. Later they fought in Korea and performed the first night drop of the war. The 92nd Infantry Division, fought in France in World War I and in Italy in World War II.
- The 365th Infantry Regiment, served in Texas and Oklahoma
- The 366th Infantry Regiment in Alabama was activated at Fort Devens, MA, a year before the outbreak of World War II, as an all-black fighting unit with black officers, an unprecedented event in the history of the United States. Prior to this time, all black units had been commanded by white officers.

- The 367th Infantry Regiment, were originally assigned in New York
- The 368th Infantry Regiment in Tennessee, Pennsylvania, and Maryland in World War I was only one of the four regiments in the 92nd that had problems in combat. The 93rd Infantry Division was to fight in France in World War I, but the four regiments that would have composed this division were sent to help the French Army. The French didn't want to give them back, so they fought the rest of the war attached to the French Army. In World War II the 93rd Division fought in the Pacific Theater.
- The 369th Infantry Regiment, the "Harlem Hellfighters," were by far the most celebrated black unit in World War I.
- In World War I soldiers of the 370th Infantry were awarded sixteen Distinguished Service Crosses and seventy-five Croix de Guerre. Called the "Black Bastards" by the Germans, the men of the 370th were mostly from Chicago and figured they were just as tough as the New Yorkers of the 369th. In World War I, the 369th was part of the 92nd Division rather than the 93rd, arrived in Italy ahead of the division headquarter units, and fought as the 370th Regimental Combat Team until the rest of the division arrived.
- The 371st Infantry in World War I consisted of men from Maryland, Massachusetts, Ohio, and Washington, DC.
- The 372nd Infantry Regiment Armored (Tank Units) originally was a part of the 93rd Infantry Division (Colored), and served with the French Army during World War I.
- The 371st Tank Battalion originally was a part of the 93rd Infantry Division (Colored), and served with the French Army during World War I.
- The 509th and 510th Tank Battalions (Heavy) was part of the Panzer Battalion. With the 509th serving in the Ukraine and the 510th served in Lithuania and fought in the Kurland pocket until the end of World War II.
- The 758th Tank Battalion (Light) was established in 1941 at Fort

Knox, Kentucky. One of the most famous members was famed baseball legend Jackie Robinson.

- The 761st Tank Battalion Army Air Corps and the 99th Fighter Squadron (99th Pursuit Squadron) became the first combat squadron of the Tuskegee Airmen. They entered combat in North Africa on May 31, 1943, and moved on to Italy. Paired with the white 79th Fighter Squadron in Italy on October 9, 1943, they moved to the 332nd Fighter Group the following July.

- The 100th Fighter Squadron, part of the 332nd Fighter Group is part of the Alabama Air National Guard, located in Montgomery Air National Guard Base.

- The 301st Fighter Squadron, part of the 332nd Fighter Group was activated on February 19, 1942 at Tuskegee Army Air Field, Alabama.

- The 302nd Fighter Squadron, was part of the 332nd Fighter Group and saw combat action in European Theater of Operations and Mediterranean Theater of Operations in February 1944 – 1945.

- The 332nd Fighter Group was formed on July 4, 1944, and composed of the 99th, 100th, 301st, and 302nd Fighter Squadrons

- The 477th Bombardment and Composite Groups were originally established in May 1943 at MacDill Field, Florida, and assigned to Third Air Force, supporting various combat missions in World War II.

- The 41st Engineers originally started as the 126th Engineer Mountain Battalion and was activated in 1942 at Camp Carson, Colorado.

- The 31st, 47th, and 48th Quartermaster Regiments were created in the 1930s, but did not activate until the 1940s. These units served in the Philippines, Japan, Alaska, and Vietnam.

- The 341st Field Artillery Regiment was activated in 1917 and has a proud history of being one of the best fighting units in the U.S. Army.

- The 76th and 77th Coast Artillery units were assigned to Fort Bragg in 1941 and received the highest praises because of the soldiers advance proficiency in mathematics, especially trigonometry.
- Field Artillery School Detachment
- Army War College Detachment
- Engineering School Detachment
- Medical Detachment, USMC
- Medical Detachment, Fort Huachuca
- 50th Military Police
- 730th Military Police
- 320th Anti-Aircraft Barrage Balloon Battalion—was the first black unit to see combat in WWII during the D-Day Invasion, June 6, 1944.
- 27th Signal Construction Company

## Sage Advice

### Lieutenant Colonel William Simmons, USAF

- Find a role model on whom you can truly depend. If he fails you, seek out another. Some of us can "talk the talk" but get confused when it is time to stand and be counted.
- Ensure you do everything you can to formulate plans for your own success. Make sure you have "all squares filled" (i.e., professional military education, master's degree) to ensure that there are no questions about your qualifications for any position in your chosen specialty.
- Stay abreast of current issues, particularly those issues that directly affect your onward and upward mobility.

### Anonymous Captain, USAF

- Never accept no for an answer.
- Don't forget who you are and that all eyes are always on you. Even though you may do your job better than anyone else despite your color, people are still going to have preconceived

biases and stereotypes. The military is truly a cultural melting pot.

- Remember the law of attraction. Share your knowledge with those who are just as hungry to aspire and seeking opportunities to excel.

## Captain Hilary R. Johnson-Lutz, USAF

- Play your position. Learn and perform your job well, because ultimately that's what it's about. This means not only learning your job but learning how to lead and finding your leadership style. This is a work in progress for me.
- Don't get hung up on race! We have a right to be whomever we choose to be. Let race be their issue not yours ("they" can be many people, including your own). I had to learn this for myself. I was always very conscious of being the only black officer in an organization, but I'm over it now because I know that I have every right to be there.
- Stay true to yourself. Don't let others influence who or what you should be or do. Do you—whatever that is. I've learned this the hard way. Generally speaking, if someone has a problem with you, it's their problem, not yours.

Those Shoulders

We stand on the shoulders of those who paved the way,
Those who took a stand in the days of yesterday.

We stand on the shoulders of those who chose to excel,
Thus we have been challenged to do just as well.

We stand on the shoulders not for self, or to be seen,
But because we have a mandate, and that is to intervene.

We stand on the shoulders with our heads held high,
Listening to their voices, you must continue to try.

Thank you for your shoulders!

(By Lieutenant Colonel Ruth Segres, Chaplain, USAF)

# CHAPTER 2
## UPON WHOSE SHOULDERS ARE YOU STANDING?

I can do all things through Christ which strengthenth me.

—Philippians 4:13

But Jesus looked at them and said to them, "With men this is impossible, but with God all things are possible."
—Matthew 19:26

None of us is responsible for the complexion of his skin. This fact of nature offers a clue to the character or quality of the person underneath.

—Marian Anderson, 1941

There is no easy walk to freedom anywhere, and many of us will have to pass through the valley of the shadow of death again and again before we reach the mountain top of our desires.

—Nelson Mandela, 1953

The success of military officers today rests squarely on the shoulders of those men and women of our past. The bravery, dedication, and leadership exhibited in the past should provide motivation for us today. When we are confronted with a difficult task, it is important to think back to the courageous acts of those who came before us. We need to clearly understand that these individuals are a significant part of our past, present, and future. In order to tap into our legacy, we need to do just as our African ancestors did and call upon them in time of need. We need to build upon their success by making them a part of our daily decisions.

African Americans can trace their military legacy to the first conflict in the Revolutionary War. If you review each war, you will find black soldiers heroically contributing to the successful conclusion of those conflicts. Many of our heroes have gone unnoticed or rarely acknowledged in history. Over the years, you learned that most of our military heroes have distinguished themselves as Buffalo Soldiers, the Golden Thirteen, Triple Nickel, black WAPS, and Tuskegee Airmen. The legacy that these great men and women left is nothing short of amazing, and their accomplishments should be preserved forever.

Knowledge is power! The power of knowing exactly who you are and what you can achieve is extremely powerful. Just think back on how many negative things you were perhaps told growing up, or unfortunately how many negative things your children face every day. You can change these events and turn these negatives into positives by merely understanding the wisdom that has been passed on. You are destined for greatness and can accomplish anything you set your mind to if you are willing to embrace the truth.

We African American officers owe a great debt of gratitude to those gallant heroes of our past. They endured hardships and suffered injustices and rarely received equal compensation to that of their white brethren and sisters. You may ask, "What was their motivation? Did they have you and me in mind as they fought our nation's wars and racism at the same time?" The answers to these questions will be addressed as we move through this section.

The way to call upon your past is to first learn about our ancestors' accomplishments. Read everything you can get your hands on about African Americans and military history. Read about how the American government used African Americans for war purposes only when they needed them to defend their interests, and, in spite of the government's reluctance, these brave souls continued to give their lives in record numbers just to be recognized and die for something more than themselves. Slaves were commonly thought of as property, nothing more than cattle or sheep, even as low as pigs. To join the ranks of the U.S. military was a big deal!

Living as a slave was the worse type of life any human could ever imagine. Only those who worked in the fields were provided with enough rations to maintain their strength to carry on the required labor. Those slaves who worked in the master's house often took advantage of their environment, cooked additional food for themselves, and would later take it home to their families. The slave environment created a natural hostility and disrespect for whites and some blacks alike. Blacks knew that, in order for them to improve their condition as slaves, they would one day have to be offered the same opportunities as whites. Living in slavery was not an option and was fought and resisted for as long as they lived.

For blacks living in America during its first three hundred years, serving in the military provided an improvement in lifestyle over living in slavery. Blacks would much rather serve in the military and die with respect than work on the plantation and die as slaves. Their motivation was freedom, dignity, and respect, and, believe it or not, total liberty— liberty to freely come and go, make life decisions, have and raise a family, and be respected as human beings. This was their motivation. The recognition and admiration given to black soldiers by other blacks were amazing. Never before, at least in America, was the black man ever viewed with more respect by his peers than the black military man. One exception to this was the black preacher. Many would argue that the black preacher continues to hold this place of honor today.

Frederick Douglass clearly understood that, until blacks were allowed to fight in our nation's wars, we would not be considered as equals. We would not secure political representation or equality in public accommodations. He lobbied for years, advocating for blacks to be given the right to actively participate in the Civil War. It is ironic that blacks had already fought gallantly in previous wars and displayed courage on the battlefield. Still the American government was unwilling to recognize their accomplishments. Even after exhibiting heroic courage during the Civil and Spanish American Wars and issued twenty medals of honor, our government seemed to forget their accomplishments.

Why the constant amnesia and lack of recognition? Why couldn't the government see that, without the unfailing support and overwhelming commitment of black people, the country would have lost every war our nation ever fought? Could they not see the inhumane treatment and unjust laws they imposed on blacks? The amnesia, in this case, was created by a superiority complex, self-determination, greed, prosperity, and a selfish need for expansion. How could our nation fairly recognize the black man's accomplishments and face the guilt and shame of eliminating Native Americans from their land? This would be too much of an emotional burden to bear, so the best thing to do was to view this episode of our past as something that had to be done. The mentality of most whites during this time was "those poor blacks and Native Americans were better off being subservient to whites than being in control of their own lives." It was believed that blacks and Native Americans were less civilized, helpless and savage.

Who better to save these docile people from their dismal existence but white Americans? This belief was dominant in most circles during this time. If you were not white, then you could not possibly be right, or entitled to equal treatment. History shows us that blacks and Native Americans were doing just fine before encountering the white man. The white man's introduction to indigenous people around the world has always been faced with an air of superiority and need to improve the native's standard of living. Most often each encounter has been challenged, resented, and resisted.

The mere fact that African Americans were transported to America against their will and forced to build a nation without receiving recognition or compensation truly amplifies the determination white Americans held. Blacks performed everything they were asked or that was required. They endured a meager existence, and they were punished if they complained. These courageous people resented every day of these horrible conditions yet pushed on, fighting for justice any way they could, even if it meant fighting for the very nation that kept them in bondage.

The accomplishments of those who came before us were nothing short of amazing, remarkable, and refreshing. These people lived in an environment where they knew the conditions would never improve in their lifetime, but they maintained a certain spirit, character, and pride that embodied faith and a promise for their collective future. Many of these early African Americans were separated from their siblings and parents at an early age, which caused a void in knowing their individual family history. Blacks grew up without knowing exactly who they were. Many times they did not know their birth parents, uncles, aunts, brothers, sisters, or any record of their family's origin. Without knowing your immediate family's background and history, it becomes difficult to understand your past, traits, characteristics, and potential talents.

Even with the many limitations and restrictions black Americans faced, they embraced their conditions and charted new ground. Each successive generation was determined to do better than the previous. From the early 1600s through much of the 1800s, it was illegal for slaves to know how to read and write. Still many were able to escape slavery, move north, secure freedom, and learn how to read. Many times some of these free blacks moved south with the purpose of teaching slaves how to read and write. Some blacks who lived in the big house on plantations were taught to read by working as nannies for white children. These nannies were often tasked with allowing these children to practice their reading while their parents were busy doing other things.

In spite of the many limitations, blacks were committed to doing better. How did they endure these terrible conditions and unjust laws? They internally knew that things had to get better and that their situation could not be any worse than they were. During Reconstruction, some blacks were given the opportunity to purchase land and build schools, churches, and homes. These pioneers took advantage of this opportunity and created America's first black neighborhoods. Many of these areas were developed from slave quarters and later would become our nation's underprivileged communities and ghettos.

The center of the black community has always been the black church. The church was the only place during this period where a black man (the preacher) could exhibit any authority. Even during slavery in the early

1600s and 1700s, blacks would congregate together for worship and discuss community matters that pertained strictly to them. The black church became more than a place of worship; it was the community center, the political forum, the hospital, the community refuge in times of homelessness, the wedding chapel, the complete focal point for black life. The black church still serves the same purposes today as it did during the settling of our nation.

Before engaging in battle, black soldiers were known for hosting "prayer meetings," where they would engage in singing, praying, and worshipping into the wee hours of the morning. These early pioneers were strongly connected with their faith in the Lord and religion. Even though many of these men could neither read nor write, they would memorize passages from the Bible and commit them to memory. Living daily in harsh conditions caused by injustices provided a natural reason to believe in God and commit to religion.

In July 1794, Richard Allen became the pastor of St. Thomas African Episcopal Church. St. Thomas African Episcopal Church was renamed African Methodist Episcopal Church in 1799. This was the first official predominant black church in the United States. Over the next one hundred years, membership had grown to over four hundred thousand parishioners. Up until this point, most black churches in America were small storefront-type arrangements. Many people would hold church meetings and worship service inside a community leader's home.

As mentioned earlier, worshipping God has always been the center of black life, primarily because the only hope of a better life was to occur in the afterlife. Life for African Americans was full of suffering, social hardships, political injustices, little or no education, in many instance borderline starvation, and a lack of dignity regardless of one's age. Even elderly black men during the early days would be referred to as "nigger" or "boy." White Americans did not give black Americans any respect regardless of their age, political or social status, or accomplishments. "A nigger is still a nigger, regardless of who he or she is" was the tone in most of America at the time.

Free blacks have always been in America. Even with their limited access to education and regardless of their accomplishments, they were still oftentimes relegated to the second-class treatment in those times. It would take blacks over four hundred years of struggling in America to earn equal access to public accommodations, the right to vote, and the opportunity to gain a decent education.

The implementation of affirmative actions of the 1960s and 1970s brought significant changes in America. These sweeping changes were not welcome by the white majority. The National Association for the Advancement of Colored People (NAACP) was founded in 1909 by a group of black activists who were determined to pioneer changes at the highest levels of our government.

President Woodrow Wilson was a staunch white supremacist. He allowed many of his cabinet members to establish official segregation policies in most federal government offices. His administration imposed full racial segregation in Washington, DC, and ousted blacks from most federal positions. This action outraged members of the NAACP, and they went to work with their first public protest, speaking out about the lynching and lack of job opportunities. Finally, in 1918 President Wilson conceded and made a public statement against lynching. From the time of the signing of the Emancipation Proclamation in 1865 to 1920, over 286 blacks were hung by whites. Justice was not pursued by local officials because lynching was an accepted practice. African Americans did not have any protection under the laws of the land. If a white citizen felt like murdering or raping a black person during this time, there was little to stop him other than his conscience.

At the turn of the twentieth century, blacks were terrified and lived each day in complete fear. Many blacks clearly understood the dangers and horrors of living among whites, and each day they were uncertain of whether they were going to live. They could only depend on their faith in God. This strong belief in God elevated the perceived power of the preacher or pastor. Religious ministers were given more respect from other blacks because they often had more education and represented the hope that resided within the community.

W. E. B. DuBois, the NAACP president, campaigned for President Wilson in 1918. He was offered an army commission and would be in charge of dealing with race relations. DuBois failed his army physical and could not serve. In 1914, President Wilson told the *New York Times* that "if the colored people made a mistake voting for me, they ought to correct it." In speaking on the Ku Klux Klan, President Wilson stated that the Klan "began to attempt by intimidation what they were not allowed to attempt by the ballot or by any ordered course of public action."

Black communities started expanding during the Reconstruction period. Blacks came together and started speaking out throughout the 1800s. They created newspapers and abolitionist groups. Many times these groups met inside community churches. The church was the community center for political advancement and other civic venues. Many of these civic organizations provided job skills and networking opportunities. Blacks quickly learned that there was strength in pulling together.

They learned to take pride in each other's accomplishments and push relatives and friends in attending college, joining the military, or pursuing other professional endeavors. These black successful enclaves could be found in Tulsa; Richmond; Rosewood; Atlanta; Nashville; Memphis; Montgomery; Birmingham; Washington, DC; cities throughout the South; and more new developments in the West. These communities were not limited to the South; huge efforts were made in Detroit, Boston, Chicago, Harlem, and Philadelphia. These communities were purchased, built, and sustained with black dollars and produced our nation's first successful African American merchants, preachers, bankers, teachers, entertainers, and other professionals.

These communities were soon destroyed by prejudiced and jealous whites who felt that these blacks were becoming too lofty. Unfortunately, through Jim Crow laws and the Ku Klux Klan, they took action by destroying many of these neighborhoods. Laws were changed to prevent blacks from publicly assembling, voting, running for public office, and securing loans to purchase homes and businesses. Life in America for African Americans was difficult, to say the least, but they continued to exhibit the tenacity needed to excel. ·

It is important to remember the struggle of our past. It may not be glamorous and filled with fame and fortune for all, but it is securely wrapped with determination, struggle, challenges, perseverance, prayer, and ultimately accomplishments. These are the elements that provide the will and determination for our leaders today. This is where our abundant energy and patience to endure come from. Our past is filled with a legacy of accomplishments. You merely need to be made aware of your history and the significant accomplishments of our past.

Meeting Colonel (Ret.) Lee Archer (the famed Tuskegee Airman and WWII ace) would be a milestone in anyone's life. He embodies the success and tenacity from which today's officers can draw leadership, courage, and perseverance. After initially meeting him for the first time, he shared with me this statement: "I can rest comfortably now because I can see the types of officers that are being produced. Today's officers are more prepared, and determined, and educated than we Tuskegee Airmen." We are more prepared, but do we truly understand what we need to do to maintain that edge? Do we exhibit the strength and preparation where everyone can see our preparedness and determination? We must understand the accomplishments and successes of the past to ensure we have a bright future.

Each day when you go to your office, attempt to do a better job than you did the previous day. Work a little harder; read a little more; or send a letter or e-mail, thanking someone who did something nice or rewarding to you or your unit. There is an old saying in the air force: "You are only as good as your last sortie!" We need to remember that each day is an opportunity to excel and do great things. Who knows what opportunities will be presented to you? Major General Johnny Weida, USAF, while commandant of cadets, continually inspired cadets with the phrase, "You find success where opportunity meets preparation." Each day you have to train to be ready for the next challenge. Who knows what opportunity will come your way? But you must be ready for the challenge.

The key to success is constant training. The Army trains continually. When they are not training, they are cleaning equipment, checking records, and reviewing procedures to ensure they are mission ready. Colonel Peter Champagne, US Army and former United States Forces Korea provost marshal, trained his entire unit by properly preparing his soldiers for war, honing their combat skills, and getting them in tip-top physical shape. His troops intensely participated in live-fire drills and exercises, urban assault courses, sniper fire competitions, and a very rigorous physical fitness program called the "Iron Watch Dog Challenge." As a commander who cared about his troops by raising their standards and demanding excellence at every corner, he developed officers of character with high moral integrity. His constant saying was to "be tough but fair." Even the most astute and polished officers had difficulties meeting the demands placed on him under Colonel Champagne's supervision. After serving with this senior leader, you had a new profound respect for what being the best is all about.

Excellence is a journey, not a destination. When you make doing your very best your goal in everything you do, you are setting yourself up for success. You are conducting operational risk management techniques and looking for ways to improve. You don't allow yourself to settle for mediocrity or anything other than your very best. Giving your all is difficult to do, especially on a consistent basis. There are always limits, concerns, and restrictions to halt progress. This is the primary reason you have to clearly understand what has been accomplished before, so you can draw strength from those who have come before you. Once you have embedded successful traits and developed them into habits, the less you will view restrictions as adverse. You will embrace your new way of living and set even higher standards.

The best way to learn about your past is to immerse yourself into our history by visiting museums and historical monuments that focus on black life and our heroes. You will be surprised at how many national historical sites exist and the significance they played in our development. Take advantage of your surroundings by getting to know the many heroes who reside in your neighborhood or special monuments in the areas while on temporary duty.

Upon whose shoulders are you standing? Do you know your history? Are there veterans in the local area that you can draw strength from and serve as your mentor? I guarantee you, securing a mentor is worth its weight in gold. Design your career and allow a senior officer within your field to review your intentions. I am certain they will assist you in vectoring your career toward success.

Good luck with your endeavors!

## Historical Landmarks, Museums, and National Monuments

### Alabama

- The Birmingham Civil Rights Institute, 520 Sixteenth Street North, Birmingham, AL 35203 (205-328-9696)
- Tuskegee Institute National Historic Site, 1212 West Montgomery Road, Tuskegee, AL 36083
- Dexter Avenue Baptist Church, 454 Dexter, Montgomery, AL
- Swayne Hall, Talladega College, 627 W. Battle Street, Talladega, AL 35160

### Arizona

- Fort Apache-Old Fort Museum, 73 San Carlos Reservation, Fort Apache, AZ (602-338-4625)
- Fort Huachuca, 556 Auger Avenue, Fort Huachuca, AZ 85613-7011

### Arkansas

- Little Rock Central High Visitors Center and Museum, 14th and Park Streets, Little Rock, AR

### California

- California African American Museum, 600 State Drive, Exposition Park, Los Angeles, CA 90037 (213-744-7432)

### Colorado

- Black American West Museum and Heritage Center, 3091 California Street, Denver, CO 80205 (303-292-2566)

**Connecticut**
- First Church of Christ, 250 Main Street, Wethersfield, CT 06109

**Florida**
- British (Negro) Fort, Apalachicola National Forest (a short distance from State Road 65, near Sumatra, FL)
- Bethune (Mary McLeod) Home, 640 Mary McLeod Bethune Boulevard, Daytona Beach, FL 32114

**Georgia**
- King-Tisdell Cottage (Museum of Black History), 514 E. Huntingdon Street, Savannah, GA (912-234-8000)
- Tubman African American Museum, 340 Walnut Street, Macon, GA (478-473-8544)
- Martin Luther King Jr. Center for Nonviolent Social Change, 449 Auburn Avenue NE, Atlanta, GA 39312 (404-524-1956)
- Sweet Auburn Historic District, Elwood Avenue, Atlanta, GA
- Stone Hall (Fairchild Hall), Morris Brown College Campus, Atlanta University, Atlanta, GA
- King (Martin Luther Jr.) Historic District, 2 Martin Luther King Jr. Drive, Atlanta, GA 30334-4600

**Illinois**
- DuSable Museum of African American History, 740 East 56th Place, Chicago, IL 60637-1495 (773-947-0600)
- Abbott (Robert S.) House, 4742 South Martin Luther King Jr. Boulevard, Chicago, IL
- DePriest (Oscar Stanton) House, 3140 S. Indiana Avenue, Chicago, IL
- Wells-Barnett (Ida B.) House, 3624 S. Martin Luther King Jr. Drive, Chicago, IL
- William (Daniel Hale) House, 445 East 42nd Street, Chicago, IL

- DuSable (Jean Baptist Point) Homesite, 401 North Michigan Avenue, Chicago, IL

## Iowa

- Fort Des Moines Provisional Army Officer Training School, Building 87, Military Reservation Motor Pool, Des Moines, IA 50303

## Kansas

- Brown v Board of Education National Historical Site, 424 South Kansas Avenue, Suite 220, Topeka, KS 66603-3441 (913-354-4273)
- Nicodemus Historic District, Graham County, KS

## Kentucky

- Monument to Kentucky's African American Civil War Soldiers, Old State Arsenal, East Main Street, Frankfort, KY (502-564-3265)
- National Underground Railroad Museum, 115 East Third Street, Maysville, KY, 41056 (606-783-2668)
- Lincoln Hall, Berea College, 110 Lincoln Hall, Berea, KY 40404
- Young (Whitney M. Jr.) Birthplace and Boyhood Home, southwest of Simpsonville, KY, off US Route 60 on the campus of the Old Lincoln Institute, now the Whitney M. Young Jr. Job Corps Center

## Louisiana

- Anna Bontemps African American Museum and Cultural Arts Center, 1327 Third Street, PO Box 533, Alexandria, LA 71301 (318-473-4692)
- River Road African American Museum, 3138 Highway 44, Darrow, LA 70725 (225-562-7703)
- The Amistad Research Center, Tilton Hall-Tulane University,

6823 St. Charles Avenue, New Orleans, LA 70118 (504-865-5535)

- Yucca Plantation (Melrose), Melrose Plantation, 211 Kyser Hall, NSU, Natchitoches, LA
- Port Hudson, 236 Highway 61, Jackson, LA 70748
- Dillard (James H.) Home, 1555 Poydras Street, New Orleans, LA 70112

## Maryland
- The Pan African Historical Museum USA, 1500 Main Street Tower Square, Springfield, MD 01115 (413-733-1823)

## Massachusetts
- Museum of Afro American History, 46 Joy Street, Boston, MA 02114 (617-739-1200)
- Frederick Douglass Memorial, outside New Bedford City Hall, 133 William Street, New Bedford, MA 02740
- Boston African American National Historic Site, 14 Beacon Street, Suite 506, Boston, MA 02108 (617-742-5415)
- African Meeting House, 14 Beacon Street, Suite 719, Boston, MA
- Baldwin (Maria) House, 196 Prospect Street, Cambridge, MA
- Cuffe (Paul) Farm, 1504 Drift Road, Bristol County, MA
- DuBois (W. E. B) Boyhood Homesite, Great Barrington, MA
- Nell (William C.) Residence, 203 Nelson, Boston, MA 02127
- Trotter (William Monroe) House, 97 Sawyer Avenue Dorchester, MA

## Michigan
- The Motown Museum, 2648 W. Grand Boulevard, Detroit, MI (313-875-2264)
- Museum of African American History, 315 E. Warren Avenue, Detroit, MI 48201-1443 (313-494-5800)

## Minnesota

- Roy Wilkins Memorial, John Ireland Boulevard (midway between the State Capitol and St. Paul Cathedral), St. Paul, MN

## Mississippi

- Delta Blues Museum, 114 Delta Avenue, Clarksdale, MS (601-624-4461)
- Oakland Memorial Chapel, Alcorn State, Claiborne, MS 39096

## Missouri

- George Washington Carver National Monument, 5646 Carver Road, Diamond, MO 64840 (417-325-4151)
- Jefferson National Expansion Memorial (old courthouse), N. 4th Street, St Louis, MO 63102
- Mutual Musicians Association Building, Musicians Association Building, Local 627, Kansas City, MO 64110
- Joplin (Scott) Residence, 2658 Delmar Boulevard, St. Louis, MO 63103

## Nebraska

- Great Plains Black Museum, 2213 Lake Street, Omaha, NE (402-345-2212)

## New York

- Schomburg Center for Research in Black Culture, 515 Malcolm X Boulevard, New York, NY 10037-1801 (212-491-2200)
- Armstrong (Louis) House, 3456 107th Street Corona, NY 10368
- New York Amsterdam News Building, 2340 Frederick Douglass Boulevard, New York, NY 10027
- Bunche Ralph J. House, 115-125 Grosvenor Road, New York, NY

- Cook (Will Marion) House, 75 Broad Street, Suite 2400, New York, NY 10004
- Ellington (Edward Kennedy "Duke") Residence, Broadway at 246 Street, Bronx, NY
- Henson (Matthew) Residence, Eighth Avenue, New York, NY
- Johnson (James Weldon) Residence, 112 Colin Street, Syracuse, NY
- McKay (Claude) Residence, 180 West 135th Street, New York, NY
- Mills (Florence) House, 220 West 135th Street, New York, NY
- Tubman, Harriet Home for the Aged, 180 South Street, Auburn, NY
- Villa Lewaro, North Broadway, Irvington, NY

## North Carolina
- The Martin Luther King Memorial Gardens, Martin Luther King Jr. Boulevard and Rock Quarry Road, Raleigh, NC
- North Carolina Mutual Life Insurance Company, NC
- Union Tavern, PO Box 1996 Milton, NC 27305
- Thomas Day House, Broad Street, Milton, NC 27305

## Ohio
- African American Museum, 1765 Crawford Road, Cleveland, OH 44106 (216-791-1700)
- National Afro American Museum and Cultural Center, 1350 Brush Row Road, PO Box 578, Wilberforce, OH 45384 (937-376-4944)
- Dunbar House, 219 Paul Laurence Dunbar Street, Dayton, OH (800-860-0148)
- Oberlin College
- Dunbar (Paul L) House, 219 Paul Laurence Dunbar, Dayton, OH
- Young (Colonel Charles) House, US Route 42, Wilberforce, OH

- Langston (John Mercer) House, 207 E. College Street, Oberlin, OH

## Oklahoma
- 101 Ranch Historic District, Guthrie, OK

## Pennsylvania
- African American Museum, NW corner of 7th and Arch Streets, Philadelphia, PA (215-574-0380)
- The Delfe Museum of Afro American Culture, 7th and Dauphin Streets, Philadelphia, PA
- Mother Bethel A. M. E. Church, 419 S. 6th Street, Philadelphia, PA
- Harper (Francis Ellen Watkins) House, 6306 Germantown Avenue, Philadelphia, PA
- Tanner (Henry O.) Homesite, 2908 W. Diamond Street, Philadelphia, PA

## Tennessee
- Chattanooga African American Museum, 200 East Martin Luther King Boulevard, Chattanooga, TN 37403 (423-266-8658)
- National Civil Rights Museum, 450 Mulberry Street, Memphis, TN 38103-4214 (901-521-9699)
- Franklin (Isaac) Plantation, Gallatin, TN
- Fort Pillow, 3122 Park Road, Henning, TN 38041
- Jubilee Hall, Suite 1000, Fisk University, Nashville, TN 37203

## Texas
- The African American Museum, 3536 Grand Avenue at Fair Park, Dallas, TX (214-565-9026)

## Rhode Island

- Site of the Battle of Rhode Island, 2 Memorial Boulevard, Newport, RI 02840

## South Carolina

- Avery Research Center for African American History, College of Charleston, 125 Bull Street, Charleston, SC 29424 (803-727-2009)
- Penn School Historic District, The York W. Bailey Museum, 16 Penn Center Circle W, St. Helena, SC
- Chapelle Administration Building, County Office Building, PO Box 726, Charleston, SC 29402-0726
- Stone River Slave Rebellion Site, SC
- Heyward (Dubose) House, 76 Church Street, Charleston, SC
- Rainey (Joseph) House, 909 Prince Street, Georgetown, SC
- Smalls (Robert) House, 907 Craven Street, Beaufort, SC
- Home of Madam C. J. Walker, Vesey (Denver) House, 56 Bull Street, Charleston, SC

## Virginia

- Booker T. Washington National Monument, 12130 Booker T. Washington Highway, Hardy, VA 24101-9688 (540-721-2094)
- The Black History Museum and Cultural Center of Virginia, Clay Street, Richmond, VA 23219 (804-789-9093)
- Maggie L. Walker National Historic Site, 600 N 2nd Street, Richmond, VA (804-771-2017)
- The Alexandria Black History Resource Center, 638 North Alfred Street, Alexandria, VA 22314 (703-838-4829)
- Jackson Ward Historic District, East Clay Street, Richmond, VA
- Hampton Institute, Hampton, VA 23668
- Pittsylvania County Courthouse, Pittsylvania County Clerk, PO Drawer 31, Chatham, VA 24531-0031

- Moton (Robert) Home (Holly Knoll), 6496 Allmondsville Road, Gloucester, VA
- Waller (Maggie Lena) House, 110A Leigh Street, Richmond, VA

## Washington, DC

- Anacostia Museum, Smithsonian Institution, 1901 Fort Place SE, Washington, DC
- The African American Civil War Memorial (subway entrance at 10th Street and U Street NW), Washington, DC
- Mary McLeod Bethune Council House, national historic site, 1318 Vermont Avenue NW, Washington, DC 21005 (202-332-1233)
- The Frederick Douglass National Historic Site, 1411 W Street SE, Washington, DC 20020-4813 (202-426-5961)
- Howard (General Oliver Otis) House, 2400 Sixth Street NW, Washington, DC 20059
- Saint Luke's Episcopal Church, 2001 14th Street SE, Washington, DC
- Bruce (Blanche K.) House, 1337 10th Street NW, Washington, DC
- Cary (Mary Ann Shadd) House, 1421 W. Street NW, Washington, DC
- Grimke (Charlotte Forten) House, 608 R Street NW, Washington, DC
- Woodson (Carter G.) House, 1538 9th Street NW, Washington, DC
- Drew (Charles Richard) House, 2505 South I Street, Washington, DC
- Terrell (Mary Church) House, 326 T Street, Washington, DC
- Octavius Augustus Williams Home, 338 U Street, LeDroit Park, Washington, DC
- Dr. Garnet C. Wilkinson Home, 406 U Street, Washington, DC
- Walter Washington Home, 408 T Street, Washington, DC

- Willis Richards Home, 512 U Street, Washington, DC
- Dr. Jesse Lawson and Dr. Anna J. Cooper Home, 201 T Street, Washington, DC
- Reverend Jesse Jackson Residence, corner of Fourth and T Streets, Washington, DC
- Julia West J Hamilton Home, 320 U Street, Washington, DC
- Major Christian Fleetwood Home, 319 U Street, Washington, DC
- Duke Ellington Home, 420 Elm Street, Washington, DC
- Paul Laurence Dunbar Home, 321 U Street, Washington, DC
- Honorable Oscar De Priest Home, 419 U Street, Washington, DC
- Senator Edward Brooke Home, 1938 Third Street, Washington, DC
- General William Birney Home, T and Second Streets, Washington, DC

## Canada
- Buxton Historic Site and Museum, North Buxton, Ontario, Canada (519-352-4799)
- John Freeman Walls Historic Site and Underground Railroad Museum, Lake Shore Township, Windsor, Ontario (519-258-6253)

This list is not complete, and some may have been unintentionally overlooked. Some of the national landmarks are not opened to the public year-round. It is advisable that you contact the National Park Service before you attend.

## Sage Advice

### Major Elaine R. Washington, USAF
- Know the commanding officer: God himself. Seek His counsel and direction. (You have been predestined to succeed. You just have to walk in the right path).

- This world order, this military life, and its trials and tribulations are to conform us to the image of God, His way, His timing, and His glory.

## Major Jacqueline Randolph, USAF

- Never disappoint your mentors.
- Nothing is impossible with God.
- Do not compete with others. Compete with yourself. Do the best that you can do, which usually exceeds what others are doing. Go the extra mile. Do the extra task, because you know you can! Compete with yourself. During one of the extremely rare times I was not on temporary duty (normally three hundred days a year), I was told to clean the bathroom and toilets. I was an airman first class, and my goal was to clean the toilets so well that God himself would refuse to use any toilet except those I had cleaned. I was so diligent that my senior master sergeant told me to stop cleaning the bathroom in the middle of my work, and he never asked me to do it again.
- Regardless of where you are assigned, reach out and embrace all races and new experiences. There is nothing off-limits to black people or women. Don't believe that lie. I own a cabin and 2.5 acres in a mountain community. I've never seen any other black people in my county in the four years I have lived here. I constantly get teased by my black friends who won't visit me because the Klan lives there or black people are supposed to live in the city. I am happy with my home, neighbors, church, and community. Recently, I was very sick. My neighbors arrived at my house and tried to forcibly remove me and bring me to their home to care for me. Somehow, I had enough strength to refuse. They brought soup to my house for days until I recovered.
- I recommend that a new lieutenant find a SNCO/NCO and latch onto him. They can make or break you and can make you shine! As a young Airman First Class, two black SNCOs, Master Sergeant Packard (chief loadmaster) and Senior Master Sergeant Slaughter (chief flight engineer), latched onto me (the

only black woman in the squadron) and rebuked, praised, molded, and mentored me continuously. When my squadron commander told me he was sending me to Officer Training School (OTS), I was very resistant. I absolutely loved my job and could not believe I would be paid to have fun! These two SNCOs cornered me in a wall-to-wall counseling session and told me I was going to OTS or suffer their wrath. Needless to say, I didn't want to find out what that meant!

# CHAPTER 3
## REACHING YOUR PEAK PERFORMANCE!

My son, pay attention to your wisdom; Lend your ear to my understanding, That you may preserve discretion, And your lips may keep knowledge.

—Proverbs 5:1–2

There are 110 secrets to success: Don't waste time looking for them. Success is the result of perfection, hard work, learning from failure, loyalty to those for whom you work, add persistence.

—General (Ret.) Colin Powell, 1989

When opportunity knocks you want to be fully dressed.

—Major General Charles "C. Q." Brown, USAF

Being a member of the United States military is truly one of the noblest professions known to mankind. Being an officer in the United States military is one of the highest privileges that a person could ever achieve. Understanding this fact is paramount in reaching the pinnacle of success in your career.

Reaching your peak translates to striving for perfection. We all know that success or excellence is a journey, not a destination. Once you board the success train, there is no getting off. Well, once you are on, you do not want to intentionally get off. This chapter introduces several strategies that will aid you while you are on your success train.

Learning to be the best at anything takes hard work and consistent practice. If you are going to be a successful military officer, you have to want it, and you are going to have to want it *really bad*.

Okay, you are probably saying, "I'm not afraid of hard work," but I caution you that effort is only half the battle. You perhaps have to change your thinking, what you read, and the people you hang out with, and immerse yourself in being the best officer you can possibly be. *Oh, no,* you are probably thinking, *how do I embrace my heritage and at the same time change who I am?* I am not completely suggesting you change who you are as a person, but develop yourself into a better you!

Our ancestors had enormous obstacles to confront daily, yet they found that burning desire to be the best they possibly could be. They learned not to complain about trivial matters but to press on toward accomplishing their goals, striving toward bettering conditions for their family and themselves. There are thousands of black heroes that we can use as examples for how to overcome difficulties, rise above our circumstances, and succeed in spite of everyone telling you that you will never amount to anything.

Success does not occur by happenstance; it takes a concerted and focused effort to hit the target consistently. It requires you to embrace everything about yourself. That means knowing your past, executing success habits in your present, and pinpointing planning for your future. It takes hard work. For example, when you were in school, being a good student meant doing all your homework and giving 100 percent in class, and you were most likely going to receive an A for the semester. Almost every military officer is a *good* officer, but you want to be a *great* officer, and that means giving 150 percent each and every day of your existence.

Giving 150 percent means being competent in your duties, arriving early, and going home late in an effort to be the best officer assigned to your unit. It means learning how each sister service operates and deals with whatever you are working on. It means researching what corporate America is doing and how to apply lesson-learned and benchmark practices to make your unit better. You will find that military officers are very talented and motivated individuals. In order to stand out above your peers, you have to go the extra mile by learning more than what your peers know, and learning how to apply those principles to reach your goals.

Learning to reach your peak performance consistently and embed excellence in all you do takes work. Stephen Covey states that the space between stimulus and response identifies where you find happiness. When young people make decisions they typically make faulty, quick decisions without fully considering the repercussions or consequences of their actions. The more mature a person becomes the shorter that space between stimulus and response. It is important for officers to make sound, prudent decisions on a consistent basis. Subordinates and superiors alike depend on your every decision, so learning to make good, well–thought out, and thorough decisions early on will serve you well.

After many years of making mistakes and talking over professional problems with fellow officers, the following success strategies were validated. There is no particular order to any of them, because all stand on their own merit and serve their unique purpose. Learn each of these strategies, write them down, personalize each one, and adapt them to your daily life. Keep a positive attitude. Have you ever heard the phrase that "your attitude determines your altitude"? Reaching your peak performance is more about possessing a positive attitude than anything else.

The right attitude will put you in the appropriate frame of mind to properly handle and address the challenges of the day. The proper attitude eases confrontations and relaxes preconceived notions and biases. Additionally, being competent in your duties and responsibilities builds confidence in you, your peers, and your supervisors. Professional and technical competence will quickly elevate you above your peers, and will cause your supervisors to learn to rely on you in times of crises. Competence will assist you in having a positive attitude and feeling good about your environment.

Having the right attitude is contagious and will make others desire to be around you. No one wants to be around someone with a bad attitude for too long. Smile when appropriate, and enjoy the moment and your time in the military. Being an officer is a tremendous privilege and will present rare opportunities for you. Take advantage of this time, and keep a positive attitude.

*Find a good mentor.* Regardless of your rank, mentorship is vital and will help to eliminate barriers you encounter and offer solutions to resolve conflict and adverse situations. Do not limit yourself to mentors who look like you. White officers have always commanded African American officers, and those black officers who have reached senior levels can quickly look back and identify numerous white officers who supported them in their climb to the top. It always helps to have a mentor in your career area, but do not allow this to hinder your search. Senior officers are always looking to assist younger officers trying to make a positive impact on the military.

Be careful in your selection, because selecting the wrong mentor can have a devastating effect on your career. All officers need to have mentors, so do not delay and find someone who is willing to take you under their wing and offer good, sound, honest advice that will support your career. Be advised that you will not always agree with sincere and honest assessments from your mentor. Perhaps, sometimes you will have to agree to disagree, but for the most part your mentor is speaking from years of experience and has lived through the challenges you are confronting.

*Take tough jobs.* Don't be afraid of taking on tough duties and responsibilities. It is too easy to remain in your comfort zone and not step out of your safe environment. Jobs that require long hours and frequent temporary assignments are often rewarded with positive annual evaluations that will secure your future promotion. Your supervisor is always looking for young officers willing to stand up and be challenged. They take pride in officers with the courage, tenacity, and confidence to take on tough duties. When young officers are assigned the toughest duties, their supervisors learn to call on them for future critical assignments. Each success builds on the next, and the more experience and exposure you receive, the better apt you are to make critical decisions when needed.

Be on constant alert for those long temporary duties and assignments above your current rank. Don't worry about not being ready for a tough job. Step up to the plate, toss your name into the hat, surround yourself with people who are willing to assist you in the task, and then learn from them. These professionals will provide you with the assistance, guidance, and support that have made them successful throughout their career. Be confident. No one wants you to fail, so step out on courage and faith, and know that success is yours merely for the asking.

*Build professional competence (read everything in sight).* Technical competence is the one thing that no one will ever be able to question or take away from you. Your coworkers and supervisors will come to rely on you. Read everything you can get your hands on about your profession and the history of its development. Smart officers pride themselves on being able to think outside the traditional box. Create a personal and professional library with books, magazines, and journals relating to your profession. Know who the pioneers are in your career area. Be able to apply different techniques in an effort to resolve professional problems. Technical competence will serve you well over the years and create a unique blend of discipline that will assist you in securing your future as a military officer.

*Take classes every year (be a lifelong student).* Technical competence comes from a variety of sources. Local colleges and universities will serve you well in gaining the insight needed to excel in your profession. Online courses are recommended for military members, because they can be taken during your off-duty time. Continually enroll in classes that are related to your chosen career area. These classes will expose you to new horizons and introduce you to current philosophies in your profession. Always be on the lookout for new ideas and methods to increase efficiencies.

*Personal appearance is never forgotten; no one should ever have to remind you.* Each morning you put on your uniform, you need to take pride in knowing that you look the best you possibly can. It takes hard, consistent work to look good. You need to invest ample time to ensure you have uniforms that properly fit and are serviceable. Your uniform should always be clean and showcase the appropriate badges, rank, and insignia. No one should ever have to tell you that you need a haircut, and, ladies, you need to know the standards and adhere to them. Grooming standards are vitally important, so do not take them for granted. Of course you have heard the old adage, "You only get one first impression." This old saying is true, and the impression you make often determines how people treat you and interpret the things you say and do. Physical fitness is another area on which you need to continually focus. No one wants to follow an obese officer, and being overweight will prevent you from maintaining the competitive edge needed to compete with your peers. It is imperative to remain within fitness standards. Take pride in yourself, and use the gym facilities on your base to remain in shape.

*Keep copies of your records and awards. Documentation is everything!* When you least expect it, you will need a copy of your records. Your supervisor will assume that you have copies of your records. In preparing awards and annual reports, you may need immediate access to your personnel records. Military personnel centers sometimes lose copies of personnel records or reflect inaccurate information. It is your responsibility to ensure your records are correct. Do not take this responsibility lightly; your future promotion may depend on its accuracy.

*Collect biographies of senior officers.* On your service website you can find the biographies of every flag officer. Make copies of those general officers you meet and serve under so you can see firsthand how they got where they are. You need to know their previous assignments and promotion timing. After reading over biographies for years, you will eventually learn to clearly see those salient assignments that had a pivotal impact on getting that officer to the general officer ranks. Most generals will tell you that the most important assignment is the one in which you currently are. If you do a great job in the position you are in, then it will serve you for the next two to three assignments. Always do your best and learn from general officers who have risen to the highest levels within their service.

I started collecting senior officers' biographies when I was a young captain, and it proved to be invaluable. What I learned after reading and studying biographies over the years is general officers have five common accomplishments: 1) professional military education was completed in residence, 2) at least one promotion from major to colonel was below the zone, 3) they served one assignment as a senior officer's executive officer, chief of staff, or special assistant, 4) they served on the joint Staff, and finally 5) they were deployed to war. While there are no guarantees and established receipts in getting promoted as a general officer, I have learned these five items offer a good foundation in reaching the senior officer ranks.

*Create a file of both your and your peers' performance reports and awards.* It is important to talk to your friends and associates on how to write performance reports and awards. If your friends are willing to give you a copy, then place it into a file and hang onto it throughout your career. You will find as you journey through your career these documents will become important and assist you in creating ideas or serve as a template to get your writing jump-started.

*Writing and speaking will become your best friends.* Learning to communicate effectively is vitally important to the success of your career. College writing and professional writing are two completely different arenas and should not be confused. Talk with your supervisor about writing style and how to organize thoughts and ideas. You will find that briefing preparation is a skill that takes time to master, and you will be well advised on perfecting PowerPoint and other computer applications.

Being able to convey your ideas to notes and checklists, and accurately interpret your commander's intent is critical to your success. Take classes to learn correct grammar and proper usage of the English language. Military jargon is rare and can be considered a language of its own. Learn to master it, because it will become your best friend. You can only be as effective as you can communicate. Many of the lessons that I have learned over the years are summed up in the list below. Remember you cannot recall the spoken word, so once it's said there is no going back to clean it up. When you submit something you write, have a coworker review it before submission. Your writing and speaking skills are a direct reflection of you, and if you don't make a great impression initially, you may not receive a second chance. Take your time to grow your skills, and be thorough in this pursuit because it is vitally important to your career.

Spend time with senior leaders to learn their style and techniques. Gathering their perspective will prove critical to your success. Practice writing on your own, so when you are tasked with an assignment you are properly prepared.

## Major Rules for Preparing a First Draft

- Work to understand your sources.
- Think about where you are going before you begin to write.
- Write to illuminate, not to impress.
- Write for your classmates and for your future self.
- Make a statement and back it up.
- Always distinguish fact from possibility.
- Don't plagiarize.
- Allow time for revision.
- Stick to the point.
- Say exactly what you mean.
- Never make the reader back up
- Don't make readers work harder than they have to.
- Be concise.
- Proofread!

## Preparing Oral Presentations

- Do not simply paraphrase.
- Be selective.
- Delete extraneous details.
- Focus your talk on the results.
- Draw conclusions as you present each component of the study.
- Plan to use the blackboard.
- Summarize the major findings.
- Be prepared for questions.
- Know what you're going to say and how you're going to say it.
- Don't rush.
- Make visual aids work for you.

- Write unfamiliar lines on visual aids.
- Don't mumble.
- Try to sound interested in what you are saying.
- Don't end abruptly.
- End your talk gracefully.
- Do not allow your presentation to exceed the time allotted.

*Always use your chain of command and effectively communicate!* There will be times that you need to talk or work out an issue with your senior staff. You may feel that you have a good reputation and your commander knows exactly who you are so you have the right to approach him or her directly without going through your immediate supervisor. Don't do it! Regardless of how urgent and important you believe your issue is, you need to include your immediate supervisor. There may be rare occasions that you have to go directly to your commander, but this should be reserved for exceptional moments. Even on these rare occasions you need to follow up with your immediate supervisor. Overlooking or going around your immediate supervisor undercuts his authority and belittles his ability to remain informed. Your actions displays to your commander that your supervisor has little control of his section or unit.

*Complete your professional military education (PME) as soon as you are eligible.* PME is designed to take you to the next level by providing you with the knowledge, skill, and competence to successfully operate at the next higher rank. PME will introduce you to strategic and critical thinking, an overview of military history, basic required knowledge for officership, and expectations of the next higher rank.

Ensure each of your performance reports clearly recommends you for the next higher level of PME; this will increase your chance of being selected to attend in-residence. Each service has certain requirements; it boils down to you completing the necessary basic requirements expected for the officer to achieve the next higher rank. Once you are in school, immerse yourself in your studies. Maximize this opportunity by realizing that there is a reason for you being selected, and you must make the most of this experience. You will encounter many officers who will make great grades with little or no study. Perhaps these officers are service academy graduates and spent the last four years studying the subject matter, and PME is nothing more than a refresher. Don't allow yourself to take this experience lightly or for granted by not studying or reading every assignment. What is good for others is not necessarily good for you!

It is vitally important that, if you did not learn how to properly study during your undergraduate years, you learn it now. You will find that you will depend on it as you continue to climb up the ranks. Many senior officers may be required to read five hundred to a thousand pages per night to prepare for a briefing or testify before Congress, and these talents are not learned overnight. It takes practice! So take this advice to heart, and learn how to write and improve your memory techniques now.

The following techniques were taken from cadet training at the United States Air Force Academy.

## Increasing Your Memory

- *Organize.* List facts in alphabetical or chronological order. Get a general idea of the material. Note that both simple and complex facts in logical order are much easier to remember.

- *Make it meaningful.* Look for connections in what you are studying. For example, packing a parachute by itself can be boring; however, the excitement of jumping out of a plane gives a whole new meaning to this process. Focusing on the big picture helps provide meaning to the learning process and stimulates us to remember.

- *Create associations.* Associate something new with something you already know. This creates a building process in your memory bank. If you already know a Bill Smith, think of the Bill you know and associate him with the new Bill Smith.

- *Learn it actively.* People remember 90 percent of what they do, 75 percent of what they see, and 20 percent of what they hear. This saying is very accurate, as action is a proven memory enhancer. Move your hands, pace back and forth, and use gestures as you recite a passage. Actively involving your body will help you to remember.

- *Relax.* Eating proper foods, avoiding caffeine before an exam, and getting proper exercise will help you relax and feel more confident. Relaxing will enhance your ability to recall facts faster and with more clarity, and you will feel better overall.

- *Create pictures.* Draw diagrams or make up cartoons. Use them to connect facts and illustrate relationships. When abstract concepts can be "seen," they are much easier to remember. You can be as creative as you want, as long as you understand your scribble.

- *Recite and repeat.* When you repeat something out loud, you anchor the concept better by using two or more of your senses. Repetition is the mother of learning. If you use more than one sense, you create a synergistic effect, which is a powerful memory technique. If you recite out loud in your own words, memory is enhanced even more!

- *Write it down.* Writing notes to ourselves help us to remember. If we write down an idea or a passage several times in different areas, we increase our chances of remembering it.

- *Reduce interference.* Find an area free from distractions. Studies show that most students study more effectively in a quiet area in one hour than in a noisy area in two hours.

- *Overlearn.* When you think you've got it, don't quit. Don't miss a chance to review just one more time. Did you ever hear the expression "I beat that subject to death"?

- *Review notes the same day.* Studies prove that, in order to store information long term, it must be reviewed within twenty-four hours. By getting in the habit of the same-day review, we increase the chances of remembering by over 70 percent!

- *Use daylight.* This method is particularly effective for weekend study and review. Study the most difficult subjects during daylight hours. For many students the early-morning hours can be especially productive and will stimulate the memory process.

- *Distribute learning.* Research suggests marathon study sessions (three hours or more) are not as effective as light study sessions (one to two hours), which are distributed at different times during the week. Take frequent breaks. Some students can study for fifty minutes or more, while others need to stop after thirty minutes. Try to distribute your length of study in the same rhythm as your classes. One popular study strategy is to study for 50 minutes, rest for 10 minutes, and then study again for 50 minutes. I call this My 50/10/50 Study Plan. Give yourself rewards. You've earned them!

- *Keep a positive attitude.* Studies prove that, if you repeat to yourself negative feelings about a subject, you increase your chances of failing. Since we all want to succeed, replace the negative thoughts with positive ones. For example, replace "I can't do it" with "It's not easy, but I am tough and I accept this challenge." Prove you can, and you will! This is a self-fulfilling prophecy, as attitude directly affects the memory.

- *Go on an information diet.* Just as we avoid certain foods, we can choose what information not to retain. Extract core concepts, study what you will be tested on, and abbreviate large passages of information into easy-to-digest phrases. This will help you remember.

- *Combine memory techniques.* All of the memory techniques work better when combined. You can overlearn a formula, sing about a famous person, think positive thoughts about subjects, and use sight, sound, and other methods to sharpen your memory.

- *Remember something else.* When you are stuck and can't remember, think of something related to the information. For example, if you cannot remember a name, think about what the person did, the period in which they lived, or with whom they associated. Write down what you do know, and soon it will trigger facts that you are trying to recall. This technique really works!

- *Note when you don't remember.* If you tried some memory techniques that do not seem to work, it's all right. Experiment with other techniques, and use what is best for you, not what works for a classmate. Be a reporter, get the facts, and find out what works and what doesn't. Congratulate and reward yourself when you do remember.

- *Use it before you lose it.* Information stored in the long-term memory may become difficult to recall if you don't use it. Simply read it, write it, speak about it, and/or apply it. This is especially effective when you have to recall formulas or facts from a previous course. Retain all notes, and keep the information fresh with a review.

- *Affirmation of your good memory helps you to remember.* When you are sharp and recall all the facts, accept compliments! When you do not recall the facts, take a little time, think hard, then relax and the facts will come to you. You may have to use various techniques to help you remember, but never give up. You truly never forget. Those facts will eventually come to you. If not, keep studying, try again, and they will!

Understand the Uniform Code of Military Justice (UCMJ) and the discipline process. As an officer you will be expected to clearly understand how to encourage and maintain discipline in your subordinates. The best primer is reading the UCMJ and conferring with a staff judge advocate on the finer details of the military discipline system. There is a time and a place to implement discipline. In an effort to administer the appropriate level of discipline, you must know the extremes and limits under which to operate. The UCMJ outlines the discipline system for the armed services. Take advantage of your legal office, and get to know the ins and outs of this important document.

Volunteer for at least one project two levels higher annually than you are assigned. Each year you will hear of many tasks that come down from headquarters for which they are looking for volunteers. Raise your hand and take on these challenges and new opportunities, because they will teach you valuable organizational skills, introduce you to the critical skill of staffing and coordinating, expose you to networking, and give you a rare chance to interact with senior officers. Remember it is not who you know, but who knows you. By doing well on one of these large projects, the experience will offer you potential future opportunities to take on duties with greater responsibility.

Taking on big projects will assist in honing your professional skills and learning administrative techniques that will serve you in the future. Ask your supervisor to submit you for officer of the quarter/year whenever possible. Your goal is to separate yourself from the rest of your peers. Be a standout from the pack!

What better way to do this than taking on the toughest duties early on in your career. You need to come in to work early and plan on leaving late. You should learn to read to comprehend. You need to become an expert in your craft. That translates into knowing the whys and whens of your profession. You are going to have to consult with SNCOs and officers with much more experience than you to learn the finer points of your profession. Conduct comparison analysis with other installations and similar units to see how they conduct business, and draw from this experience.

Your supervisor is critical to your future success, so this officer has to be made aware of your skills and talents. Having your supervisor recognize you by nominating you ahead of your peers will help you solidify a place for future advancement. Complete your master's degree as soon as possible. You don't want to wait for someone to tell you that you need to go back to school. You need to already process the initiative, drive, and professionalism to discipline yourself to return back to school. Returning to school is a lot easier today than ever before. You have available to you tuition assistance that will pay up to 75 percent of your tuition. With the number of online courses, there is no excuse for not completing your education, regardless of the number of hours you work and your extensive deployments.

Taking classes while deployed will allow you to take advantage of your time away from home and focus on something important that will serve you well in your future. Having a master's degree will increase future employment options when you have completed your first tour and you're trying to decide on whether you are going to remain in the military or become a civilian. Without this degree, your options are tremendously diminished. As soon as you complete your basic training, you should set your sights on working on your master's degree. Most master's degrees require thirty-six credit hours or more. This degree will give you the finishing touches of professionalism. You will be required to write papers and read hundreds of pages on a weekly basis. Be prepared to dedicate a minimum of twenty hours per week to be successful.

Do not sacrifice your family for the mission. Some senior leaders may disagree with this philosophy, so make up your own mind. It is vitally important that your spouse and children clearly understand and appreciate what you do in the military and support you in making the daily sacrifices that will be required. The mission of your unit is vitally important and will get done with or without you. Before you were assigned, your unit operated efficiently, and it will continue once you are reassigned elsewhere.

There is nothing more important than your family, so take time out and cherish this blessing. When your son or daughter has a recital or school play, or some other special event, schedule time off and plan on attending, it will mean the world to your children, and it should be the world to you. As your children grow older, your presence will instill confidence and pride in them, and provide lasting memories for the rest of your life.

Eventually, your children will grow up, and if you were rarely around during their formative years, it may play out in adverse behavior or poor grades in school. You need to take time out to spend with your spouse, as well. Schedule a date at least once per month and do something special. Great relationships are established by developing lasting memories. In order to remain in a healthy and happy relationship, you have to keep your relationship alive and ensure your spouse knows that you love her. One old saying is "If you want to remain married, you have to act like you're married." Your military career will most likely cause you to deploy several times during your first five years. In order to successfully survive this episode, you must have a great relationship with your family. You can't perform at your maximum level if you have severe personal challenges at home. The military wants you to be successful, and the best way to do that is to keep your family matters in order. If you take care of your family, then you will also take care of your career.

Get involved with the community. The communities in which you reside and work are vital to the success of your installation. Make it a point to join various civic organizations and positively contribute to the health and welfare of your community. Military officers have a long and rich legacy of supporting community organizations and making a positive impact while assigned. Research your local Big Brothers, Big Sisters organization, chamber of commerce, Masons, Shriners, Rotary, school advisory committees, parent booster clubs, or local youth team.

Make yourself stand out in the community by getting involved. Most communities are lacking young, energetic, honest men and women who are willing to contribute to local organizations. Volunteerism is not as prevalent as it once was. You will find community leaders eager to accept your talents and will put you quickly to work. Another added benefit of supporting local communities is creating a positive image for the military and expanding your professional skills.

Join professional organizations. Joining professional organizations will keep you abreast of modern advancements in your profession. It will provide a network of like-minded professionals all trying to make a name for themselves and sharing the latest and greatest in your career field. Most professional organizations publish a journal that will assist you with benchmark material that can be used as a template in refining your core professional knowledge. Synchronizing your skills and talents with civilian professionals will make you legendary in your pursuits.

Attend trade shows and conventions to expose you to new career updates. Read journals of experiments and surveys that are being conducted to determine if there are applications that are relevant to your duties. Being a part of an organization larger than your traditional circle will only assist in your further development. Make it a point to know the industry leaders and which companies are major shakers. Learn which companies are operating in the global market and what share of the market they control. Go as far as writing articles for your professional trade journal, sharing highlights of how your unit is contributing to your profession. Ensure you gain approval from your commander and public affairs office before submitting your article for publication.

Join Toastmasters within the first five years of service. There is no other training in your professional career that will serve you more than learning how to speak in public. Toastmasters is an international organization that teaches people how to control themselves while speaking publicly. It hones your organizational skills and teaches you delivery tactics, how to control and energize your audience, and most importantly how to get over any internal fears you may harbor about public speaking.

## Speaking Tips

- Prepare your speech. Take time to research the topic on which you are going to speak. In an effort to ward off potential questions about your topic, you need to know associated issues concerning your topic. Know your facts!
- Know your audience beforehand.
- Get plenty of rest the night before your speaking engagement.
- Dress appropriately.
- Speak loud and clear.
- Be concise. People tend to remember the content from shorter speeches than they do longer ones.
- Have a brief introduction and logical conclusion prepared.
- Know your subject matter or topic inside and out.
- Make eye contact with your audience.
- Use your hands to emphasize important points.

## Social Training

When you were a young child, your mother would always remind you which fork to use and, if you visited someone's house, to always be on your best behavior. It is important to remember these traits, because your image and reputation may depend on it. While in the military, you will be invited to several senior officers' houses for dinner or social events, and it is vitally important that you remember those little lessons your mother taught you. If you forgot, here are a few reminders when dining.

## Dining

- Always present a tip consisting of 15 to 20 percent of your meal. It is important to reward your server for good service. Your tip should be based on the before-tax subtotal.
- There are three types of dinners: family Style (all meal items on the table and passed from individual to individual), buffets (a smorgasbord of food from which to choose), and formal dinners (served already plated). For formal, semiformal, or coat-and-tie/dress events, do not wear jeans or sandals. Menu cards will be on the table.
- Before you leave, always say good-bye to the host/hostess.
- For military functions, stay until the event is over, if possible. Or at least stay long enough to mingle with all guests present.

## Professional Image

- The higher ranking or position of prominence is called first because the other person is being introduced to them. "General Smith, I would like to introduce to you my mother, Lieutenant Colonel Julia Green."
- A man is always introduced to a woman. "Gloria, I'd like you to meet my cousin Danny."
- A young person is always introduced to an older person. "Grandma, may I introduce to you my girlfriend, Cheryl."
- A less prominent person is always introduced to a more prominent person. "Professor Johnson, meet my nephew Robert."
- Handshakes should always be done with a firm grip but not a vise grip. Place name tags on your right so that you can easily read them when shaking hands.
- Hold your drink in your left hand. To start conversation, ask general questions, and speak with as many people as possible.
- At sporting events, exercise good manners; do not throw objects;

do not use disparaging terms, words, or phrases; and keep your gestures clean.

- While traveling or on temporary duty, be aware of and respect cultural differences, do not offend with language or gestures, and obey local customs.

## Common Courtesies (Being a Guest)

- Always RSVP by the date requested.
- Adhere to the dress code.
- Respect others' property; don't snoop!
- Do not smoke in the home, and don't excuse yourself to smoke.
- Always thank the host/hostess.
- Follow house rules.
- Help around the house.
- Use appropriate language.
- Dress conservatively.
- Send a thank-you note within forty-eight hours after the event, thanking the host or hostess for inviting you.

Don't ever forget your spirituality. This book is not a religious book, nor does it attempt to sway you toward a particular religion. However, most blacks will agree that if it was not for God's grace we would not be allowed the freedoms and opportunities available today. With the many obstacles our ancestors had to overcome, one must marvel at the tenacity, drive, and determination they required to keep on keeping on. Successfully navigating through life without being lynched, raped, or mobbed required a certain type of skill. When you read about how Benjamin O. Davis Jr. was silenced during his years at West Point, you have to wonder how he made it. Only by the grace of God do any of us survive. All good things come from above, and the Heavenly Father deserves all the praise and recognition for your continued success.

As you walk into your next training session or staff meeting, look around the room and determine if you are the only black officer. Say a prayer that your peers and supervisors don't look at you only as a black officer but as a competent professional who has something positive to contribute. Remember your spirituality, because you will find that you are going to need it when you don't have anyone else. There will be times in your career when things are just going great. This is the time to say a big "Thanks you, Jesus!" There will also be times when things are not going your way and you find yourself in over your head. Find it in yourself to again say, "Thank you, Jesus!" If you don't have tough times or down periods in your life, you won't really appreciate those great periods. What would life be if there were no challenges? Your spirituality empowers you to accomplish anything you set your mind to. With God on your side, who can be against you? There is nothing you cannot achieve. Knowing whom you serve and for whom you are working makes life so much easier. Being spiritually grounded puts things in perspective, and you will find yourself smiling when others are frowning or beside themselves.

Keep your focus, and realize whom you belong to and, most importantly, whom you serve. So when things are not going your way at work, look at your peers and supervisors, smile, and just say, "Thank you, Jesus!"

Be cautious in raising the race card. It is too easy to say that you are being treated a certain way because you are black or that your boss doesn't like you because you are a few shades darker. Just because things are not going your way does not mean it is because of your race. Keep an open mind and critically analyze what is going on. Seek out advice from your mentor, senior officers, and SNCOs on your installation. Sometimes it is important to talk to someone in a different unit to gain a fresh perspective on matters.

When you constantly use the race card you will develop a reputation for being a chronic complainer or not being a team player. Just because things are not working out for you or you did not get selected for a certain assignment does not mean that your supervisor or commander is prejudiced. You may not have the skills required to accomplish a certain thing or your timing is off.

You may not be in the right place at the appropriate time, or you may just have an adverse attitude and your boss wants to take more time in mentoring and developing you. Most senior officers and SNCOs know the discrimination and harassment rules better than you and understand the penalties of committing such a crime. The armed forces have strict policies against discrimination and, if found guilty, will uphold the strictest punishment possible. If you feel you are being discriminated against, after receiving counseling, seek out the inspector general to lodge your official complaint. Be sure you have all your facts documented over a period of time and can prove your allegation.

As mentioned earlier, it is just too easy to list an adverse action as being discriminatory. Work to find the win-win solution, and learn to work within the guidelines of your service. There is nothing more important than securing a good reputation and being known for fair treatment and a bright and energetic attitude. If you are professionally competent and exhibit an insatiable thirst for knowledge, you will find yourself being nominated and recommended for more duties than you can handle.

Embrace your race by being the best that you possibly can be. The promotion system is designed to recognize competent officers who exhibit professionalism and impeccable integrity. This has to become your way of life; if not, you will not be successful, and it is not because of your race!

Drink responsibly. Have no more than two drinks at any social event. Tradition has made alcohol into what seems an integral part of the military social setting. You must, however, behave in a fashion that illustrates you are not drinking to get drunk, even if this was your habit while in college. Drink to refresh yourself. Make it an internal rule that you are not going to allow yourself to get drunk in public. If you do, it can very likely mean the end of your career. Every safety briefing you receive will caution you against the horrors and penalties of drinking and driving, so take heed! If you are out for any engagement or military function, you need to find a suitable substitute for alcohol. Suggestions are tonic water, juice, or soda. Drinking alcohol needs to be reserved for the privacy of your home or that special dinner.

As an officer you are now a member of an elite group that controls your life on and off duty. If you cannot control your off-duty behavior, then you will not find tenure as a military officer. The best thing to do when going out, if you plan on drinking, is to plan for success by having a designated driver. You need to ensure that you use the buddy plan every time you decide to go out. Some of the best-made plans are spoiled when your buddy decides to engage in drinking or you succumb to having more than you intended.

There is no bigger killer to a career than a DUI or drinking irresponsibly. Most people lose their inhibitions when under the influence of alcohol. Don't put yourself in this situation. Control your destiny by living responsibly and placing limits on how many drinks you are willing to consume. Good luck, and live responsibly!

## Sage Advice

### Lieutenant Colonel Avis Headen III, USAF
Setting Priorities: Mission, Prepare for the Fight, Learn, Love, and Leave a Legacy (MPL-3)

- *The mission has to be job number one.* We must do whatever it takes to accomplish our mission. We stand ready to pay the ultimate price for ensuring our mission is met. Prepare for the fight. The most basic requirement of preparing for the fight is maintaining physical fitness and keeping your human weapon system "fit for the fight." Are you physically fit?
- *Learn.* Excellence is enhanced by reading and enriching yourself and your family with different experiences. I challenge you to learn more about your profession by reading professional journals, completing appropriate professional military education, and attending courses in your field of expertise. Then, I challenge you to stretch beyond your comfort zone and learn about something with which you are unfamiliar—a new culture, a new hobby, or an influential person from our past or present. The pursuit of excellence and commitment to lifelong learning strengthens your self-confidence and better prepares you for leading. Try to know what you don't already know!
- *Love.* Lots of lip service is given to the word "love," especially as we

get closer to holidays. Dr. Stephen Covey, author of *Seven Habits of Highly Effective People*, states that the word "love" is a verb. We all need to understand and employ this concept. The feeling of love can only be realized by taking action and demonstrating your love for a person. In time, you realize the fruit of love (the feeling). You cannot possibly show your children you love them without participating in their lives. So I plead with you to make loving your family a priority. Plan ahead (notify your chain well in advance) to attend soccer games, plays, and important events in your children's, spouse's, and significant other's lives. You will never regret taking the time to show them your love. That being said, there will inevitably be times when you are not able to make one of their activities, due to mission requirements. For this I apologize. When everything is said and done, remember you will come back to these important people. My prayer for you is that they will welcome you with open arms and have no regrets about your service to our great nation.

- *Leave a legacy.* I have had the opportunity to work for many commanders in my twenty-year career. There is always one thing that separates the average commander from the extraordinary commander: vision. The good ones always knew where they wanted the unit to be in two to five years, and they eventually got there, leaving positive can-do troops to carry on the legacy of excellence. Figure out how you can contribute to the vision and where you want to be in two, five, or twenty years, and write this down! This is called your legacy statement or vision. Reference your legacy daily or, at the very least, weekly. Remember always this is your map to excellence. Trust your map, and never chase the issue of the day.

## Captain Avonne D. Rosario, USAF

- You are part of the world's greatest and most powerful military. There are people who would love to be where you are right now. Appreciate that fact, if nothing else.
- Know your job. Do your homework (reading regulations and

policy letters, etc.). People may not like you, but they can't say that you don't know your job.

- Accept challenges. We learn from our scar tissue, not by obtaining trophies.

# CHAPTER 4
## STRIVING FOR PERFECTION

As for God, His way is perfect; the word of the Lord is proven; He is a shield to all who trust will Him.

—Psalm 18:30

It's better to be prepared for all opportunity and not have one, than to have all opportunity and not be prepared.

—Whitney M. Young Jr., Civil Rights Activist

I was raised to believe that excellence is the best deterrent to racism or sexism. And that's how I operate my life.

—Oprah Winfrey, 1989

American citizens expect military officers to be the persona of perfection and professionalism, be in good physical shape, and have above-average intelligence. Immediately, after taking your oath of commissioning, you do not instantly become this superhuman of professionalism, nor are you expected to know everything about your assigned career field. The military will provide the necessary training required of you in the finer points of officership, military strategy, and history. You will eventually become the professional military expert America demands of you after years of honing your skills and working alongside other professionals with similar experiences.

Your initial basic officer training will introduce you to the many tenets of officership (e.g., how to salute, understanding your chain of command, marching, basic military traditions, etc.), which includes wearing the uniform. You need to pay close attention to everything being introduced, because it will become the foundation of learning new and more complex concepts in the future. You will be given minor responsibilities, and you will be exposed to stress in very unique ways. After succeeding at these minor tasks, you will be given additional tasks that will stretch your imagination and challenge your talents. All of these experiences are intended to introduce you to new concepts and to ensure your transition from civilian to military officer is successful.

There are several new concepts and organizational structures that will be initially introduced. Many of these new concepts have been tested and tried over years and are in place to ensure you are able to think on your feet, take orders, and act properly without hesitation or doubt. It is during this hesitation, that millisecond of doubt, that can cost you or one of your comrades his life. As a military officer you will be expected to make clear, conclusive decisions that are sound and well thought out. You will be called on to lead America's youth into combat and return them home without injury. This takes years of training to be successful. You will be sent to challenging schools that will teach specific skills and introduce unique concepts. These training opportunities will enhance your performance and provide you with the confidence needed when the specific talent is required.

As an officer, your integrity is expected to be sincere and reliable. You will be given many chances to test your honesty, and each time you will be expected to shine even brighter. If you fail, you will be potentially labeled and your reputation will follow you to future assignments. Not adhering and completely embracing your service's core values truly is the kiss of death to your career. The US military has a deep tradition immersed in high values and seeks Americans with the highest character and integrity.

The core values of our nation's military are very similar. Each military service is listed below. Most Americans were initially introduced to these values by their parents or grandparents. I like to call them "Grandma values," because they are the types of lessons that your grandmother would teach you when she took you to the corner store and you, unbeknownst to her, picked up a piece of candy. Once brought to her attention, without hesitation she spanked your bottom and made you take it back and pay for it. These traits are reinforced in elementary schools, churches, and civic organizations across our great nation.

The basics of strong moral values start in the home. If your home did not convey these teachings, then hang on to your hat, because the US military is truly steeped in them and they will have to become a part of your everyday life. If you ever spent time in scouting, you will remember being tested in each of these values and receiving merit badges when successfully completing the assigned task. Completely embracing these values is essential if you are going to be successful as an officer. There can never be a time that you relax your values to accommodate personal, professional, or relational gain. *We do not compromise our values for anyone at any time!*

## US Military Core Values

### Air Force
- Integrity First
- Service Before Self
- Excellence in All We Do

### Marine
- Honor
- Courage
- Commitment

### Navy
- Honor
- Courage
- Commitment

### Army
- Loyalty
- Duty

- Respect
- Service
- Honor
- Integrity
- Courage

Most will agree that these values are appropriate for all Americans, especially professionals, to embrace. In some professions these values are merely given lip service and are treated only as a label. In the military they are more than a label or trend; they are the very foundations of leadership and courage, and they demand your total commitment. If you have a hard time with any of these values or cannot completely grasp these concepts, then perhaps a career in the military is not for you.

As you closely examine our armed forces' core values, you will see that they are spiritual in nature and influence. These values or traits have a common bond with religious faith in the sense that they inspire and mandate the individual to be a good and decent citizen and neighbor with admirable qualities. The military is a secular organization with spiritual values. You will find that many civilian organizations embrace spiritual values. This commonality allows God's fingerprint to be embedded on our military and the way that we carry ourselves. Most will agree that God is involved in everything. Our military is no different. Aligning your personal values with God's spiritual values will ensure your success.

If you are committed to becoming a military professional you will quickly realize that you belong to a special breed of people and that a career in the military is a calling, not merely a profession. You will be called to put your life and the lives of those people assigned to you on the line. This is an awesome responsibility and one that should not be taken lightly. If you have any doubts, then the best thing for you to do is to start your separation papers as soon as possible.

As your rank and responsibilities increase, more demands will be placed on you, and your noncommittal attitude can have serious adverse consequences. Possessing these core values is just the beginning. You need to ensure that you have the traits expected of an officer. You need to dress as an officer or person of responsibility and be a person of good character and accountability both on and off duty. Remember you are always on parade!

As an officer you need to maintain a neat and professional appearance. You need to ensure you are properly groomed, cleaned, and dressed conservatively when in civilian attire. While in military uniform you need to ensure your hair is cut to military standards and your uniform is clean, properly fitted, and outfitted with proper military insignias. Boots or low-quarter shoes need to be highly shined and presentable. If you're wearing camouflage or the battle dress uniform, then they need to be cleaned and properly fitted. No one should ever have to tell you that you are not within standards. Consistently exceeding standards is tough to achieve yet will be expected in every forum and venue you will find yourself.

Stephen Covey states that the most successful people, including military officers, need to live a principle-centered life. Principle-centered living means living with a sense of purpose, by including honesty in your daily living, making thoughtful and productive decisions, and seeking win-win solutions to confrontations and problems. By embracing this lifestyle you often eliminate superficial and trivial problems that many encounter. If you do encounter problems, you are equipped with the balance and know-how of resolving issues in an expeditious and thorough manner.

Immaturity and naive perspectives will sometime cloud your judgment and hamper your ability to make sound decisions. You will often find yourself as the only African American assigned to your unit or attending certain meetings. As you continue to get promoted and climb the ladder of success, you will find yourself being surrounded by white officers. Do not fret or become uneasy. Realize that you belong there just as much if not more than your colleagues.

Successful African Americans have had to operate in professional environments for generations. You too will be successful if you pay close attention to what is going on around you and, more importantly, learn your job. Job competence cannot be overstated. It is essential to military success.

It is universally assumed that military officers possess the highest integrity, and your performance consistently exhibits excellence in everything you do. Society looks to the military officer as the standard when it comes to high ethics and morals. When young officers initially confirm the oath of office, they rarely think of the true meaning of being a professional officer.

Below Lieutenant Colonel Richardson, USAF, a combat veteran pilot with over three thousand flying hours offers critical, sound, and timeless advice to his subordinates. If these tenets are completely embraced, it will surely lead to your success. If not, then you will have a difficult time adjusting to military life. Sit back and listen to his sage wisdom!

The first step to becoming a military officer is to graduate from college. Following are a few words of advice for achieving this goal. If prospective students were to ask me for advice as they are preparing for college, I would first of all tell them to start the preparation process early. By this, I mean that they should start ensuring that they develop themselves according to the "whole person" concept well before their senior year.

Next, I would encourage them to find someone in life who is where they want to be, and do what they did to get there. Recruit that person's help if at all possible. Next, I would let them know that the most valuable asset they can bring to college is the determination to succeed. They will experience obstacles, but it's their response and reaction to those obstacles that will determine their eventual success or failure. Finally, I would encourage them to get connected to the resources that are at their disposal at the earliest opportunity. Colleges are typically not in the business of seeing how high they can get their attrition rates. Once you get accepted into a college, it is sometimes harder to get out than it was to get in. To fail out of a college academically, one must intentionally ignore all of the well-meaning instructors, counselors, centers, and organizations that are in place to ensure their success. The sooner the new college freshman learn to build their web of support around them, the sooner they will realize that a threefold cord is not quickly broken. The single thread that tries to exist and succeed on its own is easily snapped.

What I went through to get into and succeed in my college experience is a testament to the fact that despite the roadblocks one may find, there always a way to succeed and reach your educational dreams. Whether meeting obstacles during the application process, student support services, personal or interpersonal relationships, or the curriculum, there are always people and resources around that are dedicated to the person who refuses to quit.

Have a mission and vision statement that resonates with the defined purpose and people within. Your organization lays our expectations that they can expect from you and that you expect from them. Let them know early on what you like and dislike. Here's an example....

## Seven Standards I Expect from You

1. *Maximize your potential across the board with high standards of professionalism.* Mediocrity did not get you into this fine institution. Do not accept it for yourself, and don't let your buddy accept it either. A squadron is only as strong as its weakest link. No weak links entered the academy, and none should graduate from it. This experience, like all of life, is what you make of it. The more you put into it, the more it returns back to you.

2. *Be your brother's or sister's keeper.* The concept of looking out for each other is part of the profession of arms. This is not always a pleasant

task. Sometimes it involves taking the car keys instead of just asking for them. The ability to do this is what binds us together as brothers and sisters in arms.

3. *Balance loyalty.* A "buddy" who asks you to compromise your integrity and ruin your character may not be a true buddy at all. Your oath was to your branch of service and nation. Be a person of your word. Character and integrity are not on sale at Wal-Mart. You can't just go pick up another batch once you've lost them. Think about it.

4. *Foster mutual respect for each person in the squadron.* Everyone has redeeming values. Our military values the gifts, talents, and abilities of each of its members. The Golden Rule should govern your treatment of others. Treat them like you'd want to be treated. Take the time to know, appreciate, and affirm the worth, value, and importance of discrimination of any kind.

5. *Encourage unity, teamwork, and participation.* These are oils that keep the machine running. They are central to esprit de corps and high morale. Foster them and make them a key part of your squadron's identity.

6. *Know what you should know. Do what you should do.* Ignorance is no excuse. Know, live, and enforce all standards.

7. *Know the difference between a mistake and premeditated wrongdoing.* Turning around quickly and knocking over a vase is a mistake. Feeling sorry for getting caught when doing something that you knew was wrong is not. Don't confuse the two, because I certainly won't.

## Seven Standards You Can Expect from Me

1. *Provide the vision, and set the environment.* "Where there is no vision, the people perish" (Proverbs 29:18). I will ensure that my vision is clear and that our mission is defined. Enforcing high standards of excellence across the board, as well as cultivating a deep mutual respect for everyone

in our organization, is critical to creating the environment necessary to accomplish our mission and fulfill our vision. My core definition of a leader is one who removes the barriers that keep you from maximizing your potential. You can expect that, as a commander, my primary focus will be to remove the barriers that keep us from accomplishing our mission and fulfilling our vision.

2. *I provide a balanced example of officership in all areas of life.* I am a happily married man with three wonderful children. I go to church regularly and love to camp, ski, fish, and work out at the gym. You will see all facets of my life as a commander. I will not simply be a figure behind a computer monitor.

3. *Focus on leadership development.* Leadership development, to me, involves giving you the freedom to fail and make mistakes. I won't let you fall off the end of the earth in your decision making, but I might let you get close a time or two.

4. *I maintain loyalty to my superiors and my military branch's mission.* I took an oath just like you did. I am committed to keeping that oath. I trust my superiors, and you can expect that I will be loyal to them. I'm not a yes-man, because that's not what they were looking for when they hired me. My superiors encourage my input and value my ideas, but once the decision is made and the command given, I am a "yes, sir" man, because that's the mark of a true military professional.

5. *Mistakes are a part of being human.* The only people who don't make them are dead. I will make them, and so will you. The military is not a one-mistake organization. In some cases making a mistake can be costly, and even considered a crime. When mistakes happen, the best thing we can do is to own up to them, make restitution when we can, and then move on.

6. *Empowerment is key.* The privilege of your command and leadership opportunities comes with responsibility and accountability. You have

the ideas about what it takes to fix what's wrong. I will not do your job for you, but I will equip and empower you to succeed and hold you responsible and accountable.

7. *Operational focus in my approach to mentorship.* We are members of the number-one military force in the history of the world during a time when our nation is at war. That is my focus, and it will come through every time we interact.

## Seven Deadly Sins

With the following seven items, if committed, you can expect the hammer to fall. I want to make it clear that these behaviors will not be tolerated. Without exception, you fully know how grave these infractions are. Of course, I will obtain a full and complete investigation of all of the facts and circumstances involving each incident and react accordingly, but the best thing you can do is to steer clear of these items entirely. You have been warned!

1. *Alcohol and drug incidents.* Illegal drug and steroid use, to include the unauthorized use of prescription medication, is a crime and will be dealt with accordingly. Alcohol abuse often leads to criminal behavior. Think smart, act safely, and manage risks *always*!

2. *Discrimination.* Our military has zero tolerance for this type of behavior. Our strength is in our diversity.

3. *Sexual harassment.* No one can perform effectively in a hostile environment. We have to be at the leading edge of eradicating this cancer from our culture.

4. *Integrity issues.* Say what you mean, and mean what you say. This is basic to leadership.

5. *Dereliction of duty.* Be where you're supposed to be, when you're supposed to be there, doing what you're supposed to be doing.

6. *Failure to go.* Read number five again.

7. *Toleration of wrongdoing.* The ability to keep each other on the right track is central to succeeding in the military culture.

## Seven Basic Responses I Love to Hear

1. "Sir, I made a mistake."
2. "Sir, I have an idea."
3. "Sir, I can help with that."
4. "Sir, I need your help."
5. "Sir, let me repeat that back to you so that I'm sure I understand."
6. "Sir, I'm prepared to take responsibility for my actions."
7. "Sir, I think this would be really fun."

## Seven Pet Peeves

1. *Weasels* improperly use legal hairsplitting of words to justify wrongdoing. If you mess up, own up to it like a true professional.

2. *Hermit crabs* hide when they see me coming. I'll be out and about, visiting where you work, eat, and play. I'll bring my open-door policy to you.

3. *Piranhaa* eat up and destroy others to advance themselves. You won't score any points with me this way. Teamwork makes the dream work!

4. *Sloths* are lazy and apathetic. Do your full duty. Laziness and apathy are contagious cancers that will destroy our unit.

5. *Crazy owls* ask "why" (instead of "who"). Ask "why" for clarification, not as a form of rebellion.

6. *Mangy dogs* are ragged in appearance and disposition. Take pride in your uniform, and allow that pride to shine through. You're part of a noble profession.

7. *Venomous snakes* are deceitful and dishonest. Don't tell me it's food designed to make me wise when you know it'll get me kicked out of the garden.

And here are some creatures worth emulating.

## Seven "Commander's Pets"

1. The *eagle* is the symbol of a dependable, agile, daring, and faithful conqueror. The freedoms we enjoy are worth protecting. In the air force, second best is not an option.

2. The *ant* is the smallest of creatures, but an ant can carry things many times its weight. Always remember: if your dreams are big enough, the facts don't count.

3. The *rhino* doesn't run from the threat. It charges and defeats it. Leaders of character charge toward what's right and make their stand. If you don't stand for something, you'll fall for anything.

4. The *beaver* is the most industrious of creatures, dedicated to its cause. Build bridges; don't destroy them. Build legacies; don't destroy them. Build people; don't destroy them.

5. The *giraffe* reaches to the top of the tree and ignores the low-hanging fruit. Any loser can grab the low-hanging fruits of mediocrity and failure. Winners stretch themselves and reach high for the gold standard of integrity, service, and excellence.

6. The *bumblebee*, aerodynamically, shouldn't be able to fly, but nobody ever told it, so it flies. Don't make excuses as to why you can't achieve. Have a goal, and persevere.

7. The *falcon* is the world's fastest bird. It is majestic, magnificent, powerful, and full of dignity. You are members of the best military in the world. Be your best to keep us the best!

My mentors exist on the personal and professional side. My most personal mentors are my parents. My father is an inspiration because he has achieved enormous success as an entrepreneur. My mother is an inspiration because she has achieved her goal of getting her GED and continues to be strong, loving, and giving. I believe I have adapted well to life because of the influence of family, culture, and, most importantly, my Christian faith and values.

My mother's determination to keep our family together when we were young has made a profound impression on me, as it relates to keeping my family together today. I think that I can confidently say that this family-of-origin priority was passed down from her. I am very pro-family in that I will try to maximize my time with them instead of putting in a few extra minutes at the office. If given the choice of them over my career, my career would be a distant second.

As it relates to relationships, most of my life, I've been pretty much a loner. That's one big reason I did not date much. My wife has become my best friend and someone who I am privileged to let know every detail of my life. She shares my ups and downs, as well as my hopes and dreams. She has helped me to develop a life of intimacy that far exceeds the drudgery of a life of isolation.

Marriage has proven to be a phenomenal experience. The reality of my relationship with my wife and the wonderful children we have has far exceeded my wildest expectations. She is not just my best friend; she is the most wonderful person I've ever met. Our children are absolutely mind-boggling. To this day I still stare at them in disbelief that I could have something to do with such amazing creatures. My dream for them is that they will maximize the wonderful potential God has given to each of them. We have already begun saving money for their college education. This is something that we feel fortunate to be able to do. Hopefully this will enable them to start their lives with more of a leg up than I had. My values are God, family, and then everything else. I received this precious perspective as a gift from my family of origin. This axiom has affected my contribution to my family at all levels. My Christian faith is where I find my esteem and identity. My roles as a husband and father far exceed any other role I have. They make my past make sense and my future worth living. I firmly believe that the next chapters of my life will be more valuable and worthwhile because of what I received from my family of origin and because of what I've learned while serving in the military.

Lieutenant Colonel Richardson has served as a squadron commander and will be a senior leader in the air force in the coming years. Being selected to command a unit is the highest privilege an officer can achieve. Being legally responsible for people and resources is an enormous opportunity and should not be taken lightly at any point during your career. As a commander you will be trusted with the awesome responsibility of supervision, mentorship, training, and equipping the professional men and women of your unit. Apparently, you have demonstrated the professional competence, trustworthiness, integrity, vision, and potential for leadership during your career. All of these traits will serve you well in executing your duties as commander.

One senior leader once stated, "To hold on to your hat, you are getting on the wildest ride of your life!" The largest compliment an officer can receive is being selected to command. Command is a special honor, and those few officers receiving this privilege should not take it for granted and should make the most of each opportunity while executing their authority. As a commander you have the direct responsibility of challenging everyone assigned to achieve new heights and molding them into the best officers and NCOs they can possibly be. The challenges you will face will be as diverse as each person assigned. As the commander you are charged with the responsibility of accomplishing the mission by motivating each troop in completing your vision.

The duties of a commander are an awesome task. There is nothing more fulfilling and satisfying than assisting those within your command to accomplish their personal and professional goals. Being a unit commander allows you the opportunity to fulfill your professional vision for your unit by creating realistic goals and hard-hitting objectives. Every organization needs improving, and it should be your goal as the commander to identify those unit shortcomings and develop a fix-it plan by delegating essential tasks to responsible subordinates.

As a new commander you are not expected to know everything,

but with the assistance of your staff and fellow peer commanders, you will have the support to complete any mission requirement assigned. Commanders need to be organized and professionally competent. Typically, commanders have at least five to eight years of experience before being selected to this prestigious position.

Command at each level is more challenging than the previous level. To accomplish your expectations and ensure success, your vision needs to be clear, concise, and based on principle-centered goals. Stephen Covey, author of *Principle-Centered Leadership,* clearly defines the tenets of leadership based on achieving excellence for everyone involved in the process. Win-win solutions should be sought in confronting controversial issues and not terminated with matters that leave one holding the short end. Unit goals should be well thought out and communicated to the lowest levels to create collective buy-in. It is important for everyone assigned to have a clear understanding of what the unit standards and expectations are. All standards and expectations should be aligned with the commander's vision and unit mission.

The commander should take time during commander calls or other official functions to recognize subordinates that positively support the mission and make both professional and personal accomplishments. Recognizing subordinates is one of the greatest benefits and joys of a commander. Presenting awards and recognizing personal accomplishments build unit morale and pride. The commander builds his professional reputation and expands his influence by showing humility, respect, and admiration for those individuals successfully accomplishing the mission.

As a commander you are responsible for both the discipline and morale of the unit. With the high operational tempo (OPSTEMPO) of most units and rapid deployment responsibility, maintaining good morale and low discipline problems is difficult, to say the least. It would be too easy to spend most of your time with discipline problems and wayward subordinates, and not focusing on the mission or recognizing those subordinates who are making a positive impact.

Many commanders will admit that they spend about 40 to 50 percent of their time with only 10 percent of their troops. These 10 percent are those who have personal issues and cause the unit constant frustrations. As a commander you need to learn to rely on your first sergeant and other senior NCOs to deal with these problem subordinates. Most issues of a personal nature can be resolved at a much lower level than the commander. The commander needs to be made aware and remain informed of all issues within the unit, yet delegate as much as possible to qualified senior staff members to free you for more taxing and complicated issues.

There is nothing more satisfying than watching your unit grow into a fine-tuned, combat-ready unit that clearly understands its mission and how it fits into the total battle plan. Getting your unit to this level takes strategic planning and accurate execution. Your focus needs to be on communicating up and down your chain of command. Subordinates need to know that they have a boss who clearly understands his or her duty and has the respect of the installation's senior leadership.

The commander has many issues to balance and must find the right level of involvement. Only the well-seasoned commander can accomplish all that is tasked and make it look easy. Possessing this level of calmness takes strong organization skills and a conscious communication effort. Your supervisor needs to have the confidence in you that you are professionally competent, have the admiration of your subordinates, and are willing to take the calculated risk to complete the mission.

The unit commander should have the compassion of knowing how to respond to subordinates' personal issues and problems. A commander needs to know the strengths and weaknesses of his key staff. If your people have personal problems, it may prohibit them from focusing on accomplishing the mission. For example, it is good for the commander to know how many children his key staff has, or whether key subordinates are having marital problems, if higher education is a personal goal, as well as personal hobbies and goals being pursued. These issues allow commanders the opportunity to get to know the personal side of their key staff. This may prove essential when assigning important critical tasks, because it allows the ability to play to people's strengths.

There are several books written on leadership, and this should be one you put in your professional library. There are many leadership styles that are popular, and each is appropriate at certain times. Knowing when to use these various styles is essential when directing your troops to accomplish a task or attempting to influence them in a controversial matter. Many have described successful or effective leadership as the art of influencing people in accomplishing something the masses normally would not do without your input.

Leadership is having the talent, technical know-how, respect, and, most importantly, the professionalism to effectively manage and operate an organization. It takes a unique talent to develop the confidence and respect of your troops immediately. To build this type of reputation you must know your strengths and weaknesses. You must become a master communicator, be confident in your abilities, and not mind admitting your faults. You must be willing to sacrifice your personal time for the sake and good of the mission and unit, be compassionate about finding tough and accurate solutions to complex problems, be willing to take the blame for others' mistakes, and be humble enough to pass credit to your people for doing a good job. Many would say that a leader with all of these traits is impossible to find, but if you look really closely you will find that, although rare, this person does exist, and it might be you!

A military officer is the American example of moral courage, physical fitness, impeccable integrity, and deep wisdom. In order to hone these skills you must pay close attention early in your career. You need to be willing to volunteer for tough assignments and to work long hours when everyone else decides to go home. You must be willing to read everything about your profession that you can get your hands on. You must be willing to study foreign militaries and have a good understanding of their culture and history. It is desirable to speak a foreign language. Speaking a foreign language may prove a benefit if you are ever deployed to another country.

Being a military officer can be difficult at times, and will prove to be challenging because you will be stretched to the limit in a variety of ways. You will receive have many tasks, and you may not know where to start in gathering the solution or answer, but do not fret! Any task you are ever given has a support network that can provide the answer. The real issue is knowing where to find that support network. It is important to develop your own support network of military professionals that will assist you with finding your starting point.

It is critical to join the Company Grade Officers' Council if there is one on your base or post. If there is not one at your installation, then talk to fellow company-grade officers about starting one and select a senior officer to be your adviser. This organization is always a great start in surrounding yourself with other military professionals all striving to learn more about their profession. You will quickly learn that the military and other professional organizations are built around relationships. It is not about who you know, but who knows you! Successful careers are enhanced by having a good reputation and equally strong relationships.

Take time out to collect and learn the biographies of senior leaders on your base. They can serve as a guide in making future career and assignment decisions. No two military officers' careers are exactly the same, but by collecting several biographies you will be able to see the types of jobs and timing of each position of those who came before you. Use this knowledge to design your own assignments, and seek council from local senior leaders.

## Taking Command

As an officer it is your duty to be as professional as possible. If you are ever given the opportunity to command, then take it! Commanding is not a popularity contest, so do not start this job looking to make friends with everyone assigned within your command. One fatal mistake new commanders often make

is initially attempting to win over their subordinates by befriending them with gifts (i.e., always buying pizza, giving excessive time off, or going light on punishment). Initially you may think that you are boosting morale, but in the long run you are only setting yourself up for failure, because you are creating false hopes for many of your troops. Engaging in this type of behavior slowly deteriorates unit morale and may start adverse rumors.

A commander is the legal authority in the military. A commander is the unit's senior leader and should not attempt to be overly concerned about becoming anyone's friend or impressing superiors. Focus on learning the strengths and weaknesses of your unit. Search out whom you can rely on. Every unit has those officers and NCOs who are the backbone of their organization. Look for these individuals, and challenge them by giving them tough assignments. This opportunity will allow the individuals to grow in their profession, as well as enhance their reputation by working on new tasks and confirming their value to the unit.

It is imperative to give recognition when it is due. Create the opportunity to reward hard work, dedication, and innovation. By properly rewarding your troops, you will find them willing to work even harder because you share their accomplishments with both their peers and superiors. As a commander you build unit pride and esteem within your organization by giving yourself to your troops. It is vital for you to remain as professionally involved with your troops as possible. You will find the more time you spend with your troops, the more you will learn about them. They will take advantage of this time by coming to you with their personal problems, as well as keep you informed about what is really going on within the unit.

A commander who spends most of his time behind his desk without interacting with his troops is an ineffective commander. Most organizations within the military operate twenty-four hours per day. It is your duty to take time out and visit those individuals who work the swing and evening shifts. You will find that most of your best workers work the evening shifts and rarely receive the recognition they deserve. They need you to spend just as much time with them as you do in the normal workday.

To increase your effectiveness you need to fully understand the mission's requirement, internalize it, and turn it into your own vision. You will be required to share your vision with your troops so they can execute it. Your primary purpose as commander is to ensure that your troops are successful and can faithfully discharge their duties. It is imperative that you create a successful environment where the mission can be accomplished without interference or hesitation. Additionally, you are the person who supplies the resources to get the job done, including training, so each person clearly knows their expected duties.

One of my graduate instructors once stated, "He who controls the budget controls the future of the organization." This statement remained with me for a long time, because it summarized a very important truth; it pointed out the importance of sound fiscal management. As commander you will be entrusted with a budget, albeit small, but a budget nonetheless. How well you manage that budget and meet your financial obligations, as well as training requirements, will be merely one aspect of your effectiveness as a manager/commander.

Fortunately, you will have assigned a resource adviser (RA) who will be your unit financial manager that is trained on the fundamentals of financial management and budgeting. You should request a monthly update from your RA and limit the amount of funds the RA can approve without your signature. Almost all expenditures over a certain threshold will require your signature. Be on notice that not paying close attention to fiscal matters is one of the quickest ways to ruin your tenure as commander. Your supervisor will expect you to keep him or her informed of fiscal needs and requirements of your unit. Twice per year you should sit with members of your key staff and review expenditures for the year. Your staff will take pride in knowing that they have a say in new acquisitions and purchases.

You have several fellow commanders that you need to meet and make it your professional duty to get to know. Some of those fellow professionals work in military police, medical, personnel, logistics, communications, supply and logistics, the office of the staff judge advocate, and the office of criminal investigations/special investigations. You will find that a personal relationship with these fellow commanders will prove to be invaluable. Offer to take them to lunch and get to know them. You will see them at most meetings that you attend, and you'll be able to develop and solidify your relationship during those brief encounters.

Remember, it is not who you know, but who knows you! Your reputation will precede you in every encounter and endeavor. Your peers and superiors will make assessments about you based on your reputation, even before meeting you. Treasure your reputation and keep it in good standing. Your reputation is only as good as you make it. This means that you need to be on your best behavior all the time. You can never take time off and engage in minor nuisance-type behavior. Your actions and behavior will be scrutinized by everyone. You are always on parade!

## Sage Advice

### 1LT Rakanem Milligan, USAF

- Only you control your career. If you don't do anything you are going to be stuck in a job in which you are not happy. As William E. Henley said in "Invictus," you are the captain of your fate and the master of your soul.
- Education is the key. Use the military tuition assistance program in order to obtain your master's degree. Eventually when you get out you will have something to fall back on and continue to live happily.
- Manage your money. I have a budget sheet that includes my base pay, Basic Allowance for Housing (BAH) and Basic Allowance for Subsistence (BAS). I also include deduction information in my Leave and Earning Statement (LES). Add them up and subtract your expenses. (It's better if you spend a little more on bills that cause the company to carry a credit than to be short on paying your obligations.) You will have an accurate estimate of how much you have in your pocket.
- Network! The more people you know, the much easier it is to do your job.

### Captain Cedric E. Way, USAF

- Continue to ask God for wisdom, knowledge, and the ability to recognize opportunities.
- Be versatile, informed, and prepared for the mission.
- Look for opportunities, and be willing to stretch yourself in order to grow but not to break.

**1LT Isaac A. Wright, USAF**

- Get in the game. Know your job, the rules, and the ways of your service.
- Get an education. Personal improvement is physical, mental, and spiritual.
- Give back in military and community service.

# CHAPTER 5
## WHAT THEY REALLY THINK ABOUT YOU

Yet if any man suffer as a Christian, let him not be ashamed; but let him glorify God on this behalf.

—1 Peter 4:16

Respect commands itself and can neither be given nor withheld when it is due.

—Eldridge Cleaver, 1968

Power at its best is love implementing the demands of justice. Justice at its best is love correcting everything that stands against love.

—Martin Luther King Jr.

White officers have always led and commanded black troops. This is a collection of what they really want to say about you and to you to ensure your success. Listen to what they have to say. You might be surprised. This chapter is a collection of many senior military leaders' thoughts and feelings that put things in perspective for you and about you.

If you are waiting to have a black supervisor or commander, then plan on waiting for a very long time. It is one thing to take pride in having a black commander or supervisor. The primary goal should be to appreciate the wisdom, intelligence, and support your current commander offers, regardless of his race or ethnic background. You see, it really does not matter what race your supervisor or commander may be but how prepared you are to accomplish your mission. It is very likely that you will complete your entire career without ever working directly for an African American or having a commander or supervisor who is black. There are just not enough of us, so get used to it, or do something about it! Get promoted and recruit other black professionals!

White officers have always supervised black troops and always will. The successful African American officers who we admire contribute a large portion of their career's success to white commanders and supervisors. Many young black troops feel that they are not going to receive fair treatment or opportunities to excel in their career if supervised by white officers, but nothing could be further from the truth. White officers want African American troops and all other troops assigned to be as successful as they possibly can be. The primary duty of a commander is to be successful, both in your personal and professional life.

Major General (Ret.) Roosevelt Mercer contributes a lot of his success to white commanding officers who saw talent and potential in him and pointed him in the right direction. General Mercer reports, "Many of these senior officers had plenty of young white officers to choose from, but they chose me and I took these opportunities serious and made the most of each." Hard work and clearly understanding what's expected of you are the keys to success.

Major General Johnny Weida, while commandant at the USAF Academy, said it best: "It is not about the color of one's skin, but how productive one can be! It is about the contributions that each person makes. The primary focus is on mission oriented results!" Today's senior leaders understand the strength of diversity and the power that it brings both to our workplace and the nation as a whole. White commanders' focus is finding the best person for the job. There is an old saying: "It takes more to get you where you want to go than it took you to get where you currently are."

During the 2005 USAF Academy's black history celebration, General Weida in his closing remarks asked for everyone to close their eyes;

Imagine that you were flying a combat mission over North Korea, and while dodging surface to air missiles, you find yourself in trouble and in need of assistance because you have two enemy aircraft on your tail in hot pursuit. Shortly after calling for assistance you see two friendly aircraft swiftly climbing up from behind. These two aircraft quickly engaged the enemy and with precision timing take aim and shoot down one of the enemy aircraft. You still do not know the identity of these skilled pilots, but you are eternally grateful for their presence and amazing skill. You feel a sigh of relief and you return to base safely. You cannot wait to personally thank your wingman, because they saved your bacon! When you finally land you see that your hero is a black pilot, who you have never met, but it really does not matter, all that matters is that this person, this officer was competent when the skills were needed. Open your eyes and see that it really does not matter what color you are, but can you perform? Can you embrace the critical challenges you have been given? If you can, then you are the officer I want to have in my unit, because I can count on you!

Major General Weida's story reminds me of the many stories I have heard firsthand from the Tuskegee Airmen. This story reinforces everything this book is about and was the reason it had to be written. What really counts when holding leadership roles is professional competence and being able to influence the environment with what is needed when it really matters. This is what striving for perfection is all about, and it is the essence of why this book had to be written. I am not sure about you, but throughout my professional military career I never came across a book written and designed to assist African Americans in better understanding the military professional landscape they are operating.

All commanders, regardless of background, want one primary thing, and that is to be successful in accomplishing the mission. They are not concerned about who executes the mission, as long as it is completed thoroughly and without hesitation. Commanders normally make it a point to get personally and professionally involved with their troops because they want to make a positive impact on their lives. Additionally, they typically want to develop trust and respect with everyone assigned within their command so each individual can feel comfortable resolving any issues that may arise.

Brigadier General Dana Born, USAF Academy dean, stated that she works hard to ensure that, first, everyone is treated fairly and, second, the environment is inviting to all. She stated that "the Air Force Academy has a ways to go in getting their faculty to look like the rest of society and representative of the racial diversity in the Air Force, but they are working on it. It is vital that cadets of all races possess a feeling that they can be successful. We make it a point of reducing all barriers that prohibit any cadet from being successful."

Most commanders care deeply about their troops and will do anything to reduce frustrations and chaos in their lives. They are concerned about mentoring and coaching you to be your very best. Commanders normally push their troops toward civilian education, as long as attendance does not conflict or hamper the mission. So what are you waiting for? Start your education today, not tomorrow!

Your tomorrow starts today! Lieutenant General Daniel Leaf, USAF, while vice commander of USAF Space Command, had a passion for motorcycles and reported that, while assigned to the Pentagon, one evening after having dinner in a really nice restaurant he saw a guy ride up with a Harley Davidson motorcycle. As he got closer he could tell that the bike was in perfect condition and that the owner had taken amazing care of this machine. When the motorcycle rider took off his helmet, he could clearly see that the rider was a rather large black man, and he walked up to the man and complimented him on the bike. The two engaged in a long conversation about the motorcycle and then parted. The point that General Leaf makes is that it really did not matter about the race of the two gentlemen, but what they collectively had in common. The motorcycle allowed them to transcend any differences and focus on what was important at the moment: the motorcycle.

General Leaf went on to explain that if society is to cure the racial ills in this country, we need to focus on our commonalities and not our differences.

Many white commanders will shy away from racial issues because of the controversial nature of this topic. They normally do not want to deal with such issues, and they know that taking an unpopular stance on such a controversial issue can cause deep-seated tension within their unit. White officers will typically avoid commenting on such topics and only stick to the facts surrounding a situation because it is a safe zone. Many times when African American troops experience problems with their unit's leadership, they claim that they are being discriminated against. The only way to refute these claims is to use facts surrounding the case. A commander needs to ensure that all accusations are well documented, and that he clearly communicates to his staff his actions to clarify and help reduce suspicion of intentional wrongdoing.

Be cautious about using the race card. Labeling your commander or anyone else in your unit as a bigot or racist will surely lead to creating more tension than it may be worth. I am not saying not to report cases where a senior leader is clearly discriminating against or treating you or someone else unfairly, but realize that labeling someone a racist or bigot comes with a price, and that price may be your reputation if you cannot clearly and very accurately prove it.

Most claims of racial discrimination are never substantiated, and the accuser is labeled a complainer or troublemaker. To avoid this, talk directly to the individual or supervisor with whom you are having trouble. You will find that a frank, honest discussion, even if the two of you conclude to agree to disagree, is the best way to go. Spirited conversations of this nature will very likely establish a unique relationship between you and your supervisor.

Okay, you are saying, "This is easier said than done." You are absolutely right! In times like this, go to your first sergeant or another officer and meet with the person you accuse of exhibiting discriminatory practices. Ask a close confidant to accompany you to the meeting. Nobody said you have to go it alone in attempting to resolve this issue.

Use people in your military unit to assist in resolving this problem. What you will find is that many times the person making allegations is not normally aware of his actions or things are truly miscommunicated. Confronting these sensitive issues head-on takes a lot of courage and polished communication skills. If you have your act together and you have built a reputation of respect and admiration, you have nothing to fear but fear itself. Remember that *right* will always outshine, out-power, and outlast *wrong* every time. If you have good documentation, you will be able to substantiate your case and allegations.

More often than not, a situation relating to racial discrimination creates an emotional defensive response. Resist getting emotionally tangled in racial issues. Remain professional, and stick to the facts surrounding the case. Don't give in to speculation about how your supervisor feels about you or the situation. Do not engage in spreading rumors about controversial issues—or any issues, for that matter. Speak the truth all the time, and let excellence be your guide. Look for the positives in everything, because it is always too easy to see negative.

African Americans only comprise less than 20 percent of today's military and only 6 percent of the officer corps. As you progress in rank, you will learn that in many of the meetings you attend there will only be white officers and NCOs and you will find yourself as the only black officer in the room. It is typical for people of color, before entering a room, to look around to see if there is anyone else in the room who looks like them. Don't fret or feel dismayed because you are the only minority in the room. Make the best of the situation by contributing value to this meeting and every meeting you attend. Work on developing a positive attitude that is contagious. Many of your coworkers will strive to have you on their team or just want to be around you.

If you are the only minority in a room, you can bet that people are paying attention to you when you speak. So speak up! Make your presence known by actively contributing to each topic being raised, if appropriate. The only way to make a positive impact in each meeting you attend is to properly prepare by researching the agenda and topics being raised and develop questions before getting there. When you speak, speak with authority. You want everyone to listen because you are contributing value to the meeting.

Don't be alarmed when you are the only minority in the room or at a staff meeting. Tap into this isolation, and view it as a benefit. If you get into the business of counting heads, which is clearly the wrong sight picture, you will find yourself taking on feelings of loneliness and isolation. According to Dr. Samuel Betances, "diversity is not so much about counting heads as it is about making heads count."

The few minorities that are assigned to the unit and attend staff meetings need to make every effort to contribute value to the organization. African Americans are only 20 percent of the military's population, perhaps even lower in some career fields. You may or may not see blacks in some areas, especially more technical career fields. If this is your concern, then do your best to encourage our youth in your neighborhood and family to embrace subjects in science, technology, and math and work to change it. Mentor young boys and girls, and encourage them to take on the toughest academic subjects, because our nation desperately needs them.

As you continue to climb the ladder of success you will find that your environment becomes even more isolated racially. Step out of your comfort zone and get to know people of all racial backgrounds. You will find that your contemporaries will be very accommodating in welcoming you into their close circle because of your openness and professional competence. Focusing on race is not as important as focusing on merit and competence. If you are constantly adding value to the organization, your reputation will improve and your merit will become a valuable asset to the unit.

White commanders are no different than black commanders when it comes to making mission accomplishment a priority. Focus on how you can assist mission accomplishment in everything you do. Develop a passion for your profession. Do this by reading everything you can get your hands on about your duties, joining professional organizations, and attending seminars and other training about your craft.

Most white officers do not focus on you being the only black troop in the room at staff meetings. They may obviously see this, but it is not a matter to be pondered or considered on a regular basis. Racial representation of a unit oftentimes is not a dire concern to white officers and only becomes an issue if a black troop makes it one. Some white officers do not see a need to increase minority representation if it does not adversely impact or affect the unit.

While racial diversity is important, it is not the single most important issue of concern to our military. What really matters is mission readiness. To this end, are blacks and other minorities being treated fairly, or is there an unusually high amount being punished, singled out, or treated unfairly? Are the numbers of folks being discharged from your service or unit primarily black and Latinos, or is this number representative of the overall population and society as a whole? Fair treatment is a serious concern in our military, and it is your duty to ensure that commanders are pulling their weight in this regard. Learn to hold your senior leaders accountable!

Senior Department of Defense officials are looking for ways to leverage diversity by making the military more powerful and tapping into our collective differences. America is the most powerful nation in the world, because it is richly populated with people from across the globe. Our military is leading the way in innovation, finding more ways to harness and galvanize our diversity by identifying cultural competence and maximizing the talents of all.

There are many cautions that black officers need to clearly understand about white officers and American society as a whole. White officers and American society want to diversify the workplace but truly do not understand how. It is up to you to enlighten them by introducing cultural competence to them so they may assist you in fostering diversification and upward mobility. As mentioned earlier, diversity is more than merely counting heads; it is about making heads count. The one way to make heads count is to familiarize white officers with the way African Americans think, the places we go, the things we like and don't like, and the organizations we support. Only by understanding why we are and who we are can they fully appreciate our culture.

It is necessary to mention the critical importance of micro-inequities. Micro-inequities are those small things that white people do and say that makes you feel uncomfortable. You can't really label it as racist or outright discrimination, but you know it makes you feel uncomfortable.

An example of a micro-inequity is when a white colonel gets up behind a black general officer and remarks, "We sincerely appreciate General So-and-So's comments today. They were appropriate, and he spoke with clarity and was very articulate." What would you expect from a general officer, whether black or white? Would this colonel make the same comment if the general was white? Probably not, because it is expected for white officers to speak with clarity and to be articulate. Another example would be if you were the senior officer with a group of your subordinates, visiting a contractor's site, and during the initial greeting the host automatically bypassed you while asking for you by name and intentionally shaking one of your subordinates' hands. Naturally, you would excuse this matter and chalk it up to your host not knowing your identity, but deep within you are thinking, *He was not expecting a black officer from our office.* There are many examples that can be given to explain micro-inequities.

Another would be you having lunch with four other black officers at the officers' club, and a white officer walks up and makes a wisecrack: "Are you all planning a riot or something?" Or worse yet, "You all are up to no good!" Nothing is normally said about the many white officers who sit together and have lunch, but put more than two black officers together and something negative has to be said. The black officers are looked at differently. At least we think people are talking or thinking about us. *What are my colleagues and superiors going to think about all the blacks sitting together?* Get over it! Truly, you are not the subject of everyone's thoughts, so get over yourself! It is okay for you to have friendly meetings with fellow black officers in public.

Many times whites unconsciously do or say something that can be considered a micro-inequity, and unless you bring it to their attention they may never know. Most of the time when you experience a micro-inequity, you merely walk away and think to yourself, *Wow, I cannot believe that they did that. I know they knew that they were wrong!* And you think that your silence is a clear sign to them that you were upset or angered by their actions. Nothing could be further from the truth. Most of the time when micro-inequities occur, no one pays any attention to them but you! So make it a point to bring it to your commander's or supervisor's attention.

You may find that they harbored no ill will; it may just be something they are used to saying or an old habit from their past that they have not eliminated during their professional journey. Either way, be professional enough to approach the subject with them and contribute value to their life, as well as yours, by not attacking the person but addressing the issue. Always suggest changes by discussing how the comment made you feel, and ask to assist that person in overcoming the indifference.

What happens when micro-inequities are not addressed and they are allowed to go unchallenged? You get frustrated, return to your inner circle of friends, and talk about it. This causes rumors, and you build up negative energy that eventually turns to anger. After a long period of time this anger turns to hatred, and then hatred impacts your behavior, giving you a bad attitude. There is nothing good that can come of allowing micro- inequities to exist. You owe it to yourself and your supervisor, or the one who made the comment or behaved adversely, to deal with it swiftly.

Along with encouraging white officers to understand black life, you need to make a conscious attempt to understand them a little better. Take time out to learn their history and heritage. Learn what celebrations are important to them and why. Diversity education is not a one-way street; it is learning about all cultures so we can move together toward building successful high-performance teams.

It is critical to know that performance is what counts and very little else. There is an old adage, "No one can argue with success," and this is true for the military, as well as all society. When an officer of any rank consistently brings value to the unit by positively contributing to mission accomplishments, then everyone—supervisors, peers, and subordinates alike—pays attention. Success is infectious, and everyone wants a part of it.

Maintaining a positive attitude is a force multiplier. People like being around positive and successful people. Securing your future in the military is no different. If you are looking for success, keep a positive attitude and work your boss's agenda. White officers and commanders desire the same thing you do, and that is efficiently accomplishing the mission.

Even though you may be the only minority assigned to your unit, don't be dismayed. Embrace your peers and focus on learning your job and trying to become the best that you possibly can be. Nothing matters more than being successful and effectively completing your duties.

"Diversity is not just about counting heads, but ensuring every head counts!" Ensure that you are bringing value to the unit and actively working your boss's agenda. White commanders and supervisors want to see you succeed, and they are going to eliminate as many barriers as required to ensure that success. Don't expect things to be fair all the time, and if it turns out that things are unfair, then work to improve the situation. Sometimes bad things occur to good people, and when they do, understand that you may or may not have had anything to do with it. There may be times that you are overlooked, and that is okay! Don't flip out and lose your professional composure. Remain calm, and know that it is just a matter of time before you will be allowed to strut your stuff and show your professional wares.

Many times you will not be responsible for your environment. Your job is to be the best follower and leader as possible. Serve your commander with as much faithfulness and loyalty as possible. Your commander needs to have the confidence in you that, when given a task, you will accomplish it to the best of your ability and support him or her without hesitation.

Your past is full of examples of black officers succeeding in times of unusual adversity. Officers who have displayed remarkable courage in times of despair and unfair treatment excel consistently. Learn your past, and allow it to serve as a daily reminder of where you came from and how far you can go. Tap into the real potential you have deep inside of you. Patience is a virtue that you are going to have to call upon from time to time to remain professional. Silence does not mean that you are giving in or giving up. It means that you are smart enough to know when to fight particular battles. Many times your secret weapon is going to be calling on a mentor who has been through what you are going through a time or two.

White officers want you to succeed just as much as you do. Realize that they are not going to treat you any different just because you're black. Collectively we have not been treated fairly throughout the generations, so learn from this experience and allow those spirits to make you stronger and more prepared. Make your mark by contributing value to your organization and exhibiting pride and professionalism every day of your career.

## Sage Advice

### Major (Dr.) Renee K. Finney, USAF
- Treat your relationship with the military as you would any other benefactor.
- Make sure your personal and professional needs are being addressed.
- Never let them see you sweat!

### 1LT Perry Lyonel Russell
- Organize your life into three spheres (write it down): personal, professional, and spiritual. Take the time to map out where you are in each area and where you would like to be.
- All that glitters is not gold. Always remember to be flexible in life. Pick your battles. Be sure to always remain professionally marketable, get your education, and network.
- Accept that life is unfair. Move on! Even if you have to claw your way, accomplish everything you start. Do it to the best of your ability. Someone is always watching. You represent more than you could ever imagine.

### 1LT Frankie A. Locus, USAF
- Be well-balanced and well-rounded, not drifting to the extremes. And if you're neither well-balanced nor well-rounded, it is best that you become that way.

- One thing to love about black people is our confidence. Be confident, not cocky or arrogant. Never act like you know it all. But when you know something, speak up with confidence.
- Take pride in every task that you are given. Try not to feel like you always get the short end of the stick, even though nine times out of ten you will. Keep in mind that it only takes a spark to ignite a fire, and it will take your end of the stick to set it all ablaze.

# CHAPTER 6
## SAVING UP FOR TOMORROW

Finally, brethren, whatsoever things are true, whatsoever things are honest, whatsoever things are just, whatsoever things are pure, whatsoever things are lovely, whatsoever things are of good report; if there be any virtue, and if there be any praise, think on these things.

—Philippians 4:8

People pay for what they do, and still more for what they have allowed themselves to become. And they pay for it very simply; by the lives they lead.

—James Baldwin, 1961

We have a powerful potential in our youth, and we must have the courage to challenge old ideas and practices so that we may direct their power toward good ends.

—Mary MacLeod Bethune, 1955

Serving in the military will provide financial stability and modest investment opportunities. If you are smart, this section will assist you in understanding the many different types of pay, as well as how to invest your pay once received. It will be just as important to know the legal rules that all military personnel are subjected to: the Uniform Code of Military Justice (UCMJ).

African Americans are one of the largest groups of consumers in

America. It has only been in the last forty years that black money has been capitalized in a more robust way on Wall Street than ever before. This chapter teaches you about the importance of saving money and investing. Now that you are on active duty and have a promising career, it is time to start taking advantage of your financial stability and invest a portion of your salary.

There are several important concerns that you need to focus on in this chapter. The primary focus is on your finances, and the secondary focus is on the UCMJ. Not completely understanding either of these principles can lead to an unsettling career and even stymie promotion potential. As an officer you will not be given the latitude and freedom of routinely bouncing checks. By the way, intentionally or unknowingly issuing a check where funds are insufficient is illegal. So understand that military officers don't commit crimes! If you do, expect to get caught and held accountable for your actions.

There is nothing more crucial than having financial stability and learning to take advantage of time. As a rule, you cannot afford to take serious risks in handling your money. This book will introduce you to basic investing, but to find out more contact your local family readiness center and ask to speak to the installation's financial counselor. Your local library is an excellent source of financial resources, as well as monthly financial magazines, such as *Kiplinger, Forbes, Businessweek, Wall Street Journal, Investment Business Weekly*, and *Investment Weekly*, etc.

One of the first things you need to do is to develop a monthly budget. This budget will allow you to visualize how much your monthly liabilities are compared to your income. As a rule of thumb, you never want your monthly liabilities to exceed 25 percent of your monthly income. Keeping your bills low will allow you to prepare for emergencies because crises will surely come. Invest a respectable amount on a regular basis to ward off uncalculated emergencies. You need to be committed to regulating your bills and reducing your spending habits. The easiest way to cause constant headaches and stress is to mishandle your finances.

Try to control impulse buying, or "keeping up with the Jones"–type spending. As an officer you will be required to attend official functions (i.e., graduation ceremonies, promotion ceremonies, and the like). You will be required to have certain uniforms in ample supply, and you will not receive a clothing allowance. Your monthly income is all you have, and it is up to you to manage it properly.

Your monthly budget will create some controls by showing you exactly what needs to be paid first. If you are having a problem with impulse spending, you might want to write down every expense in a small booklet for about a month, regardless of how large or small. It may prove difficult initially, but within a week you will be able to see exactly where you can reduce extraneous spending. Hopefully, this routine of jotting down your expenses will become habit forming and assist you in thinking about exactly where your money is going.

Here are ten helpful hints in creating a sound and successful budget:

- Create categories that fit *your* personal situation and your spending habits, not somebody else's.
- Use accurate income projections.
- Create enough categories to give you a meaningful picture of where your money goes and where you might be able to cut costs, but not so much detail that tracking is a chore that you'll soon tire of.
- Include expenses that don't occur on a monthly basis, such as auto maintenance, homeowner's insurance, personal property taxes, service contracts, etc.
- Regularly review all categories to determine if you need more or fewer, review expenses, and brainstorm ways to trim costs in each category.
- Use cash expenditure tracking and recording. Cash spending is the biggest leak in most budgets. Cash disappears quickly, and if you don't write down everything you spend, you'll have a distorted look at your spending record.
- Use a line item for savings so you treat a contribution to your savings account just as you would a bill you owe.
- Have realistic written goals. Budgeting isn't about tracking

your costs; it's about setting financial goals (e.g., saving for a down payment on a house, buying a new car, getting out of debt, saving for retirement, putting your kids through college, traveling) and finding ways to meet them. Without goals, your budget is just a pair of handcuffs.

- Without identifying your spending patterns you will not be able to track your spending.
- Have a positive attitude toward meeting your financial goals. After establishing a monthly budget, it is vitally important to create an emergency fund that eventually equals at least three months of your base pay. This fund is only to be used for those dire times.

The emergency funds can be maintained in a money market account, certificate of deposit, or another instrument that you will not routinely use. After you develop your emergency fund, you need to start thinking about how much you can invest on a routine basis. The earlier you get started investing, the more money you can accumulate. You remember the old saying that time is money. When it comes to investing, this principle is especially true. Take advantage of your early years, and look at your investments as something that has to be done and not as something optional. Protecting your future starts today, and it is up to you to invest your money wisely.

Stuff happens! And it usually costs money when you least expect it. If you don't have an emergency fund equal to three to six months' worth of basic living expenses, you're living on the edge. There's no time like the present to get started. Your success in building your emergency fund depends on your consistency in socking away money on a regular basis and your ability to resist digging into your emergency fund for non-emergencies. Without an emergency fund, you may be forced to incur credit card debt that could take you many years to pay off and end up costing you much more in the long run. You never want to be in the position where you have to buy daily necessities like food, transportation, and housing on credit. Imagine still making payments on groceries you bought (and ate) three years ago, at 14 to 24 percent interest. Pretty depressing!

Whether you serve an initial four to five years in the military or you do a full career of twenty to thirty years, time will surely pass, and you don't want to have to wonder where your money went. How you use this time is essential to the preservation of your future. By investing a small amount on a regular basis, over the years you will be surprised how much it will grow and entice you to invest more. To illustrate the value of time as it relates to money, we will use the rule of 72. Here you will see that over a short period of time your money will double in short order.

The rule of 72 is a pretty simple concept. The rule says that to find the number of years required to double your money at a given interest rate, you just divide the interest rate into 72. For example, if you want to know how long it will take to double your money at 8 percent interest, divide 72 by 8 and get 9 years. You can also run this formula backward if you want to see how long it will take to double your money in six years. Just divide 72 by 6 to find that it will require an interest rate of about 12 percent.

It is equally important to understand the concept of risk. You need to know how much risk you are willing to accept with your money. In financial terms, risk is defined in a variety of ways and will have different meanings for each individual. To find the appropriate level of risk for you, it is vital to consult a professional. In investing your money, you need to be comfortable with the interest rate and the type of return you are going to receive.

Some financial instruments will give you a better rate of return than others. Trading in the stock market offers little more risk than investing in mutual funds, CDs, money markets, passbook checking, and savings. Each of these instruments has appropriate utilization and will be explained in detail below. The more risk you are willing to take will normally translate into a higher return. You need to ensure you have the tolerance for watching severe roller-coaster rides in your funds. Many will boast that they are quickly making huge amounts of money in the stock market and won't share with you that they have also lost a lot. You need to be careful of those officers or locker-room investors' advice.

You are going to hear outlandish stories of how much money some of your peers are making. This should be a sign that you need to learn as much as you can before leaping into similar ventures as these storytellers. Investing is a very serious business and should not be left up to amateurs. You need to seek the professional advice of people who are licensed to engage in this activity. If you do not, you may watch your savings disappear in a flash! A quick review of your local phone book will provide local financial counselors and brokers. Again, a visit to your installation's family readiness center should be your first stop.

Another critical issue you may want to consider is establishing life insurance outside of the military. Servicemen's Group Life Insurance (SGLI) was recently increased to $400,000 and can be assigned to go to whoever you want to be your beneficiary. If you are married you may want to assign your spouse as your beneficiary to ensure your family is taken care of in case of your unexpected demise.

If you are single you may want to assign your parents or some other relative, as required. Having the right amount of life insurance is just as critical as investing on a regular basis and should be a vital part of your investment portfolio. There are various types of life insurance that you need to be made aware of. Whole life, universal life, and term policies are the three basic types. When it comes to life insurance, a solid position is to have at least four to five times your annual salary.

It is important that once you leave military service you have the option of either keeping your SGLI or terminating it and merely keeping your civilian policy. It makes sense to purchase your life insurance early, because it will increase in cost as you mature. The older you are, the more expensive life insurance will be.

There are many types of civilian life insurance products available to meet the differing needs of each individual and family. In order to evaluate which life insurance policy will meet your needs, it is important to discuss the matter with a professional agent or adviser. Some of the many factors you should consider before purchasing life insurance include your age, marital status, number and ages of your children, medical history, earning capability, debt ratio, and anticipated financial needs.

Universal life insurance is a variation of whole life insurance. The difference is that with universal life, the term life portion of the policy is separate from the investment or cash portion of the policy. The investment portion of the policy is invested in money market funds, as opposed to stocks, bonds, and mutual funds. The cash value portion of the policy is an accumulation fund to which investment interest is credited and from which death benefits are paid. With universal life insurance the insured can vary the amount of his annual death benefit and annual premium payments. Insured people may also make partial surrenders of the policy and/or take policy loans against the cash value of the policy. A partial surrender is when an insured person withdraws some of the funds that have accumulated in the investment or cash portion of the policy.

Whole life insurance provides coverage for the entire life of the person insured, regardless of how long that person has the policy or how much has been collected in premium payments that keep the policy in force. Premiums may be paid throughout the insured's life or for a portion of his life. Also, premiums may be paid in lump sums when the policy is taken out. The cash value portion of a whole life insurance policy belongs to the insured and may be taken out as policy loans or when the policy is cashed in. With whole life insurance, part of the premium payment goes toward the insurance portion of the policy, part of the premium payment goes toward administrative expenses, and the remainder goes toward the investment portion of a whole life policy, which is usually tax-free until withdrawn.

Term life insurance provides a specific amount of life insurance coverage for a designated time period. Currently, the available policy lengths for term life insurance are one year, five years, ten years, and fifteen years. If the insured person dies within the time frame in which the policy is in effect, the insurance company pays out the face value of the policy. If the insured person lives longer than the term of the policy, the policy expires and pays nothing. Term life insurance does not build any type of equity. It is often one of the least expensive types of insurance and is available in several forms. Term life insurance is typically purchased as a means of temporary protection or when an individual can't afford the cost of other forms of life insurance. Some people prefer to invest their own money elsewhere and feel they can obtain higher yields without having to use a life insurance plan.

Variable life insurance is also a form of whole life insurance. As with whole life and universal life insurance, part of the premium payment goes toward the term life portion of the policy, part to administrative expenses, and part to the investment or cash value portion of the policy. There is a major difference between the investment portion of variable life and that of other forms of life insurance. With variable life, the insured person is able to choose how to invest the funds in the investment portion of the policy. The insured may select from investments such as stocks, bonds, and mutual funds, as long as they are within the insurance company portfolio. Variable life insurance is generally more expensive than other forms of life insurance. So be careful, because the death benefits may go up or down depending on investment performance. However, there is usually a minimum level for benefits, so they will not drop below a certain level.

It is vital to consult with a professional adviser to gain accurate insurance and investment information that fits your goals and lifestyle. The primary goal here is to provide you with the basics so you are informed and can start thinking about your personal fiscal matters. Remember time truly is money! There are a variety of ways for you to invest your hard-earned money. Naturally, there are individual stocks, bonds, and mutual funds. Again, your best bet is to consult a financial professional and find the right investment for you. As a good primer, it is important that you understand how mutual funds work.

Mutual funds are investment companies that pool money from investors at large and offer to sell and buy back its shares on a continuous basis and use the capital thus raised to invest in securities of different companies. The stocks these mutual funds have are very fluid and are used for buying or redeeming and/or selling shares at a net asset value. Mutual funds possess shares of several companies and receive dividends for them, and the earnings are distributed among the shareholders.

Purchasing a home is a very natural investment military people typically make. You will find many of your coworkers purchasing homes at each assignment. Many times military people hang on to these properties and rent them after departing for the next assignment, creating additional income. Some folks decide to sell at the end of the assignment, hoping to make a quick profit and reinvest the profit at the new location. You will see that your basic allowance for quarters (BAQ) normally pays the mortgage payment, as it is designed to do. So as long as you are willing to make repairs, pay utilities, and are not required to live on base, take the dive.

You need to understand a few basics about purchasing a new home before you take that important leap of home ownership. Purchasing a home is typically a sound investment, but it can quickly sour if you do not do your homework. One of the primary reasons people purchase a home is for the tax benefits. The interest you pay on your mortgage and your property taxes are both tax deductible, so basically the government is essentially subsidizing your home purchase.

Let's say you bought a $200,000 house, and you did not pay cash for the home. You received a mortgage and you decided to put 20 percent down, equaling an initial investment of $40,000. At an appreciation rate of 5 percent annually, a $200,000 home would increase in value $10,000 during the first year. That means you earned $10,000 with an investment of $40,000. Your annual return on investment would be a whopping 25 percent. Fortunately, the government is subsidizing your purchase of your home. One of the most important facts you can remember is all of the interest and property taxes you pay in a given year can be deducted from your gross income to reduce your taxable income. When you rent a home, naturally you do not receive any tax deductions and you can expect your rent to increase each year, if not more often. Whatever property taxes you pay in a given year may be deducted from your gross income, lowering your tax obligation.

One of the wonderful things about home ownership is that your home appreciates annually. The average appreciation on a home varies but at the time of this writing is approximately 5 percent, although it will vary from year to year. There will be some years that your home will depreciate, so be careful in your financial planning. Over time studies have shown that home ownership is one of the best investments a person can make.

Consult a professional realtor to determine your goals. Remember the realtor works directly for you and has your interest at heart. Securing the right realtor is vitally important in achieving this important investment. A realtor will assist you in securing funding if needed, finding the right house for you, and ensuring you do not pay too much for your initial purchase. Good luck in your journey!

## The Uniform Code of Military Justice (UCMJ)

You do not have to be a lawyer to understand the UCMJ. Take time to get to know your local staff judge advocate, order a copy of the UCMJ, and spend time reading it, as well as attending court martial proceedings when available. This exposure will prove to be invaluable to you over the course of your career.

On June 30, 1775, the Second Continental Congress established 69 Articles of War to govern the conduct of the Continental Army. On April 10, 1806, the United States Congress enacted 101 Articles of War, which were not significantly revised until over a century later. The military justice system continued to operate under the Articles of War until May 31, 1951, when the UCMJ came into existence. President Harry S. Truman signed into law the UCMJ after Congress passed it on May 5, 1950. The word "Uniform" in the code's title refers to the congressional intent to make military justices uniform or consistent among the armed forces. As an officer, it is imperative that you understand the document because you will be charged with enforcing it as you increase in rank, especially once you become a commander. Take time now and get to know this important document. Most military installations have law libraries that you can visit to view this document.

The UCMJ can be found in Chapter 47 of the United States Code, Title 10, Subtitle A, Part II. Read through to become familiar with it, and if you are a lawyer, then learn it like you know your name. Most importantly, learn the case law surrounding many of these codes and the historical patterns of many of their applications. You want to know how these laws have been interpreted and applied to unique situations in the past.

There is no need to try to memorize these articles, because when you need to deal with any of these crimes you will be required to consult a military attorney. Familiarize yourself with each article, and sit and talk with your local JAG officer if you have any questions. Before you are allowed to take command, you will receive training on the UCMJ, your authority, and proper proceedings. Again, good luck!

## Sage Advice

### Major General Charles "C. Q." Brown, USAF
- Figure out how you define success.
- Mentorship, not sponsorship, is what counts. Sponsors eventually leave; mentors do not.
- The job you are in sets your future assignments for the next two to three duty locations, so do it well!
- You are responsible for your future success.
- Ask a lot of questions.

### Lieutenant Colonel Baron D. Canty Sr., USAF
- Develop a relationship with God and a strong prayer life, and find a good church home away from home that increases your Bible study habits.
- Learn what it means to be committed in a relationship, and practice it.
- Don't take every bad comment that is made by a white person and classify it as racist. Take the critique or comment, step back, and see if there is any truth to it. If so, work on correcting it by all means possible. If the comment is not true, then move on and pray for and learn to love and forgive the person who made the comment in spite of what you think of him.

## Lieutenant Colonel Joseph C. Richardson, USAF

- Building and cultivating successful relationships is the cornerstone to a successful life and career. Your relationship priorities should encompass God, family, friends, and your comrades in arms.
- Never sell your integrity short. Always look the person in the mirror square in the eye and be proud of what you stand for.
- The most important command you'll ever have is the one that involves leading your family. To fail here and succeed in other areas is a net failure.

# CHAPTER 7

## DEALING WITH DIFFICULT SUPERVISORS!

For the eyes of the Lord are on the righteous, and his ears are open to their prayers; But the face of the Lord is against those who do evil.

—1 Peter 3:12

Fear of something is at the root of hate for others, and hate within will eventually destroy the hater.

—George Washington Carver

You're either part of the solution or part of the problem.

—Eldridge Cleaver, 1968

We can go on talking about racism and who treated whom badly, but what are you going to do about it? Are you going to wallow in that or are you going to create your own agenda?

—Judith Jamison, 1994

It would be ideal to be able to personally select your commander or supervisor and determine how that individual treats you. Every now and then you will experience a bad supervisor or someone who does not have your best interest at heart. When you have these rare situations, you need to equip yourself with the essential tools that will enable you to be successful. Having a respected and credible reputation is just one way to deal with your troublesome boss. Most supervisors will have your best interest at heart and work to develop your skills and professionalism.

This chapter will introduce you to new horizons in managing your career by providing you with key tools and essential methodologies that will allow you to confront adverse situations and find a successful resolution. As you continue to lead and receive promotions, you will be given increased responsibilities and status. "To whom much is given, much is expected." As you continue to climb the ladder of success, you will be challenged beyond measure and given increased responsibilities. In order to be prepared for these increased responsibilities, you need to constantly learn everything you possibly can about your duties and responsibilities.

By molding your reputation, you build confidence within yourself. By building your confidence, you actively work toward contributing value to the organization. Regardless of how good you are, you are going to experience tough times at certain periods in your career. Many of these tough times will be in the form of a supervisor who is willing to challenge you at every turn. In difficult times it will be very easy to interpret these rare occasions as your supervisor picking on you or singling you out. This may not be the case, and you really need to look at the bigger picture (your boss's perspective or the commander's intent) and not merely focus on your end of the spectrum.

## Seek Advice

By leaning on your own understanding or personal perspective of what is occurring, you may completely miss what is actually happening or your boss's intent. When things are not working out for you on the job, or you feel your supervisor is picking on you, seek private counseling of a senior officer (field-grade level or above). There are sure to be issues surrounding your treatment that you do not completely understand or are aware of. Allow wisdom from more senior officers to enlighten your horizons and enhance your understanding.

There is an old saying that "you can only understand and comprehend information of those things that you have previously been exposed." If you have never experienced certain issues, conditions, or situations, you may have a difficult time understanding the requirements and expectations of those duties. When you are confronted with something new, it makes more sense to have a little knowledge about expectations of that task. Without some experience or exposure, you will find yourself ill-equipped to relate to expected requirements. The best way to deal with those things you do not know is to read as much as you can and discuss these matters with supervisors or others who may have more experience than you.

It is immature to think that you can complete a task without proper training. You need to be the most knowledgeable person in your office concerning the tasks that are assigned to you. One way to obtain this knowledge is by reading career-related journals, attending professional training, and participating in discussions with your peers. By talking with your peers, you will learn the finer points or unwritten rules surrounding your career. Realize that there is a lot that you don't know about life, your profession, and professional relationships. The sooner you know these hidden agendas or unwritten rules, the sooner you will be able to navigate your way successfully through your career.

## Creating a Plan

We have already mentioned micro-inequities in previous chapters, and what you will find is that it is the small inconsistent things that will occur and knock you off-balance or cause you to doubt your potential when compared to your peers. Many times you will find that your boss may make decisions, which in your opinion adversely impact you. If this occurs, don't automatically assume that he is holding a personal vendetta against you, doesn't like you, or has it in for you. Most officers do not allow their personal feelings to interfere with their professional decisions. This separation is designed to keep an unbiased view on matters. This statement really translates into "your boss does not care about your emotions, only accomplishing the mission," so if you interpret a decision to be adverse, then you need to view the situation from a mission-focus perspective and bring it to his or her attention.

When young officers typically encounter a similar situation, they tend to be overly sensitive about the issue and to prematurely place labels on the event, categorizing it as being "racial" or something else that is typically personal. Young officers normally discuss their discontent and misgivings with other coworkers, which can create rumors that may or may not be true. You should expect for these rumors to get back to your boss or supervisor in short order, so watch what you say at all times!

The other way that young officers tend to deal with adverse information is to let it slide and do nothing, acting as if it does not matter or does not personally bother them. Eventually, as time goes by, this feeling of wrongdoing builds up and creates a feeling of hatred or dislike for the commander or supervisor. It is important to note that there are no certified mind readers within the armed forces. So do yourself a favor and make an appointment with your commander, supervisor, or first sergeant and air your concerns. It does not make sense to harbor ill feelings toward anyone. So speak up and be heard! Naturally, you should expect to be nervous, but your approach should be direct yet respectful. You will have a profound impact on your leadership growth by clearly understanding adverse issues and how to professionally deal with controversial matters.

Your supervisor will normally explain to you the reason surrounding his decisions, or he will politely tell you it is none of your business. If the latter is the response, then you need to return to your desk or office and document the event, including your meeting, and then remain silent about the matter and get on with your professional duties. There is nothing to gain by constantly talking about the issue or belittling your supervisor in the workplace. This course of action will surely lead to your professional demise.

Be on guard from this point on, and start a private daily journal of all issues, both good and bad, that occur in the workplace. Find a mentor and discuss these occurrences to gain a better understanding of professional ethics. It is too easy to request a transfer, and if you do, it will most likely be denied. You cannot run from your situation, and this is why you need to learn to professionally confront adverse issues. The best defense you can ever have in dealing with a difficult supervisor is maintaining clear, unemotional documentation. Report only the facts, not how you interpret your supervisor's actions. Remember, we typically understand adverse issues from our own personal perspective and not from our supervisor's. Tell your supervisor that if things do not change for the better, you are going to use your chain of command to address the matter with your commander. Share the fact that you have documented each occurrence and that you merely want to be treated fairly. If a pattern of adverse actions continues by your supervisor, you need to confront your supervisor one last time. If you do not have success, take it to your commander to resolve. If your issues are with your commander, then meet with him or her personally. If the issues are not resolved or properly addressed, then inform him that you plan on visiting the inspector general or his commander to discuss the issue.

When discussing this matter with your commander, bring your documentation to assist you in explaining your position. You should discuss your concerns with your commander, not confront him or her! Try to remain unbiased and unemotional. Getting too close to the issue emotionally is not going to do anyone any good, because it will only cloud the primary issue. Take your time and clearly articulate your position by reviewing each incident.

Allow your commander time to resolve the issue. Understand that your commander may or may not close the loop with you on the issue or let you know that the matter has been discussed with your supervisor or with whomever you have concerns. Remember that stress is always in the eyes of the beholder and not the one potentially causing the perceived stress. What may cause one troop to stress out may not cause even a ripple of concern to another. The key to dealing with stress is knowing the specific stresses in the work environment that you are particularly sensitive to and the warning signs in your own body and mind that signal stress overload. Once you have identified your vulnerability, you can create ongoing stress management strategies to cope with the issues.

It is not your place to question your commander, so don't! Your commander is a professional officer and will handle the issue the best way he sees fit. As a subordinate you need to have trust in and be loyal to your commander regardless of your differences. Questioning his actions or decisions may be viewed as insubordinate, and you can be sent to jail for violating any infractions. Tread cautiously from this point on, because you have now exposed your hand and may have labeled yourself as a complainer or disrupter. The way to eliminate the label as a complainer is to show that you are a team player. Start immediately by volunteering for the toughest task and unusual opportunities.

Get yourself actively involved by contributing positively to your unit. You want to clearly understand your commander's vision for your unit. Talk to coworkers and superiors about new issues that the unit is taking on, and volunteer to join or lead the effort. You may want to volunteer to deploy or do other special projects that will display you in a more positive light. These actions will prove that you are, in fact, a team player and not a complainer. It is important to acknowledge the negative adverse actions, but try hard to concentrate on the positive things that occur, not the negative. Work to develop a respectful and positive relationship with your supervisor. It may take a period of time to be successful, but you may find that your supervisor's earlier actions may have been warranted for unknown reasons and not truly targeting you.

## Dos and Don'ts
- Do the best job that you possibly can do.
- Do act professionally at all times.
- Do prepare yourself for the possibility of all your efforts backfiring.
- Don't whine, complain, or brag to coworkers.
- Don't expect everything to magically improve.
- Don't go above your boss to his supervisor.

## Seek Win-Win Solutions
There are always two sides to every situation, especially adverse issues. Eliminating yourself from emotional concerns will allow you to see the issue more clearly. Adverse issues sometimes occur even in the best of times. Even when contingency plans are developed and you anticipate adverse issues occurring, there will always be the element of surprise for which you cannot prepare.

Just as you create contingency plans for adverse incidents, you should also prepare for dealing with controversial supervisors. Think actively about what you should do when confronting controversial issues. Seek the advice of more senior officers, and ask what they would do in a similar situation. Realize that you need to sometimes set your pride aside and not be overly concerned about people disrespecting or dissing you. As long as you are in the military, expect to get your feelings hurt by superiors. Always remember you are not as important as completing the mission. Your supervisors and senior officers are always viewing matters from a mission-focused, not personal, perspective.

As long as you endeavor to work through tough issues, you are bound to encounter obstacles. There may be times that you speak out of turn, trying to assist the discussion or the problem that needs to be resolved but not clearly understanding the totality or impact of the issues. You just do not have enough experience to weigh in on every situation, so sometimes you need to be seen and not heard.

Seek first to understand and then to share knowledge. Be hesitant about leaping into new territories you truly do not understand. Seek advice and understanding from every corner you possibly can. Read books you typically do not understand or would not normally read. After reading, ask questions to experts in those select fields. Improve your understanding of professional matters by creating relationships with other professionals. Surround yourself with professionals who are experts in their chosen career fields.

Building solid relationships and working to learn as much as you can about your craft will establish you as a professional. Once this reputation is established, you will have created an expected standard that others respect and admire. Both superiors and subordinates will seek you out to resolve their toughest and most controversial issues. You will find that no longer will you be the brunt of adverse jokes or rumors, but the talk now will be how professional and competent you are and how you can be relied on.

Creating an impressive reputation that precedes your arrival will assist in warding off adverse actions or images of supervisors and subordinates alike. A good reputation will show that you have proven your professionalism and can be relied on to get the job done. By developing this reputation you create a win-win environment that makes completing your duties a whole lot easier.

This win-win solution will prove to be the bedrock of your success. Adverse situations will now be viewed as environments of learning. Take advantage of these situations, and use them as leadership and growth periods. You do not know everything, and it is not expected for you to. In the military you oftentimes have no time to think about the orders being presented; you merely have time to react. Your split-second actions will reflect your attained knowledge and training.

It is not the professional position for military subordinates to question their superiors, but it is their duty and responsibility to know the difference between right and wrong. Learn to trust your superior's judgment, and learn to respect his decisions. Seek win-win solutions at every turn, and you will find that you will gain an understanding and your supervisor will learn to respect you even more, especially when you have concerns about something he did or said.

Tristan Loo, an experienced negotiator and expert in conflict resolution, identifies ten salient solutions on his website StreetNegotiation. com.

- Always have a plan B.
- Never react to verbal abuse or harsh criticism with emotions.
- Discuss rather than confront.
- Manage the manager.
- Know that you can do little to change a difficult person.
- Keep your professional face on.
- Evaluate your own performance.
- Gather additional support.
- Don't go up the chain of command unless it's a last resort.
- Encourage good behavior with praise.
- Document everything.
- Leave work at work.

Tristan Loo provided valuable insight on how to deal with difficult bosses and adverse situations. It may take years to master these techniques, but by knowing them at least you are well on your way to becoming an effective officer. Over the years these strategies will prove invaluable to you as your rank and responsibility increase.

Good luck!

## Sage Advice

### Captain LaMont A. Coleman, USAF

- Learn how to write and speak the air force language quickly. Put yourself in positions where you will be heard either verbally or with your pen. Get your name out there. Next, seek opportunities in which you can excel from day one. Don't wait on someone to tell you about opportunities; make your own. Also, become innovative and courageous no matter what obstacles you face (do ordinary things extraordinarily). Don't accept the stereotype that African Americans are flawed: less intelligent, lazy, looking for handouts (this term is often confused with affirmative action, whose premise is not based on handouts, but leveling the playing field), bad with our money, and late to work. Invest monetarily in your future, and raise the bar in your professional work environment.

- Develop your personal values. Ninety-nine percent of the air force knows our core values ("Integrity first, Service before self, and Excellence in all we do"), but the average African American officer cannot tell you his personal core values. My core values are family, education, and work ethic connected through love and fighting.

- Be yourself. This is often overlooked. People will see through your facade. You can only fool people some of the time, but the true person has to come out, to be seen, and to be respected (I use this term loosely) for who you are, not who you believe others want to see. When this happens you will have arrived as a person. You will be comfortable and clear about what your mission is—to humbly lead by conviction the greatest group of Americans in our armed services.

## Captain Brendan Epps, USAF

- Grasp every opportunity you can as another chance to excel.
- Give the enlisted corps your best (leadership and mentoring).
- Pass along what you've learned to junior officers by teaching them, not by setting it up for them.

## Captain Braden E. Friday, USAF

- Know who you are. You won't be intimidated.
- Be flexible, but don't compromise. Possessing character is more important than being one.
- Always remind yourself where you came from.

# CHAPTER 8
## A JOURNEY, NOT A DESTINATION!

If then you were raised with Christ, see those things which are above, where Christ is, sitting at the right hand of God. Set your mind on things above, not on the things on the earth.

—Colossians 3:1–2

Train your head and hands to do, your head and heart to dare.

—Joseph Seamon Cotter Jr., 1898

It is not light that we need, but fire; it is not the gentle shower, but thunder. We need the storm, the whirlwind, and the earthquake.

—Frederick Douglass, 1852

There are no foolproof methods to getting promoted to the next rank or having a good career, but there are positive things you can do to increase your chances. The things listed here should come as no surprise, but serve as reminders and perhaps refreshers in helping you along your very promising career and enduring successfully on a daily basis. You will have to determine what a successful career for you is going to be. Many officers desire to make the rank of colonel or general, while others decide that merely reaching twenty years is their pinnacle. If your goal is to become a flag officer and you are planning on completing a thirty-year career, then you need to associate with positive people who understand the military, and you need to develop excellent traits all along your career journey. One important note to remember is that what got you to your current rank may not be enough to move you on to the next level; it may take extraordinary skills and a very strong support system.

There is nothing more important than your integrity and completely embracing your service's core values. Living a clean and trouble-free lifestyle should be the desire of everyone. But sometimes no matter how hard you try, the harsh realities of life arrive and you are forced to make several tough decisions. There was once an officer whose career was on what many would consider the fast track. As a captain in the air force, he was already selected to command a squadron. At the time of taking command, he had severe financial problems that he kept to himself, and after a year of taking command, his child died of a rare disease. He was bewildered with personal problems and grief, but he was smart enough to secure professional assistance in the form of the installation's chaplain to assist both him and his wife in dealing with the surmounting issues of grief and extensive debt. It should be mentioned that the financial problems they experienced was primarily medical bill debt incurred prior to coming on active duty.

The chaplain knew very well the installation's support organizations, and he counseled the young officer to seek professional guidance to aid in resolving his many issues. The captain and his wife met weekly with the chaplain to receive one-on-one counseling, which allowed them to work through their grief and move on with living.

The best thing the captain could have done in this situation was to not lean on his own understanding and secure professional assistance. Most professionals working within the military's support system are experienced in quickly resolving situations like this one and have most likely dealt with similar issues, so if you find yourself in a sensitive situation then consult a professional.

Face it, many of the issues facing white officers are of little concern to black officers, and issues black officers face on a daily basis are not ones with which white officers are familiar. Read this chapter carefully, and apply these strategies to your professional toolbox. Keep your eyes wide open, and be aware of your surroundings and environment. You may be surprised by many of the things you hear and see.

## Making Good Decisions

Every action starts with a simple thought. With a simple thought the Empire State Building was designed, drafted, and built. With a simple thought the Great Pyramids in Egypt were constructed. A simple thought gave scientists the ability to figure out how to send man to the moon. Great things are born out of thought and, when put into action, the magic of life and creativity begins.

In the earlier story, the officer made the right decision to get professionals involved in his life and not attempt to deal with these enormous burdens alone. In this case his support system paid off. He called in the experts and informed his commander of his situation. He effectively communicated his problems and thereby headed off the possibility of being snowballed with adverse personal issues and possibly punishment. He successfully completed his command time and went on to reach the senior ranks.

## Effective Communication

This example is a good illustration of effective communication and how confronting personal problems can be quickly tamed by being proactive and seeking professional assistance. There are several tools you need to gather as you start your career journey. Two of the most important traits are impeccable integrity and effective communication. These traits will lay the foundation and allow you to reach heights of success beyond your highest imagination.

Regardless of the sincerity of your integrity and how great your communication skills are, if you are not professionally competent you will surely lose your footing as a good officer. Professional competence is gained by reading and learning as much as you can about your craft. Take time out to learn your craft by talking to other professionals more senior than you. Take online courses to improve your understanding of the civilian side of your profession.

Enroll in seminars that will expose you to new ideas, and learn modern strategies that civilian agencies are using. Subscribe to magazines and professional journals that will allow you to gain an appreciation for what your civilian counterparts are doing in similar industries. Write articles and submit them to professional magazines and newspapers to be published. Writing is the one way you will solidify yourself as a professional.

## Professional Competence

Professional competence will give you an edge over your peers by making you more valuable to your commander and unit. You will understand complex issues and learn to apply new and innovative applications. These are the hallmarks of a professional, and it will become the foundation of your success. It is easy for seasoned commanders to assess which of their officers stand out from their peers. Being able to be that individual is essential, and the way to gain this prestigious position is to read everything in sight, volunteer for leadership tasks to gain more experience, and seek out rare opportunities to set yourself apart from your peers. Work hard to move beyond your comfort zone and grow into your profession. This takes a conscious effort on your part and will assist in transforming you into a young professional and competent officer.

There is nothing worse than not knowing your job or knowing what is expected of you. It is going to take a lot to remain on top of your game, but with concerted effort you will achieve your goal. In order to keep pace with civilian society and industry, with its ever-changing regulations and policies, you have to be aware of what is going on in the professional marketplace and industry.

Work to discover new information, and then brainstorm how to apply these new principles so that you can have discussions on these initiatives with coworkers and others who are interested. By discussing these topics you will reinforce this knowledge.

Always seek to be your best, and learn how to keep quiet sometimes. Just because you may know a particular thing does not always mean that you have to be the one to initiate change. Sometimes competence is not shown by what you say, but what you don't say. Be careful to learn when to speak and when to listen.

## Mental Toughness

Naturally, there are other traits that will prepare you as a leader and seasoned officer and will improve your abilities over time. Mental toughness is one trait that will give you the ability to know when to be sensitive and compassionate. This trait provides the drive and determination when things go wrong or your resources are low and you are expected to produce results. Mental toughness will provide the energy and motivation when all others around you are seemingly giving up. Mental toughness provides you the tenacity to remain focused when it is really needed.

There will be times that it seems like there is not enough time in the day to complete your assigned task, and to make matters worse, emergency situations that require your time and energy continue to pop up. Your boss is upset with you about something you misinterpreted, and you fell flat on your face in not living up to his expectations. Murphy has kicked into high gear, and you are feeling the pain permeating every ounce of your very soul. This is the time to call on your ancestors, by recalling the many obstacles they had to confront while living in a hostile environment and still come out smelling like a rose.

Do you have what it takes to keep the faith and work through those tough issues? Sometimes you just have to see it through. There will be times that you have to go through those difficult times. Remember the old sayings, "That which doesn't kill you will make you stronger" and "The iron that remains in the fire the longest will be the strongest." You will succeed in those difficult times; just don't lose your cool. Realize that this is only a test required of you so you can learn.

You have to have the mental toughness to endure hard times. You will be successful as long as you don't give up and don't give in. Remember you are a member of the most powerful military force that this world has ever seen. You are a part of something much bigger than yourself, and the military infrastructure, while not perfect, will assist you in becoming the very best that you can be. Be strong, and face each challenge with your chin up, knowing that your tomorrow will be better than your today. That is mental toughness!

## Organizational Skills

Another trait that will assist your success is being organized. As an officer you are going to receive endless data and a variety of raw information relating to various issues. It is important that you are able to quickly assess the data, process it, and know how to effectively apply that new knowledge and properly distribute it. Having the ability to organize your thoughts and events will serve you well. As an officer you will be given increased responsibility as you progress through the ranks.

You will have the opportunity to chair meetings and be in charge of large-scale operations during your career. In each instance you will have to brief your superiors with details of each event and provide detailed factual information for every occurrence. Planning for contingencies is a must, and knowing how to factor in operational risk management issues will prove to be essential to the success of every engagement. Learn the tenets of proper planning and the tools of hosting an effective meeting.

Effectively organizing events and motivating people to assist you will prove to be an indispensable golden nugget. Work to know the finer points of each aspect of the event you are planning. Take time out to properly coordinate with others who are assisting you and are essential to the production being a success. You will quickly find that working with people will assist you in developing professional communications and fostering relationships that you may need in future projects. Don't allow your emotions to get in the way when things don't go according to your expectations. Realize that people, not plans, make things happen. Invest time in your support staff, and they will pick up the pieces when things are not quite right to get them back on course.

## Don't Be a Careerist!

No commander likes an officer who is concerned solely about their personal career and not their subordinates. A good rule of thumb is that the best job you will ever have is the one that you are in, and the way to get promoted to the next rank is to do the best job you possibly can. There is time for career counseling from your supervisor, and you need to take advantage of those opportunities.

When preparing for those feedback sessions, you need to come in properly prepared. Bring along with you a list of duties you have completed in the last six to twelve months. Write down where you think you want to go for your next assignment and professional concerns you may have about your assigned duties and responsibilities. Don't allow this session to be a one-way discussion. Take advantage of it by asking questions of your own.

No commander wants to be hounded by younger officers trying to push their way into the limelight by nudging others aside. Being labeled as a careerist is not the kiss of death, especially if you are good at what you do, but it can mean having the commander not eagerly support your career because of your pushiness and arrogance. Tread with caution in being overly zealous about personally managing your career. You need to trust your commander to protect you and work your next assignment or promotion. You need to learn how to be humble. That means being mission-focused and not placing the emphasis on personal fulfillment. If you handle yourself professionally and learn to be selfless and create the environment for success for your subordinates, you will find yourself excelling faster than you could imagine. Zig Ziglar, the famous motivational guru, says it best: "The best way to get what you want out of life is to help someone get what they want."

## Maximizing Your Talents

There may be times that you feel like you are not being given the chance to show your stuff, or your supervisor is holding you back from reaching your true potential. When—not if—this happens you need to realize it for what it is and not panic. Work toward redirecting your positive energy to further develop yourself. Self-development is the one thing that is always in your control. Don't allow anyone to assume this responsibility. Take advantage of online courses, and attend seminars or conventions that spark your creativity and excitement about learning.

Don't allow your military supervisor to control your definition of success; you need to decide this for yourself. Things may not be optimal for you at the present time, but continue to build your résumé and motivation to conquer your dreams. Do you think that General Benjamin Davis Sr. (the first black general officer in the armed forces) merely gave up when things did not go his way or used the fact that he was black as an excuse? No way! He realized his environment, made the most of each situation, and overcame every obstacle he encountered. He realized that his tomorrow was more important than his today and that he had to make huge investments in himself to ensure he was properly prepared when opportunities came his way. He realized that not only was the whole American black race rooting for him, but most of the entire white society was watching and waiting for him to fail either personally or professionally.

Commit yourself to embracing excellence by surrounding yourself with brilliance (e.g., reading, writing, watching, listening) and supportive people. We all become products of our environments, so you owe it to yourself to become the best you. Start as hip-hop mogul Russell Simmons says: "Work on doing you!" Developing your mind through practicing successful and positive habits will allow you to maximize your talents and set you apart from your peers.

## Micro-Inequities You Might Encounter

- A coworker sees you and several black colleagues at a casual lunch, and then later at the office he asks, "What was that meeting all about?"
- You arrive at work on time, as usual. Your boss, or a coworker making the rounds, peeks in and remarks with surprise, "Oh, you're here?"
- After a staff meeting, your boss suggests, "You need to work at making others more comfortable with you. Why don't you smile more often?" Or he says, "Lighten up. Don't be so serious at work. Smile and laugh more often to make others more comfortable working with you."
- You are told you are "rough around the edges" despite your

completion of many professional development courses, and it is suggested you emulate the behavior of a white colleague.

- You continually get more responsibility but no authority.
- You arrive at an off-site business retreat dressed in business casual attire. Your white peers approach and ask why you are always so dressed up.
- You are told you are decreasing your effectiveness with your aggressive style.
- You are frequently asked why you change your hairstyle so often.
- You tell your supervisor about a problem you are having, and the response you get is "You've got to be exaggerating! I find that hard to believe."
- Your first name is arbitrarily shortened to one or two syllables without your permission.
- Walking through the hall with coworkers, you exchange greetings with two other blacks you pass along the way. Your colleague says in amazement, "My, you know so many people."
- When you walk into a room, people quickly say, "I wouldn't want to get into a fight with you!" Or they constantly claim that you are intimidating.

In dealing with any of these situations, you merely need to consider the source and say a quick prayer. If you have not figured it out yet, you will soon realize that having a successful career in the military requires a large amount of patience and prayer. Some of the incidents listed above can and will be merely overlooked, but after a while you will ask yourself, *"How much do I have to continue to deal with?"*

The answer is that you will always deal with some of these issues throughout your career; the key is to learn to understand who you are and most importantly whose you are. Connecting with your spiritualty is critically important when dealing with difficult situations. When you fully understand that we are made in the image of God the creator, you should find comfort knowing that you belong to Him. It does not matter how many obstacles anyone throws in your way, kindly acknowledge it, then move on. You are greater than your present circumstance, and you will endure many times over the amount of issues you will have to confront. You merely need to think back to our many ancestors who fought in previous wars and lived in an unjust society where prejudice was completely legal, so find your strength. By reviewing their bravery you cannot help but be encouraged by their faith and steadfastness in seeking a better life. If they did not endure their harsh realities, then surely you and I would not be in the lofty positions that we have achieved.

## Are You the Only Black at the Conference Table?

Stop counting heads to see if you are the only black in the room, because you already know that you are! This situation is going to occur more times than you can count, so get used to it. Most whites are not overly concerned about the racial mixture in the room or assigned to your unit until the roles are reversed, which will probably never happen. Make your presence count, and do not be shy about speaking up and contributing to each conversation if you have something to say. Be decisive in your comments, and don't worry about being the only black in the room.

Develop a reputation for being brilliant and aggressive. Learn to control the room with both your presence and your competence. You may be the only black in the room, so you want to optimize your presence by being viewed as an essential member of the team. Your presence needs to be missed when you are not there. Allow your supervisor and coworkers to learn to depend on you and not assume that it is business as usual when you are absent.

As you continue to climb in rank, you will begin to find comfort in this racial isolation and not be concerned about this ratio. Your rank will begin to distinguish your role, and you will be expected to live up to the responsibilities of that position. Being the only black, or one of a few in attendance, at a meeting only means that we as a nation have a lot of unfinished business in recruiting more people of color. Again, don't worry. Press on and become the best that you possibly can.

## Being Black in a White World

There has been a lot written on black achievement in white corporate America, and serving in the armed forces is no different. Some may counsel you that you need to forget about or deny who you really are by not associating with people of your race and only hanging around whites or other coworkers. While there is a lot to be said for hanging out with coworkers and strengthening those social professional relationships, there is no reason you have to deny who you are and not socialize with other black officers. You are who you are, and that fact will never change!

Hang around positive people, because they are assisting you in developing your professional skills, whether they are black or white. Don't limit yourself by associating with anyone just because of their race. Let it be because they have qualities that you admire and respect. Expand your horizons, and set your standards high. Do not allow anyone to lower them for you. Be firm in your commitment and dedicated to your success.

There have been many successful black men and women who have come before you and have paved the way for your success, so take advantage of it by realizing your legacy and inheritance of being black in America. Embrace your blackness, and exploit it for everything you possibly can. You are the only you that was born *you*—with the ancestors, ethnic background, personal baggage, professional challenges, and destiny for success. Embrace your blackness, and realize that living in a white world may be a challenge at times, but many others have made it. Even though it may be difficult at times, you too will be successful and exceed all goals that have ever been accomplished.

## Being a First in Your Family

You may or may not be the first high school or college graduate in your family, or maybe you are the first military officer. Either way, you should try to build on the success of your ancestors and improve on the legacy that they started. Work to purchase a home or receive a master's and PhD degree. Strive to obtain a White House fellowship or specialized internship. It should not be your goal to be a first in your family, but if you are, take on that title with pride and represent your family well.

Being the first merely means that no one else in your family received the opportunity to engage in this pursuit before you. It means that you are working to set a new and higher standard for your relatives who come behind you. This is important because each generation should strive to do better than the previous one and increase your station in life. Even though no one publicly acknowledged you, don't worry. Your family is quietly celebrating your accomplishments in your absence. Some people do not know how to give or receive compliments, so don't worry if nothing is said when you return home with another promotion and no one says congratulations. As you continue to rise in rank, you will find that your family may not place you on a pedestal, but they are bragging about your accomplishments to their friends and other family members. Keep up the good work, because all eyes are on you!

## Ending the Cycle of Poverty

Now that you are a military officer and receive a regular paycheck, you have the opportunity to make a decent living if you manage your money correctly. You have a chance to finally end the cycle of poverty that perhaps plagued your family because of a lack of educational or employment opportunities. As long as you remain on active duty, you can count on receiving a paycheck on the first and fifteenth of the month, regardless of where you are in the world.

In the civilian world you typically have to punch a time clock or be present for work to receive a paycheck, but that is not necessarily true in the military. If you are sick and in the hospital, you will still receive your pay on time and in the right amount. You have the rare opportunity to get yourself financially ahead if you properly budget and live within your means. Be careful of overspending or creating credit card debt. Living in debt is one of the quickest ways to ruin your stellar career, so be careful and remain committed to your budget.

If you need financial advice, secure financial counseling. No one will put you down for seeking advice, but they will surely criticize you if you find yourself in your commander's office for bouncing a check or not paying your bills on time. Don't allow this condition to occur. The number-one adverse issue facing most Americans, both black and white, is financial responsibility, so don't fall into this trap.

If you were born in a middle to low-income family, then expect family members to call and ask for money when things are financially tight. Keep your family out of your pocket! Everyone has financial crises from time to time, and not all financial crises are real emergencies. If you decide to donate money to a family member, realize that it is a gift and do not expect to get it back, unless they clearly state that they are going to return it.

Your family loves you and wants to see you climb the ladder of success. They do not intend on pulling you down. They may merely need your assistance in fully understanding your new military environment. Sometimes instead of giving funds, maybe what is really needed is sound fiscal management and education. This may be the time that you have to use a little tough love in dealing with this situation.

Even with the promise of repayment, many times situations change and it may prove difficult for your relatives to make the repayment. Remember not to be alarmed and allow yourself to get upset, because once you lend someone money you really should expect it to be a gift and not expect it to be returned. This issue can be classified as the single largest issue that creates discourse among family members, so why even put yourself in this situation? Lending money to friends is even worse than lending to family. If you value your friendship, then do not loan money to or borrow money from your friends. Once you cross this bridge, you are inviting heartache and pain, and possibly jeopardizing your friendship. Keep both your friends and family out of your pockets!

## Frustration with Family Members

Many black families are categorized as being dysfunctional. There are a variety of social reasons that our families are dysfunctional and disenfranchised. One of the primary reasons for this social dysfunction is a lack of education, which leads many family members to make inappropriate, immature, or uninformed decisions. Education is the one element that will expose you to new ideas, methods, and strategies to apply in making decisions.

Poor education is only one reason. There are several reasons that many black families still live in poverty and are incarcerated at record numbers. Whites tend to receive salaries at a rate of two to one in conducting the same or similar duties, according to the Department of Labor. Blacks typically do not invest their money in the stock market for three reasons: (1) they lack the disposable income, (2) they lack trust in the stock market, and (3) they traditionally do not understand investment rules.

Fortunately, as your education increases, you will be afforded the opportunity to become more professional and make remarkable strides in reversing any and all negative trends. It is a known fact that every decision will have a consequence. Whether a good decision or a bad one, a consequence will follow. Many times family members will make a decision without thinking completely about the pending outcome or consequence of their actions and decisions. Then once the decision is made, they will call on you for assistance. Now that you are being called for assistance, you are involved, whether you want to be or not. Your involvement may cause some frustration and anger.

When you have a family member who is a habitual bad actor, it tends to occupy your every conversation when you call or visit home. You try your best to remove the stress, but you can't because it is your family! If there is ever a time to pray and ask for encouragement, now is the time. Prayer will give you the peace of mind you need to endure these periods of frustration.

Don't allow your family to ruin your career! Take a stance and treat your relationship with your family member with a measure of control. You may have to distance yourself from it to some degree and seek counsel from your mentor or supervisor. You cannot allow a family member's actions to cause you prolonged stress that requires you to take leave or periods of absence from your professional duties.

When your family member gets on your last nerve, convert this negative energy into something positive by working out in the gym or taking a long walk and pondering your concerns, giving you the quiet time you need to think through these issues. Don't internalize these issues. Treat them for what they are, just issues! When God is on your side, there is nothing you cannot deal with if you keep it in perspective and engage it in prayer.

There is nothing more important that you can do for family members than pray for them and offer the encouragement and support needed to turn their bad behavior into something more productive. Always remember that success is contagious, and the better you do in committing yourself to these tenets of our core values and sharpening your professional tools, the more you will find others closest to you trying to emulate you. No one will ever argue with you if you are working to pull others up the ladder of success.

## Not Black Enough?

Now that you are a member of the most powerful and lethal military force the world has ever seen, those closest to you may view you a little differently. As you continue to rise in rank, you may find some of your family and friends harboring petty jealousy and criticizing you by making hateful comments. For example, "You talk too proper" or "You are not black enough!" When you first hear these comments, you will most likely react very harshly by snapping back in defense.

As you travel and gain exposure to new ideas, you should expect your knowledge to increase and your vocabulary to improve. The way that you pronounce certain words will also possibly improve. Depending on the region of the country you call home, you possibly have a tendency of saying words in a certain way. Not that your way is correct or incorrect—it is just different. After you have been away from home for a while and you return, many of your friends and family may say that you talk a little differently, or "proper." Don't be alarmed. This only means that you are developing and growing into a professional. Remember that if something remains the same, then it means that it is stagnating and not growing.

You should not expect to remain the same as you were when you originally left home; growth and professional development are positive things. Don't worry about those who criticize you. Pray for them! While praying, figure out what else you can do to improve yourself. Those who criticize you (I'm not referring to constructive criticism) are attempting to tear you down and hold you back. Don't worry about it. Just keep moving closer to your goals. In time you will have the confidence to overlook these comments and be secure in who you are and who you want to become.

Being an officer in the military will require you to dress a little more conservatively than you may be used to, so again you may receive criticism from your family and friends. As an officer, you should not dress inappropriately and identify yourself as representing the military. In order to be respected as an officer, you have to walk the walk and talk the talk, and that means dressing the part as well. Don't allow yourself to fall back into your old habits of speaking with slang, using profanity in public, or dressing inappropriately. You are a professional military officer!

As a young female officer you want to dress conservatively and never wear a top that is overly tight or too low-cut, or a dress or skirt that is too short. The most professional male officer will still be tempted and excited by your appearance if you dress in this manner. Besides this, at official functions, expect spouses to become enraged if you dress inappropriately. The same standards apply to male officers. If you dress inappropriately by wearing clothes or accessories not approved for the military setting, expect to hear about it! You are always on parade, and you need to be prepared to embrace proper dress and expected standards.

The criticisms will eventually disappear, so do not worry too much about them, as long as you comply with dress and appearance standards. You will make your own mark on life, and you are starting out by improving yourself by joining the most respected organization in the world. Be first in your commitment, and dedicate yourself to becoming the best military officer you possibly can. You will be rewarded by getting promoted to the next rank.

## Taking Vacations

For most black families, the typical vacation is returning home to spend time with family and get caught up with old friends. During your parents' and perhaps grandparents' years, the average black family could not afford to take vacations other than visiting family and friends in a nearby city or state. Blacks are now taking cruises, traveling abroad, and engaging in once-rare activities in record numbers. Being in the military will expose you to new, different, and exciting events and activities. Embrace these new activities, and try out opportunities that interest you. Who knows, you just might have fun. Don't allow yourself to remain confined to your traditional activities. Most black vacations only focus on eating, drinking, and recounting what you did in the past. Make a concerted effort to change your habits by learning how to play golf, ski, camp, hunt, or even fly-fish. Learn to have fun doing something different, by getting out and going somewhere different—not just returning home.

If you decide to go to some remote location and engage in skiing, camping, hiking, or hunting, look around and you will see that you are probably the only black face in the area. Don't worry. Take advantage of this opportunity, and relax and enjoy yourself. If you find this racial isolation too much for you to handle, then take someone who looks like you along with you and enjoy the moment. Most whites are not threatened or overly concerned if there are just a few people who look like you in the area. They know that you are just a visitor and will be leaving shortly.

Okay, you are probably thinking, *But I like going home, and who are you to tell me I need to do something different?* Stepping outside your comfort zone in your personal life will not only expose you to something different, but will allow you to learn and see places you have only read about. It will give you a chance to have something additional in common with some of your coworkers.

Your family will understand that you need a little time to yourself or just with your immediate family or friends. Take this time to create special memories, and give your children something special to cherish for the rest of their life. The thirty days you receive each year is a luxury that many civilian employees do not have the privilege of gaining without having years of tenure. This is your time, so take it and do something special! Taking advantage of your vacation time will allow you to take a break from your hectic schedule and relax in a new environment. Many times when you return home on vacation you will find yourself addressing family problems and not getting a chance to relax, so when you return to work you find yourself even more stressed-out than when you left. Take at least a portion of your leave time for you, and recharge your batteries. You will find that you will need this rest.

## Sage Advice

### Lieutenant Colonel Christopher C. Herring, USAF

- Break up the huddles on the job.
- Have lunch frequently with Tuskegee Airmen who live in your area. They have a wealth of knowledge and so much free time to kill. Your air force friends marvel over their story and benefit from the straight talk these pioneers have provided to our nation.
- Stratification is important. Learn the ground rules to achieving it early in your annual performance rating, and work hard in consistently sustaining it. Stratification offer promotion boards patterns of excellence. Make your records count by ensuring your awards and decorations are in order, and your records are properly stratified. When it comes to promotion boards, it is all in the paper!
- We are a people who always try to give back and help in our private organizations (e.g., fraternities, sororities, churches). Don't be afraid to use one-liners in mentioning your contributions to community service, but do not focus on race. Ethnic identifiers in bullet points tend to minimize the impact of the event. One way to show the impact you make as an air force ambassador is to talk about the successes. For example, discuss whether you raised $5,000 in scholarships for local children versus raising $5,000 in scholarships for children who desire to attend historically black colleges and universities. The military system doesn't have to have all of the details; they just need to know

you're productive—more so than your peer group. I also know it is good to see those private organizations send thank-you letters to your chain. Again, it sets you apart.

### Captain Derrick D. Modest Sr., USAF

- "I can do all things through Christ which strengthen me" (Phil 4:13).
- Find a mentor, preferably someone who understands the struggle you go through.
- Be productive. Learn your job, and that will help combat the doubters.

### 1LT Joseph D. Lett, USAF

- Bloom where you are planted.
- Don't succumb to careerism.
- Be a good steward.

# CHAPTER 9
## IT TAKES A VILLAGE!

But those who wait on the Lord shall renew their strength;
They shall mount up with wings like eagles, They shall run
and not be weary, They shall walk and not faint.

—Isaiah 40:31

I am overwhelmed by the grace and persistence of my
people.

—Maya Angelou, 1992

Never exalt people because they're in your family; never
exalt people because they're your color, never exalt people
because they're your kinfolk. Exalt them because they're
worthy.

—Louis Farrakhan, 1985

Anyone who thinks that you reach success by yourself is sadly mistaken.
The same holds true within the military. It is impossible to find success
and climb to the next rank without the dedicated help and assistance
of those in your support system. Many times you may find people
helping you who do not know you personally, but you come highly
recommended by your supervisor or commander. It is the credibility
and reputation of that individual that gives you the boost you need to
receive the head nod.

As you scan history, you will see that anyone who has reached success at any level had the support of others. It is important to decide who your support system will be. Are they going to be people who look like you and are closest to you, or are they going to be a team of people who barely know you personally yet embrace similar standards and values? The answer is both. It is important to have those who personally know you and a team of professionals with similar goals, backgrounds, and standards.

Throughout the history of the United States, blacks to a large degree had to depend on people in their communities and within their personal alliances to support their goals. With the approval of the civil rights legislation and school integration, more blacks are moving into suburbs and befriending whites in record numbers. Lifetime alliances are being formed, creating support systems in working toward common goals.

The history of the black church in America goes much deeper than the civil rights era. The black church during the colonial period, or more commonly called the Christianization of the slaves, was generally ineffective until the 1740s. The revivals during this period began to attract significant numbers of black converts, largely because many churches encouraged the lower classes, including slaves, to pray and preach in public. In the emotional fervor of the revival meetings, whites and blacks preached to and converted one another. Baptists and Methodists licensed black men to preach, and by the 1770s some black ministers, both slaves as well as free men, were leading their own congregations.

Black churches in the South were subjected to restrictions intended to prevent unsupervised slave assemblies. But despite occasional white harassment, southern black churches survived and provided a limited religious independence. In the antebellum years, Christianity spread gradually among the slaves. Some blacks attended church with whites to quietly nurse the children or under white supervision, but the majority of blacks had little, if any, access to formal church services. Nevertheless, slaves often conducted their own religious meetings, with or without their owner's consent.

Most will agree that there is power in numbers, and one of the first places to maximize this power in black America was the black church.

The black church was that refuge where the community could meet without interference from whites and having to deal with Jim Crow laws. The church not only was the center for spiritual renewal, but it rapidly became the local community center, meetinghouse, public school, voting place, and center of black life. Even today, it is common to see black people from all stations of life in the black Church. If you need to hear the latest news or find out how well a particular person or family is doing, you can find out by attending church.

Blacks are traditionally very conservative when it comes to dealing with homosexuality, pornography, and traditional religious standards. In recent years black society has shifted to a more liberal tone and allowed more freedoms both in and out of church. Regardless of conservativeness or liberalism, the black church is still the centerpiece for black life. Many blacks still spend the majority of Sunday and Wednesday evening in Bible class. From the earliest colonial periods in America's, history you will see that the church played a prominent role in black life. In church it did not matter if you had money or status. What really mattered was that you believed in God and it gave you hope that there was going to be a better tomorrow. People went to church to discuss life's problems and share food, clothes, job information, or anything else that really mattered in the black community. The church was the meeting spot where blacks gained insight into their inner selves and shared with each other how to read, write, organize, plan, and implement change.

The church was the safest place for blacks during this period of time, and it became the safe haven for black life. The role of the preacher was important and respected in the black community, and this individual became the designated leader and often the spokesperson for the community. Even today, when politicians need to seek out support from black communities, their first stop is the black church.

## African Methodist Episcopal (A. M. E.)

On February 14, 1760, Richard Allen was born in Philadelphia, Pennsylvania, and, at the tender age of seventeen, requested permission from his master to join the Methodist Society, which was approved. After learning how to read and write, he started preaching at twenty-two years of age at Methodist meetings. His master later determined that slavery was wrong and allowed Allen to purchase his way out of servitude for $2,000. It would take Allen five years to raise the funds. As Allen's preaching abilities increased, he was allowed to preach to both blacks and whites in New York, New Jersey, Pennsylvania, Maryland, and Delaware.

During one meeting, Absalom Jones was kneeling in prayer at the front of the church and was asked to move to the rear of the church. This action caused the Free African Society to raise enough money to create a congregation only for Africans. The African Church of Philadelphia became the first official black church in America and part of the Protestant Episcopal Church of America.

Richard Allen, along with eleven other members, took the lead and started the Bethel African Church. By 1816, there were several African Methodist churches around the country, and while uniting together they formed the African Methodist Episcopal denomination. On April 11, 1816, Richard Allen was named its first bishop.

## Christian Methodist Episcopal (C. M. E.)

In 1866, black members of the White Methodist Episcopal Church South petitioned to form a separate church. On December 15, 1870, the first General Conference of the Colored Methodist Episcopal Church was held at Liberty Church in Jackson, Tennessee, and William H. Miles and Richard H. Vanderhorst were elected bishops. In the next twenty years membership would reach an impressive 103,000. In 1954, the denomination changed its name to Christian Methodist Episcopal Church.

## Church of God in Christ

In 1896, Charles H. Mason and Charles Jones formed the Church of God. The following year, the name changed to Church of God in Christ (COGIC). In 1907, Jones split with Mason and formed the Church of Christ (Holiness) USA. In 1907, Mason became presiding bishop until his death in 1961. White ministers separated from COGIC and formed the Assemblies of God in 1914.

## Progressive National Baptist Convention Inc.

Sometimes blessings come out of chaos, and this is the case with the emergence of Progressive National Baptist Convention Inc. In 1957, the National Baptist Convention USA Inc. president, Reverend J. H. Jackson expelled ten pastors over the issue of tenure, and Progressive National Baptist Convention Inc. was created. On November 14–15, 1961, Reverend L. V. Booth formed the Progressive National Baptist Convention.

## National Baptist Convention USA Inc.

In 1880, the Foreign Mission Convention was organized in Montgomery, Alabama, and Reverend W. H. McAlpin was elected as the first president. In 1886, the American National Baptist Convention was organized, and two years later this organization transformed into the National Baptist Convention in Atlanta, Georgia, where Reverend Elias C. Morris was elected president. In 1916, the National Baptist Convention of America was reorganized as the National Baptist Convention USA Inc.

## National Baptist Convention of America Inc.

The National Baptist Convention of America Inc. has the same legacy and birth as the National Baptist Convention USA Inc. and, in 1915, was made its own entity. Phi Beta Kappa was the first American college fraternity and was organized at the College of William and Mary in 1776. Men and women of this organization adopted Greek letters to identify their new organization. Over the years college fraternities and sororities played a major role in college life. Black college fraternities and sororities did not emerge until the early 1900s. Unlike their white counterparts, the black groups have remained very active at the graduate level and have played a major role in the cultural, social, and civic life in their communities.

Civic organizations played a huge role, as well. From the creation of the early abolitionist movement and organizations and the Underground Railroad, blacks knew that if they were going to survive in America they needed to band together, even if it was viewed as illegal. Blacks had little choice other than uniting together to attempt to effect change on a society that was unfair and at times brutal. There are several organizations in existence today that maximize the talents and pursuits of well-meaning professionals.

Unlike most white college fraternities and sororities, most black members of Greek organizations will remain active with their organizations long after college. You will find many active-duty officers are enlisted members of black fraternities and sororities. Most will share with you that these organizations allowed them a safe haven to discuss the frustrations of work with close brothers and sisters who clearly understood the stresses of working in the professional world. Oftentimes, you will find military retirees who have served most, if not all, of their military career actively working in communities and actively supporting civic and fraternal organizations.

Most senior members of fraternities and sororities take time out of work with younger people in their community by providing guidance and mentorship on how best to be effective and successful, how to resolve conflicts, and how to improve their station in life. Each organization has its unique charter and impact on society. These organizations are vital to the success of our communities and establishment of professionals worldwide. Many younger members of civic organizations gain their experience in *Robert's Rules of Order* (official guidelines on how to officiate an organizational meeting), organization, and event planning. Being a member of these organizations creates opportunities in honing public speaking skills, improving writing, and overall communication abilities. These organizations are vital to the success of America in remaining the premier world power.

Take time to learn of the many black professional organizations in existence today. The list contained in this book is far from complete and only serves as a guide to get you started in partnering with other professional organizations that are dedicated to enhancing black life in your neighborhood and this country. Many of these organizations had a direct impact on the successes during the civil rights era and before, and that legacy continues today.

If you are interested in learning more about any of these organizations, feel free to contact them directly; contact information is provided. They will be glad to put you in touch with their local representative. Once you make contact, be ready to start working and making a positive difference in your community. One of the biggest advantages of becoming a member of these organizations is the teaming affect with like-minded people who are all striving for perfection and have a legacy of excellence behind their name. You will find yourself growing in wisdom and engaging in environments completely separate from the military. You will find it vitally important to remain aware of the accomplishments being made in the professional civilian communities.

Another huge benefit of joining one of the fraternities or sororities is being able to socialize with professionals with similar backgrounds. Most of these people have graduated from historically black colleges and universities and are now working hard in the professional world, struggling to get ahead just like you.

Embrace this opportunity, and watch the experiences and accomplishments you are gaining in these organizations spill over into your military life. Partnering with other black professionals will give you an additional edge to secure mentors outside of the military and learn from other time-honored black traditions.

Being in the US military already provides you the opportunity of being a member of something great and being involved in something much larger than yourself. There is no greater service than laying down your life for something in which you believe. Freedom is not free! It requires the citizens of this nation to be willing to fight for the right and liberty, which is a very special privilege. Each of the organizations listed are dedicated to supporting this fight for freedom and supporting you in reaching your pinnacle in rank.

Take time to research each of these organizations and find the right one for you. Each organization is looking to add you to their roster, because they want fresh, new, intelligent people to join their ranks. As a new member you will expose yourself to new ideas and professionals who are making huge accomplishments within their career field and making their mark on society. Many times it is hard to find military members willing to take leadership roles in civic organizations because of their frequent temporary assignments and demanding duties. If you are committed to making a difference, take time out and get yourself involved.

## Civic and Social Organizations

### National Association for the Advancement of Colored People (NAACP)
4805 Mt. Hope Drive
Baltimore, MD 21215
Phone: (877) NAACP-98
Local: (410) 580-5777

The NAACP emphasizes that people of all races, nationalities, and faiths unite under one premise—that all men and women are created equal. The NAACP is the nation's oldest civil rights organization and has changed America's history. Despite violence, intimidation, and hostile government policies, the NAACP and its grassroots membership have survived and preserved a bright future for generations to come.

### United Negro College Fund
8260 Willow Oaks Corporate Drive
P.O. Box 10444
Fairfax, VA 22031-8044
Phone: (800) 331-2244

The mission of UNCF is to enhance the quality of education by providing financial assistance to deserving students, raising operating funds for member colleges and universities, and increasing access to technology for students and faculty at historically black colleges and universities. Since its inception in 1944, UNCF has grown to become the nation's oldest and most successful African American higher education assistance organization.

### Urban League
120 Wall Street
New York, NY 10005
Phone: (212) 558-5300

Fax: (212) 344-5332

Established in 1910, the Urban League is the nation's oldest and largest community-based movement devoted to empowering African Americans to enter the economic and social mainstream. The mission of the Urban League movement is to enable African Americans to secure economic self-reliance, parity, power, and civil rights. The Urban League employs a five-point strategy, tailored to local needs, in order to implement the mission of our movement: education and youth empowerment, economic empowerment, health and quality-of-life empowerment, civic engagement and leadership empowerment, and civil rights and racial justice empowerment.

## National Black Caucus of State Legislators (NBCSL)

444 North Caucus of State Legislators
Washington, DC 20001
Phone: (202) 624-5457
Fax: (202) 508-3826

The primary mission of the National Black Caucus of State Legislators is to develop, conduct, and promote educational, research, and training programs designed to enhance the effectiveness of its members, as they consider legislation and issues of public policy that impact, either directly or indirectly, the general welfare of African American constituents within their respective jurisdictions.

## Congressional Black Caucus (CBC) Foundation Inc.

1720 Massachusetts Avenue
NW Washington, DC 20036

In January 1969, newly elected African American representatives of the 77th Congress joined six incumbents to form the Democratic Select Committee. The committee was renamed the Congressional Black Caucus in 1971. Their goals are to positively influence the course of events pertinent to African Americans and others of similar experience and situation, and to achieve greater equity for persons of African background in the design and content of domestic and international programs and services. While the CBC has been primarily focused on the concerns of African Americans, the caucus has also been at the forefront of legislative campaign for human and civil rights for all citizens.

## Blacks in Government

National Headquarters
3005 Georgia Avenue NW
Washington, DC 20001-3807
www.bignel.org
e-mail: BIG@bignet.org

A Black in Government (BIG) was established in 1975 by a small group of African Americans at the Public Health Services, which is part of the Department of Health, Education, and Welfare in the Parklawn building in Rockville, Maryland. BIG has been a national response to the need for African Americans in public service to organize around issues of mutual concern and use their collective strength to confront workplace and community issues. BIG's goals are to promote equality in all aspects of American life, excellence in public service, and opportunity for all Americans.

## Southern Christian Leadership Conference (SCLC)

One Georgia Center
600 West Peachtree Street, 9th Floor
Atlanta, GA 30308
Phone: (404) 522-1420
Fax: (404) 527-4333

The SCLC grew out of the Montgomery Bus Boycott, which began on December 5, 1955. The boycott was called out by the newly established Montgomery Improvement Association. Martin Luther King Jr. served as president, and Ralph Abernathy served as program director. It was one of history's most dramatic and massive nonviolent protests, stunning the nation and the world. Sixty people came together, representing ten states, and announced the founding of the Southern Leadership Transportation and Nonviolent Integration. Later in New Orleans, Louisiana, on February 14, 1957, the organization shortened its name to Southern Christian Leadership Conference. Today, the SCLC is a nationwide organization fighting to improve human rights around the world.

## TransAfrica Forum

1629 K Street, NW, Suite 1100
Washington, DC 20006
Phone: (202) 223-1960
Fax: (202) 223-1966
e-mail: info@transafricaforum.org

TransAfrica Forum is a center for activism focusing on conditions in the African world. It sponsors seminars, conferences, community awareness projects, and training programs. These activities allow the organization to play a significant role in presenting to the general public alternative perspectives on the economic, political, and moral ramifications of US foreign policy.

## Fraternities and Sororities

### Alpha Phi Alpha Fraternity, Inc.

23 13 St. Paul Street
Baltimore, MD 21218-5234
Phone: (4 10) 554-0040
Fax: (410) 554-0054

Alpha Phi Alpha became the first intercollegiate Greek-letter fraternity established primarily for African Americans on December 4, 1906, at Cornell University in Ithaca, New York, by seven college men who recognized the need to foster brotherhood. This vision became known as the "Jewels" of the fraternity. The fraternity created scholarship, fellowship, good character, and the uplift of humanity as their guiding principles.

Alpha Phi Alpha has led the nation in the fight for civil rights though leaders such as W. E. B. DuBois, Adam Clayton Powell Jr., Edward Broke, Martin Luther King Jr., Thurgood Marshall, Andrew

Young, William Gray, Paul Roberson, and many other prominent African Americans.

## Alpha Kappa Alpha Sorority, Inc.

5656 S. Stony Island Avenue
Chicago, IL 60637
Phone: (773) 684-1282

Founded on the campus of Howard University in Washington, DC, in 1908, Alpha Kappa Alpha Sorority is the oldest Greek-letter organization established by and for African American college-trained women. The small group of women who organized the sorority were conscious of a privileged position as college-trained women of color, just one generation removed from slavery. They were resolute that their college experiences should be as meaningful and productive as possible. Alpha Kappa Alpha was founded to apply that determination.

## Kappa Alpha Psi Fraternity, Inc.

2322-24 North Broad Street
Philadelphia, PA 19132-4590
Phone: (2 l5) 228-7184
Fax: (215) 228-7181

On January 5, 1911, Elder Watson Diggs, along with nine other college undergraduate men, founded the fraternity Kappa Alpha Nu and later changed the name to what is now known as Kappa Alpha Psi on April 15, 1915. Founded for the fundamental purpose of recognizing achievement, the fraternity united men of culture, patriotism, and honor.

## Omega Psi Phi Fraternity, Inc.

3951 Snapfinger Parkway
Decatur, GA 30035
Phone: (404) 284-5533
Fax: (404) 284-0333
http://www.oppf.org

On Friday evening, November 17, 1911, three Howard University undergraduate students, with the assistance of their faculty adviser, gave birth to the Omega Psi Phi Fraternity. This event occurred in the office of biology professor Ernest E. Just, the faculty adviser, in the Science Hall (now known as Thirkield Hall). The three liberal arts students were Edgar A. Love, Oscar J. Cooper, and Frank Coleman. From the initials of the Greek phrase, meaning "friendship is essential to the soul," the name Omega Psi Phi was derived. The phrase was selected as the motto. Manhood, scholarship, perseverance, and uplift were adopted as cardinal principles. A decision was made regarding the design for the pin and emblem, and thus ended the first meeting of the Omega Psi Phi Fraternity.

## Delta Sigma Theta Sorority, Inc.
1707 New Hampshire Avenue NW
Washington, DC 20009
Phone: (202) 986-2400

Delta Sigma Theta Sorority was founded January 13, 1913, by twenty-two collegiate women at Howard University. These students wanted to use their collective strength to promote academic excellence and to provide assistance to persons in need. The first public act performed by the Delta founders involved their participation in the women's suffrage march in Washington, DC, in March 1913. Delta Sigma Theta was incorporated in 1930.

## Phi Beta Sigma Fraternity, Inc.
145 Kennedy Street NW
Washington, DC 20011-5294
Phone: (202) 726-5434
Fax: (202) 882-1681

This organization was founded at Howard University in Washington, DC, on January 9, 1914, by three young African American undergraduate students with the ideals of brotherhood, scholarship, and service. The motto of the fraternity is "Culture for Service and Service for Humanity." The founders deeply wanted to create an organization that viewed itself as a part of the general community and was inclusive to the needs of the community.

## Zeta Phi Beta Sorority, Inc.
1734 New Hampshire Avenue NW
Washington, DC 20009
Fax: (202) 232-4593

Zeta Phi Beta Sorority was founded on the simple belief that sorority elitism and socializing should not overshadow the real mission for progressive organization—to address societal mores, ills, prejudices, poverty, and health concerns of the day. Founded on January 16, 1920, Zeta began as an idea conceived by five coeds at Howard University in Washington, DC. Arizona Cleaver, Myrtle Tyler, Viola Tyler, Fannie Pettie, and Pearl Neal were now known as the organizational "Five Pearls," who dared to depart from the traditional coalitions for black women and sought to establish a new organization predicated on the precepts of scholarship, service, sisterly love, and finer womanhood. It was the ideal of the founders that the sorority would reach college women in all parts of the country who were sorority-minded and desired to follow the founding principles of the organization.

## Sigma Gamma Rho Sorority, Inc. (Since 1922)
International Headquarters
1000 Southhill Drive, Suite 200
Cary, NC 27513
(888) SGR-I922
Phone: (919) 678-9720
Fax: (919) 678-9721

Sigma Gamma Rho Sorority's aim is to enhance the quality of life within the community. Public service, leadership development, and education of youth are the hallmarks of the organization's programs and activities. Sigma Gamma Rho addresses concerns that impact society educationally, civically, and economically.

**Iota Phi Theta Fraternity, Inc.**
Founders Hall
1600 N. Calvert Street
Baltimore, MD 21202
Phone: (888) 835-5109

On September 19, 1963, at Morgan State College (now Morgan State University), twelve students founded what is now the nation's fifth largest, predominately African American social service fraternity. Iota Phi Theta has always recognized the need for strong, effective leadership at every level of the organization. Iota Phi Theta's national governing body is the Grand Council. On April 12, 1963, Americans watched with horror and outrage as Birmingham Commissioner of Public Safety Theophilus Eugene "Bull" Connor and his officers used water hoses and police dogs against peaceful civil rights demonstrators. On June 12, Medgar Evers, NAACP field secretary and civil rights leader, was assassinated at his home in Jackson, Mississippi, by segregationists. On August 28, 250,000 people participated in the historic March on Washington and heard Martin Luther King Jr. deliver his historic "I Have a Dream" speech.

## Masonic Organizations

### Prince Hall Masons

On March 6, 1775, Prince Hall and fourteen men of color were made masons in Lodge #441, attached to the 38th Foot in Boston initiated these brave men. It was through an Irish Masonic Lodge that Prince Hall Masonry came into being. It marked the first time that blacks were made Masons in America. About a year later, since the conflict between England and America had commenced, the British Foot Infantry left with its lodge, leaving Prince Hall and his associates without a lodge. Before the lodge left, a Worshipful Master "permit" was issued to meet as a lodge and bury their dead in proper manner and form. This permit, however, did not allow them to do "work" or to take in any new members.

Under it, the African Lodge was organized on July 3, 1776, with

Prince Hall as the Worshipful Master. It wasn't long before he received an additional "permit" from Provincial Grand Master John Rowe to walk in procession on St. John's Day. On March 2, 1784, African Lodge #1 petitioned the Grand Lodge of England, the premier or mother grand lodge of the warrant (or charter), to organize a regular Masonic lodge, with all the rights and privileges prescribed. The Grand Lodge of England issued a charter on September 29, 1784, to African Lodge #459, the first black lodge.

You cannot become a Shriner until you are first a Mason. Masonry does not solicit members; no one is asked to join. A man must seek admission of his own free will. A man is a fully accepted "Blue Lodge" Mason after he has received the first three degrees, known as Entered Apprentice, Fellow Craft, and Master Mason. After that, he may belong to many other organizations that have their roots in Masonry and that have a Blue Lodge Masonry as a prerequisite.

In order to become a Shriner, a man must be a Mason. The fraternity of Freemasonry is the oldest, largest, and most widely known fraternity in the world. Members of the Ancient Arabic Order Nobles of the Mystic Shrine of North American are members of the Masonic Order and adhere to the principles of Freemasonry: brotherly love, relief, and truth.

## National Coalition of 100 Black Women, Inc. (NCBW)

1925 Adam C. Powell Jr. Boulevard, Suite 1L
New York, NY 10026
Phone: (212) 222-5660
Fax: (212) 222-5675
e-mail: NC100BW@aol.com

Founded in 1981, NCBW, a nonprofit 501(c)(4) organization, has approximately 7,500 members in 62 chapters in 25 states and the District of Columbia, with organizing groups in St. Thomas, West Indies; London, England; York, Pennsylvania; Boston, Massachusetts; and Omaha, Nebraska. NCBW's mission is the development of socially conscious female leaders who are committed to furthering equity and empowerment for women of color in the society at large, improving the environment of their neighborhoods, rebuilding their communities, and enhancing the quality of public and private resources for the growth and development of disadvantaged youth. NCBW is dedicated to community service, the creation of wealth for social change, the enhancement of career opportunities for women of color through networking and strategically designed programs, and the empowerment of women of color to meet their diverse needs.

## The Links, Incorporated
1200 Massachusetts Avenue NW
Washington, DC 20005
Phone: (202) 842-8686
www.linksinc.org

On the evening of November 9, 1946, Margaret Hawkins and Sarah Scott, two young Philadelphia matrons, invited seven of their friends to join them in organizing a new type of intercity club. A year earlier, in 1945, Link Hawkins had conceived the idea of a group of clubs composed of friends along the eastern seaboard and had spent many hours with Link Scott, thinking, planning, and discussing the possibilities of such an endeavor. The Links, Incorporated, consists of four main areas and has membership of over 12,000 professional women of color in 274 chapters located in 42 states and 3 countries. It was the intent of the founders of the club to have a threefold aim: civic, educational, and cultural. Based on these aims, the club would implement programs, which its founders hoped would foster cultural appreciation through the ruts; develop richer intergroup relations; and help women who participated to understand and accept their social and civic responsibilities.

## National Association of Colored Women's Clubs, Inc. (NACWC)
1601 R Street, NW
Washington, DC 20009
Phone: (202) 667-4080
Fax: (202) 667-2574

NACWC was organized to train and educate youth about the

responsibilities of good citizenship, and encourage them to register to vote and to understand the functions of government. The primary focus is to provide opportunities for internships at the local, state, and national levels and encourage African American women to engage in political education and voter registration, forums, and seminars. NACWC engages in research and fact-finding on critical issues uniquely affecting the quality of life of African American women and youth, and develops and advocates public policy positions at every level of government.

## National Congress of Black Women, Inc.

1224 W. Street SE, Suite 200
Washington, DC 20020
Phone: (301) 562-8000
Toll-free: (877) 274-1198
e-mail: info@npcbw.org
Suggestions: webmaster@npcbw.org

The National Congress of Black Women, Inc., is a 501 (c)(3) nonprofit organization dedicated to the educational, political, economic, and cultural development of African American women and their families. The organization serves as a national leader in providing leadership opportunities for women in decision-making positions in government, nonprofit organizations, and the private sector. It serves to identify and act as mentors to aspiring leaders among African American women. Additionally, it encourages African American women to engage in nonpartisan leadership activities in the educational, economic, social, and political arenas, the first of which is registering to vote.

## 100 Black Men of America, Inc.

141 Auburn Avenue
Atlanta, GA 30303
Phone: (404) 688-5100
Fax: (404) 688-1028

The mission of 100 Black Men of America, Inc., is to improve the quality of life within our communities and enhance educational and economic opportunities for all African Americans. The organization is committed to the intellectual development of youth and economic empowerment of the African American community based on the following precepts: respect for family, spirituality, justice, and integrity.

## Professional Organizations

### National Organization of Black Law Enforcement (NOBLE)

Hubert T. Bell Jr. Office Complex
4609-F Pinecrest Office Park Drive
Alexandria, VA 22312-1442
Phone: (703) 658-1529
Fax: (703) 658-9479

NOBLE was founded in September 1976 during a three-day symposium to address crime in urban low-income areas. The symposium was cosponsored by the Police Foundation and the Law Enforcement Assistance Administration. The goal of NOBLE is to be recognized as a highly competent, public service organization that's at the forefront of providing solutions to law enforcement issues and concerns, as well as to the ever-changing needs of our communities. The purpose of NOBLE is to unify black law enforcement officers at executive and command levels, to conduct research in relevant areas of law enforcement, and to establish linkages and liaisons with organizations of similar concerns. Most importantly, the organization articulates the concerns of black executives in law enforcement.

### National Black Nurses Association (NBNA)

8630 Fenton Street, Suite 330
Silver Spring, MD 20910
Phone: (301) 589-3200 or (800) 575-6298
Fax: (301) 589-3223
e-mail: NBNA@erols.com

In 1971, NBNA was organized under the leadership of Dr. Lauranne Sams, former dean and professor of nursing, School of Nursing, Tuskegee

University, Tuskegee, Alabama. NBNA is committed to excellence in education and conducts continuing education programs for nurses and allied health professionals throughout the year. Its mission is to provide a forum for collective action by African American nurses to investigate, define, and determine the health care needs of African Americans and to implement change to make available to African Americans and other minorities health care commensurate with that of the larger society.

**National Association of Black Journalists (NABJ)**
University of Maryland
8701-A Adelphi Road
Adelphi, MD 20783-1716
Phone: (866) 479-NABJ (toll-free)
Fax: (301) 445-7101
e-mail: nabj@nabj.org

NABJ is the largest organization of journalists of color in the nation. It was founded by forty-four men and women on December 12, 1975, in Washington, DC. NABJ is committed to strengthening ties among black journalists and sensitizing all media to the importance of fairness in the workplace for black journalists. NABJ focuses on expanding job opportunities and recruiting activities for veteran, young, and aspiring black journalists, while providing continued professional development and training.

**National Association of Black Accountants, Inc.**
7249-A Hanover Parkway
Greenbelt, MD 20770
Phone: (301) 474-NABA
Fax: (301) 474-3114
e-mail: customerservice@nabainc.org

Since 1969, the National Association of Black Accountants, Inc., has been the leader in expanding the influence of minority professionals in the fields of accounting and finance. The goals of the association are:
- to promote and develop the professional skills of our members;

- to encourage and assist minority students in entering the accounting profession;
- to provide opportunities for members to fulfill their civic responsibility;
- to ensure long-term financial stability and provide adequate resources to implement chapter, regional, and national programs; and
- to represent the interests of current and prospective minority accounting professionals.

## National Association of Negro Business and Professional Women's Clubs, Inc.

1806 New Hampshire Avenue NW
Washington, DC 20009
Phone: (202) 483-4206
e-mail: info@nanbpwc.org
Website: www.nanbpwc.org

Founded in 1935, the National Association of Negro Business and Professional Women's Clubs, Inc., is a national nonprofit organization that promotes and protects the interests of female business owners and professionals. The importance of education and economic development through entrepreneurship was emphasized as women sought to support women through community service and social activism.

## National Society of Black Engineers

World Headquarters
205 Daingerfield Road
Alexandria, VA 22314
Phone: (703) 549-2207
Fax: (703) 683-5312
e-mail: http://www.info@nsbe.org

The National Society of Black Engineers started in 1971 by two Purdue undergraduate students, Edward Barnette (now deceased) and Fred Cooper, who approached the dean of engineering at Purdue University with the concept of starting the Black Society of Engineers.

They wanted to establish a student organization to help improve the recruitment and retention of black engineering students. The dean agreed to the idea and assigned the only black faculty member on staff, Arthur J. Bond, as adviser. The organization strives to accomplish the following objectives:

- Stimulate and develop student interest in the various engineering disciplines
- Strive to increase the number of minority students studying engineering at both the undergraduate and graduate levels
- Encourage members to seek advanced degrees in engineering or related fields and to obtain professional engineering registrations
- Promote public awareness of engineering and the opportunities for blacks and other minorities in that profession
- Function as a representative body on issues and developments that affect the careers of black engineers

**National Black MBA Association**
180 North Michigan Avenue, Suite 1400
Chicago, IL 60601
Phone: (312) 236-2622

The National Black MBA Association was established in 1970 and is dedicated to creating partnerships that result in creating intellectual and economic wealth in the black community. This organization is comprised of black business professionals in a wide variety of agencies and industries. The organization gains its strength from a strong belief in community and a commitment to economic and educational development initiatives that support the global African American community.

## Sage Advice

### Chief Master Sergeant Vernon F. Boardley, USAF
- If I had any advice for young minority officers, first I'd like to say that I hope that you were lucky enough to have two loving

parents, as I did in Stephen and Naomi. More often than not, this is simply not the case in our communities, so I feel that I have been blessed to have been raised in a nuclear family. Growing up with limited resources, I have learned to appreciate the values and words of wisdom that my parents instilled in me. Although my parents had limited education, they constantly stressed that education was the key to success in life. My father used to tell me, "Never be afraid of an honest hard day's work," "Before you can lead, you have to master how to follow," and "No matter what, believe in yourself." These are very good principles that I still find myself falling back on even as I speak today.

- My road to being an air force chief master sergeant has been very rewarding, but the road was anything but easy. Quite often, just by virtue of whom you are, people just don't understand you, or you have to deal with preconceived stereotypes, as we all have them. Once again, I have to refer back to my upbringing, as my parents laid the road out that I would have to travel. Therefore, I would like to think that I was ready to take on this adventure that we call life. So, in closing, I would like to reiterate the wise words that my father once told me: Never be afraid of an honest hard day's work. Before you can lead, you have to master how to follow. And no matter what, believe in yourself. In addition, do not be afraid to make a fool of yourself from time to time. Raising your hand and stating that you would like to be the base Point of Contact (POC) or the Combined Federal Campaign can be a very scary proposition. Trust me it is scary for everyone else also. But that is a tremendous way to separate yourself from your peers, along with leading the way. I am very honored and privileged to be given the opportunity to express some of my thoughts in this effort. Good luck, and Godspeed in all of your endeavors.

## Chief Master Sergeant Paul Acron, USAF (Ret.)

- Find mentors (higher- and lower-ranking). They don't have

to look like you or be of the same gender. Positions and titles are very critical for promotion; therefore, you need the right recommendations and push statements in your performance reports. Also, find a very good SNCO to educate you on how to take care of the enlisted troops. Once they believe/trust in you, they will definitely watch your back. Their successes equal your success.

- Network. You can't be antisocial. By nature, African American folks don't like to attend functions where it appears they're kissing up. However, all of the handshakes and bargains are made at the commander's parties, officer professional development sessions, sporting events, military functions, etc. Be an active member in your local company-grade officer organizations. Sometimes just your presence goes a long way. As a chief master sergeant, this is the hardest challenge to convey to my aspiring SNCOs. Trust me on this one. Most of the things you do to display success will not be written on paper.
- Find a spiritual connection. I firmly believe there is no success without Him in your life.

## 1LT Angela C. Holmes Kinsey, USAF
- Please keep your head up, be optimistic, and do not come into the military with a chip on your shoulder.
- Don't play the race card, and don't expect a handout. Not everyone is out to get you because of your color, and no one is going to have sympathy because of your color.
- All Caucasians are not your enemies, and all African Americans are not your friends.

## 1LT Corey L. Trusty, USAF
- Find a mentor who will educate you in the ways of the military, and continue to seek them out. They are the backbone of a young officer being in the know of many things!
- Continue to educate yourself, and never turn down an opportunity to further your military education or your

professional education. Education will be vital to good performance and, hence, your success!

- Volunteer for the hard assignments and/or for those assignments no one wants, and perform well!

# CHAPTER 10

## PUSHING FORWARD FROM BEHIND

When wisdom enters your heart, and knowledge is pleasant
to your soul, discretion will preserve you; understanding
will keep you, to deliver you from the way of evil, from the
men who speak perverse things.

—Proverbs 2:10–12

A man who won't die for something is not fit to live.
—Martin Luther King Jr., 1963

Great careers don't come without sacrifice. Something in
your life will probably have to go. Decide now, what you're
willing to forfeit to get what you want.
—Cydney and Leslie Shields, 1993

The noncommissioned officer (NCO) has always been the backbone of
our military service. African Americans make up a significant portion
of our armed forces, and most of our contributions have been within
the enlisted ranks. At one point in our nation's history it was illegal for
blacks to serve as officers, and we had no other choice but serving as
an enlisted person. The majority of our heroic contributions have been
made by people who wear stripes on their arms, and this dedicated
courage should not go unrecognized or overlooked but built upon.

Capitalizing on the knowledge and valor of those who serve gallantly
in the lower ranks means paying respect to and holding in esteem the

actions, mentorship, and bravery shown by enlisted men and women since the Revolutionary War. You must recognize that not one P-51 would have flown from Tuskegee field if it were not for the professional service of the enlisted flight crew that maintained those aircraft. The majority of the members of the real unsung heroes were enlisted men. The 9th and 10th Calvary that came to the rescue of Teddy Roosevelt during the Spanish-American War in Santiago were mostly enlisted men. It is vitally important that we do not forget the role the enlisted men and women play in our personal success and the success of our organization.

Even today, in Operation Enduring Freedom and Operation Iraqi Freedom, it is the enlisted corps that stands tall and takes on the toughest missions. One army sergeant major stated very eloquently, "This war is being fought and won at the staff sergeant level. This is where the tactical-level decisions are being made that saves lives on a daily basis." It is the enlisted men and women who are putting their lives at risk daily for the preservation of freedom. Fortunately, military pay has increased over the years, but still it is the enlisted grades that receive less in retirement and while on active duty yet consistently give more.

The sacrifice that our enlisted corps continually makes is the sole reason that young officers need to heed their advice on how to succeed as an officer. These are the men and women who are looking for greatness in a leader and will take pride when they have something to do with your development. One senior officer noted that when he was a young second lieutenant, the senior enlisted manager of his unit called him in to his office and said, "L-T, you don' t have to listen to me, if you don't want to, but if you are smart, I am going to make you into a fine officer." The chief master sergeant instructed the lieutenant to come see him each day, thirty minutes before reporting to work. The lieutenant walked away a bit frazzled about what the chief wanted, specifically every day, but agreed to meet with the older man, as instructed. Each day the chief looked the lieutenant over to ensure his uniform was in order, asked what he planned on accomplishing that day, and ensured his equipment was all in working condition. The chief went as far as providing notes for the lieutenant on what to say to his troops when he got to work.

This routine for the young lieutenant visiting the chief went on for approximately six months, and during the final session the chief stated to the lieutenant, "L-T, you are well on your way. Remember this and the things I talked about, because you will need to recall them in the future." The lieutenant walked away still a bit confused but was deeply appreciative for this seasoned NCO's advice and time.

This senior NCO took time out and took personal ownership of the lieutenant, and it paid off for this officer, because he continued to use the advice and wisdom offered by the chief. He could have very easily walked away from the chief and appropriately told him, "I outrank you, Chief, and I don't have the time or interest to come to see you on a daily basis!" Instead he humbled himself and took the time to learn from someone with a lot more experience than him.

The lieutenant did not realize it, but all while the chief was holding these private sessions with the lieutenant, he was talking to other SNCOs within the unit and building a positive reputation for the young officer. This reputation eliminated barriers other company-grade officers had to encounter, and paved the road for the lieutenant. When it came time for his annual report, he received the highest ratings because he was well thought of by the entire enlisted corps within the unit.

His unit commander supported this young officer, as well, and would publicly recognize his talents and competence. Even though the chief was the reason behind the lieutenant's recognition and praises, he kept quiet and allowed the lieutenant to stand in the limelight and receive the recognition and high ratings. Fortunately, the lieutenant was smart enough to eventually realize what the chief had done, and he returned to thank the chief for his efforts and sharing his time and energy in developing him into a professional officer.

This is just one of the roles of our enlisted corps. They stand in the shadows while officers receive the recognition and promotions far exceeding them, showing humility and without complaining. Officers, on the other hand, need to recognize their role and support the efforts of their enlisted troops, because their career would surely fail without the direct support of the enlisted corps. Officers need to learn how to listen and communicate effectively. Your troops are looking to you to make clear and concise decisions. They desire officers who are willing to share the center stage by recognizing the actions and heroic feats of your troops. Take time out and find a senior NCO who you can talk with freely. Ask this person to be your enlisted mentor. You need someone who intimately knows your job and is willing to make spot connections when you are heading down the wrong path. Most SNCOs would love to take the time and share with their officers their knowledge, but many of them will not seek you out to make this invitation. So take the time and secure their service.

It takes a team of dedicated professionals to build your career and develop you into a seasoned officer with the respect and admiration from your peers and subordinates alike. You cannot be successful on your own; it takes a support team all along the way. The previous chapter discussed several civic organizations that are willing to support you in meeting your career goals. It is just as vital for your subordinates to support you as it is your superiors and peers.

The enlisted corps will push you as far as you are willing to go. Be careful that their efforts are not in vain. You need to ensure that you are fulfilling all obligations required of officership at your level. You do not uphold your end of the bargain by remaining competitive or, better yet, exceeding your peers. The gallant efforts of your NCO team will be in vain. Do not disappoint them. At times they will seem to be the only fans in your corner.

What is it that your subordinates are looking for? They want someone who is willing to lead and will not shy away from tough decisions. They want someone willing to take the blame if someone in your unit makes a mistake and provide the necessary top cover if things go wrong. Simply put, put your name on the mailbox! This is your unit, and they demand that you stand up and take charge. Develop the technical competence to know what you are doing, ask questions when you do not know, and have the integrity to say, "I don't know," if you really don't. Don't try to buffalo your way through something, because they realize when you are tap dancing, even if you don't. Remember that they probably know your job a lot better than you do, so never insult their integrity by trying to baffle your way through something. Just ask for help.

When you find your enlisted mentors, share with them your goals and aspirations. They will quickly tell you tales of previous officers they have served with who have made it and others who failed miserably. Ask them how those who made it were successful, as well as the methods, decisions, and other related matters of what made the officers unsuccessful. It is critical to your success that you know both sides. Many times officers make mistakes and don't realize it until it is too late.

Your enlisted corps wants to see you succeed, because now they have a direct impact on developing you into one of their future leaders. You may be in a position to hire them into that dream job somewhere in the future. If you remain on active duty long enough, you will find those who you have served with during your first few assignments somewhere along your journey. Make a concerted effort to remain in touch with those with whom you are impressed.

You just never know where you may end up or the talents you may need to complete a particular project. Building a network of professionals is vitally important and will serve you well as you continue in your career. You will never have all the answers, but knowing where to get the answers is just as important. Take time and archive both the temporary address as well as a permanent address of everyone you value and consider close. You may need the permanent address (of parents or siblings), because military people tend to move around a lot, and these relatives typically have a way of knowing your mentor's whereabouts.

As an officer you will be required to discipline enlisted members to enforce standards and maintain good order. Before making a career-ending decision that may adversely impact a subordinate's career, consult your senior NCO. They normally will have a vast amount of experience dealing with similar events. Taking their counsel will enhance your rapport and provide confidence in both you and your senior NCO.

*Don't hesitate in administering discipline to black subordinates.* It should be carried out without hesitation, within the prescribed procedures of your assigned unit. You should not flinch when it comes to administering discipline to anyone warranting the appropriate degree. Everyone will be watching if you show any favoritism when you take action, and if you show any signs that you are harder on blacks than you are on whites, then you will lose credibility. If you engage in actions that are anything less than professional and fair, your respect will dwindle, as well.

Everyone who looks like you is not your friend. Many times you will find that some black troops will test your professionalism by expecting leniency or favors. Be on guard if this occurs, and nip it in the bud at once. Bring in your first sergeant as your witness, and discuss the adverse actions of your delinquent troop with him. It becomes both a credibility and morale issue in how you deal with these situations.

Fairness is important when executing discipline. All eyes are on the officer each and every time crises occur and critical decisions need to be made. Are you prepared to make the tough calls? Your enlisted force is looking to you for leadership and guidance. Do you shy away from tough situations, or do you embrace them and gather together the appropriate people to find resolutions?

The bottom line is your troops are looking for leadership! They want an officer who can make an honest assessment, treat everyone fairly, and present the unit in a positive image. This may seem a little overwhelming initially, but you will find yourself growing into your boots. It takes time, *so don't expect that others will expect you to know everything.* They will expect you to take on these new challenges and find the solutions, by both doing research and networking with other professionals. Be a person of action, but realize that your actions have to be well thought out and carefully executed.

You are the motivational force that inspires. Being inspirational means that you have a positive image both on and off duty. This does not mean that you have to walk around smiling all the time and looking for group hugs, but it does mean that you need to know how to keep things in perspective and not get overly excited when things go wrong. You need to have a very silent confidence about yourself, and your people can expect to hear wisdom from you when needed.

Leaders do not get overly rattled when the bullets start flying or crises arise. They have been trained during their career to react appropriately in times of trouble and realize that a trained rehearsed response is what is needed, not a lot of emotions and unnecessary chatter about the event. Again, no one expects you to be completely uncaring, but you must possess a certain calmness and assuredness.

In time, you will become that professional that you long to be, and your subordinates will learn to admire you and desire to be around you more often than not. Be careful not to allow your head to swell because you are in a leadership position. Keep your head and humility, because everyone is watching and the one thing that they will hate to see is an officer who is arrogant and conceited, and takes all the praise and compliments when it really belongs to the troops. Don't steal their thunder!

Officers' ability to lead and influence their troops is predicated on the willingness and followership of their enlisted corps. Officers' ability to effectively lead is developed over time and hopefully under the watchful eye of dedicated NCOs. Young officers can learn a lot from members of their enlisted staff, and it behooves each of them to select a senior NCO who is willing to take them under their wing and share their unique perspective on the finer points of leadership. Senior NCOs supervise and discipline the majority of our enlisted corps and provide the continuity to create mission success. It is not easy to gain rank within the enlisted corps, and just because you, as a junior officer, may outrank every enlisted professional does not mean that you should take them for granted.

As a matter of fact, you should consider it an honor for senior NCOs to offer their assistance in nurturing and mentoring you. The secrets of leadership and success principles learned over the years do not come easily and should not be taken lightly. Professional soldiers are required to initially learn to follow orders and then serve at every level of individual and unit leadership. As junior NCOs, they are given basic stewardship over one or a few more enlisted members. Senior NCOs are given the responsibility of supervising a branch or division and often the supervision of large numbers of younger enlisted members. At every rank our NCOs receive increased responsibility and opportunities to supervise.

By gaining all of this experience over the life of a successful career, naturally they have a lot to share with our officer corps. Junior officers need to learn to listen and value the advice and contributions of enlisted members. Officers need to do everything within their authority to support their enlisted corps by writing honest and credible performance reports that will assist them more competitively in securing the next rank, as well as submitting good awards and decorations. Taking care of your troops should be viewed as critical to you as your own success and, at times, even more vital. When officers don't take the time to support their enlisted corps, the word spreads like wildfire.

Your reputation as a good and supportive leader can prove crucial to your success, as well. Many senior NCOs have the ear of senior officers, and they take advantage of this opportunity by discussing critical issues that have significant impact on the mission, including unit morale, personnel, discipline, tactical factors, and leadership. It is a privilege and honor to have immediate access to senior officers and use this time to make a contribution to bettering the organization. Younger officers need to be keenly aware of the relationship between senior officers and senior NCOs and use it as an example of how to gear their professional relationships with the enlisted corps. This relationship needs to be completely professional and fortified in the core values of each of the services.

NCOs take pride in grooming young officers and watching them grow into mature men and women. They want to see these young officers be successful. If you ever hear a NCO refer to you as his or her personal lieutenant or captain, you should take this as a sign of personal commitment and dedication. It is rare for NCOs to adopt a junior officer, but when it happens you should consider it a privilege and unique honor, because this professional soldier has made a personal commitment to you for your entire military career.

NCOs have the talent and expertise to successfully mentor any officer. When time is taken out to assist your career, you need to pay close attention. Do not be afraid of attaching yourself to NCOs at all levels, but be careful that you maintain a professional relationship. *Do not allow yourself to become too close or intimate with subordinates.* There is nothing wrong with friendliness in relationships, but you need to be cautious of fraternizing and maintaining an unprofessional relationship. Even the appearance of unprofessional relationships can cause you problems in your career, and close attention needs to be paid in all your dealings.

It is important to provide a usable definition of fraternization and unprofessional relationships, so there is no doubt in your mind what you need to avoid. What is an unprofessional relationship? An unprofessional relationship is one that detracts from successful mission accomplishment and creates the atmosphere of overfriendliness and favoritism. A sexual relationship with a subordinate is included in this area of unprofessional relationships and should never occur. Continually going to lunch with the same subordinate is not appropriate and will cause rumors within the organization. For many junior officers this is a very difficult issue to deal with, because many junior NCOs are about the same age and perhaps have similar interests and backgrounds. Do not allow yourself to become consumed by these trivial elements.

The successful accomplishment of the mission is too important to America and our allies to compromise with unprofessional relationships. Ensure you maintain a professional atmosphere in the office environment. Do not allow NCOs or any subordinates to call you by your first name without using your rank and last name. You should always require all subordinates to use your rank and last name. You should do the same if discussing a superior or peer with a subordinate. For example, if talking with an enlisted member, you should not refer to Captain Bill Jones as Bill or Jones. You should refer to him as Captain Jones. Your actions create the tone of professionalism and show your NCO that professionalism is the only thing tolerated. In turn, they will mimic your example, and professionalism will be reinforced within the unit.

NCOs want to be a part of your success. They cherish the opportunity of being a part of something special and being able to contribute positively to the successful accomplishment of the mission. Officers create the environment for this opportunity to exist for NCOs, and this authority should not be taken for granted. Officers need to include NCOs in every phase of unit accomplishment and give liberally so that they are challenged and allowed to grow.

As an up-and-coming officer, you will gain the opportunity to lead. This is a privilege that is yours for only a finite period of time. Make the most of every day as you proceed in becoming the best officer that you possibly can be. It will take the support of both your senior and junior NCOs to pull this off successfully, so get busy in fostering relationships. They want to see you succeed as much as you want to succeed. Your career as an officer will be marked with fantastic relationships you have developed throughout your entire career. These men and women are the ones who will help you shine and become the best officer our military has ever seen. Good luck!

## Sage Advice

### Staff Sergeant George Jones, USAF (Ret.)
- Military members need to learn their history and take pride in whom they are and where they have been. Once they know their history, they cannot help but want to do better!
- Read biographies of those who came before you, and don't just learn of their accomplishments; learn why they did what they did.
- Make it a point to meet retirees, because they have a lot to give and want to engage with young people who are walking the same roads they were once on.

### Chief Master Sergeant Willie Upshaw, USAF (Ret.)
- Respect yourself and the tradition that has been painfully established by your predecessors. Your personal accomplishment and appearance both on and off duty must always be above reproach. The harsh reality is that you are in a fishbowl and everything you do is under constant scrutiny. There always will be those who expect you to fail.
- Respect for your superior is crucial, but of equal importance

is respect for your subordinates. They depend on you to accomplish the difficult task. Be impartial and consistent whenever administering accolades and discipline. Showing favoritism is poison to effective leadership and respect for you as a young officer.

- Listen to and respect the wisdom of seasoned senior NCOs, especially those with the grade of E-9 with regard to enlisted and operational matters, for they have been there. Although your commission is predicated on academic achievement, which is commendable, your academic achievements are no substitute for actual experience. Arrogance and pride will most certainly prove detrimental to your effectiveness and growth as a leader.

## Chief Master Sergeant Raymond R. Campbell, USAF

- Sometimes you will have to validate yourself. You will find that leadership can be a lonely business. Follow the rule of treating people the way you would want to be treated, and validate yourself based on that principle. Whenever you find yourself making important decisions about your personnel, make sure you ask this question to yourself: *How would I feel?* This is a great vector check to ensure you are making well–thought out decisions.
- Seek out mentors who support your leadership agenda. Don't pick mentors just because they look like you.

## Chief Master Sergeant Fermon S. Reid, USAF (Ret.)
### The 3 Ls: Listen, Learn, and Lead

- *Listen.* Listen to the advice and guidance of SNCOs; they have many success stories and lessons learned to share. Beware of individuals who always agree with you and tell you exactly what you want to hear; they may not have your best interests or the interests of the organization in mind.
- *Learn.* Learn by watching the SNCOs interact with others on a daily basis and how they treat personnel. Seek out the respected SNCOs who do an exceptional job of balancing people and the

mission. They may not be liked by everyone but have earned the respect of subordinates, peers, and superiors for their proven leadership track record over the years.

- *Lead.* Lead your subordinates by setting a positive example and leading out front, while adhering to our first and most important air force core value: integrity. Never commit your personnel to a task or job that you're unwilling to do yourself. Tell them what you want accomplished, provide them the resources and authority, and allow them the time to complete the task. Run interference, and provide top cover when needed. Always ensure your words are reinforced by your actions.

# A CHRONOLOGICAL SUMMARY OF AMERICAN HISTORY, HIGHLIGHTING AFRICAN AMERICANS

The best way to appreciate the many accomplishments of African Americans is to review significant feats since their arrival in the Americas. The following summary provides a quick review of these tremendous events in American history. Take time to learn these accomplishments, and allow each event, accomplishment, and feat to serve as a motivator in solidifying your dedication to becoming your very best.

1492   Pedro Alonzo Nino, born in Palos de Moguer, Spain, and of African descent was a ship pilot and assisted Christopher Columbus sail to the Americas and was on the third voyage discovering Trinidad.

1513   Balboa's group crossing Panama had thirty blacks.

1517   Bishop Las Casas (Spain) said Spaniards could import twelve blacks each to New World.

1526   First slave revolt in what is now South Carolina.

1538   Estevanico (Little Stephen) led the expedition that discovered Arizona and New Mexico.

1620   Blacks were with DeSoto on his journey to Mississippi. The second settler in Alabama was black (from DeSoto's expedition). Blacks were among the group that founded St. Augustine,

Florida. First cargo of slaves for English America came to Jamestown, Virginia. First public school for blacks and Indians in Virginia.

1624    William Tucker, first black child born and baptized in English colonies.

1638    First slaves came to New England, most house servants, grooms, and footmen.

1639    The Virginia House of Burgesses passed the first legislation to exclude blacks from the militia.

1641    Massachusetts became first colony to legalize slavery.

1645    First American slave ship: the *Rainbow*.

1652    Because of the possibility of Indian attack, a Massachusetts law required all blacks, Scotsmen, and Native Americans who lived with or were servants of English settlers to participate in military training.

1656    Massachusetts prohibited blacks and Indians from military service because of white fears about possible uprisings.

1660    Connecticut passed a law barring African Americans and Native Americans from military service. By the end of the century, all of the colonies had enacted similar laws.

1661    First petition for freedom granted to a slave by New Netherlands (New York).

1662    Virginia law said children of slaves are slaves.

1663    First slave revolt in colonial United States in Gloucester, Virginia.

1664    Maryland prohibited intermarriage between black men and white women. Other colonies followed.

1671    Maryland legislature stated that conversion to Christianity did not alter slave status.

1672    English king chartered Royal African Company. It came to dominate world slave trade.

1688    Quakers formally protested practice of slavery.

1689    During King William's War, France and its Indian allies threatened England's North American colonies. Black militia fought and died in this imperial conflict. They also served later in Queen Anne's War (1702–1713), the second of three major confrontations between the French and English for control of North America.

1700    First antislavery pamphlet by Judge Samuel Sewall appeared in colonies.

1701    An early South Carolina law required militia captains "to enlist, train up, and bring into the field for each white, one able slave armed with a gun or lance."

1703    The South Carolina Assembly offered to free any slave who captured or killed any Native Americans considered hostile to the colony.

1704    First school for blacks in New York City.

1705    Virginia statues allowed listing slaves as "property."

The Virginia Assembly passed legislation preventing Negroes, mulattos, or Indians from holding civil, military or ecclesiastical office.

1708    Charles Town, South Carolina, employed "slave cowboys" to help protect the settlement from Indian attack.

1712    Slave revolt in New York City. Pennsylvania forbade further import of slaves.

1715    South Carolina used slaves to help fight during the Yamasee War.

1720    Jupiter Hammon, first black American writer who published (1761), born.

1729    Armed blacks helped to defend French Louisiana from Indian attack.

1731    Benjamin Banneker, born in Baltimore—scientist, mathematician, political scientist, farmer, essayist, and surveyor—died 1805.

1735    Free black militia officers in Louisiana led black troops during an Indian war.

1741    Major slave revolt in New York City, eighteen blacks hanged.

1743    John Woolman began his campaign against slavery.

1745    Jean Baptiste Pointe Du Sable born, established trading post that became Chicago.

1747    Absalom Jones born, first black minister ordained in America. The South Carolina Assembly provided for the use of blacks troops in the event of danger or emergency, and authorized the enlistment of 50 percent of all able-bodied slaves between the ages of sixteen and twenty.

1748    Prince Hall born, founder of Negro Freemasonry.

1750    Blacks helped found Los Angeles, California. Crispus Attucks, martyr of the Revolutionary War, escaped from his master in Framingham, Massachusetts.

1753    Scipio Moorhead, earliest known black American artist, born.

1756–1763

Black soldiers served during the French and Indian War, the

North American colonial struggle that pitted the French and Spanish against the British. Brazilia Lew fought during this conflict as a member of a Massachusetts militia company. He later saw action at the Battle of Bunker Hill during the American Revolution.

1758    Frances Williams, first African American college graduate in Western Hemisphere.

1759    Paul Cuffee, business leader and philanthropist, born.

1760    Richard Allen born, founder and bishop of African Methodist Church in Philadelphia.

1761    Phillis Wheatley, poetess of American Revolution, arrived on slave ship.

1762    James Derham, first recognized black doctor in America, born. Began practice in 1800.

1770    Anthony Benezet opened school for blacks in Philadelphia. Crispus Attucks, a runaway slave turned Jack-tar, and four other colonists were killed during the so-called Boston Massacre, in which British soldiers fired on unarmed men and boys who were causing a disturbance. He was first African American killed during the American Revolution.

1772    Lord Mansfield's decision against slavery in English territory effected future decisions in New England.

1773    George Leile organized first black Baptist church in Savannah, Georgia.

Bill Richmond, father of modern prizefighting, is born in New York, New York.

Slaves in Massachusetts petitioned state legislature for freedom.

1774    Continental Congress agreed to import no more slaves.

General Thomas Gage rejected the petition of Boston blacks, who offered to fight for the British in exchange for their freedom. Massachusetts began enlisting blacks in its militia companies.

1775    Benjamin Franklin became president of the Quaker Abolitionist Society.

Peter Salem, Salem Poor, Caesar Brown, Titus Coburn, Alexander Ames at Bunker Hill.

Continental Congress barred blacks from army. Royal governor of Virginia offered freedom to all slaves joining British Army.

Washington got Congress to accept free blacks. Five thousand served.

April 19: Blacks took part in the Battle of Lexington and Concord. The first armed clash between England and her colonists in North America was sparked by the dispatch of seven hundred British soldiers from the Boston garrison sent to seize colonial arms and possibly arrest rebel leaders; the redcoats encountered armed resistance instead. Pomp Blackman and Prince Estabrook were two of the black Minutemen who took part in the event immortalized as the "shot heard round the world." Estabrook was killed during the fighting.

May: Black patriots helped Ethan Allen and the Green Mountain Boys take Fort Ticonderoga, New York, by surprise.

June 15: Continental Congress chose George Washington to head the newly established Continental Army. Shortly after assuming command, Washington ordered his officers not to recruit black troops. He later rescinded this order to allow the enlistment of free blacks. Congress subsequently approved this decision in 1776.

June 17: Several black soldiers (most notably Peter Salem and Salem Poor) helped defend Breed's Hill in the Battle Hill on Charlestown Heights, overlooking Boston Harbor. Although tactically a British victory, this confrontation was psychologically significant for the colonists. The patriots met British regulars and successfully held onto their position until they ran out of ammunition.

July: American General Horatio Gates ordered his officers not to recruit "any deserters from the Ministerial Army, nor any stroller, Negro, or vagabond, or persons suspected of being an enemy to the liberty of America, nor any under eighteen years of age."

September 25: Edward Rutledge proposed that all blacks in the Continental Army be discharged. Voted down by Northern delegates, the issue cropped up again in October 1775 because of white fears that the army was becoming a refuge for runaway slaves. At that time, a committee agreed to exclude blacks (especially slaves) from the service. However, after Northern officers and soldiers strongly protested the measure, Washington reversed this decision in December 1775 to permit free blacks to serve.

November: The Ethiopian Regiment was formed in Virginia after about eight hundred blacks responded to the royal governor's offer of freedom to all male slaves who joined the British forces.

November 28: Continental Congress formally established the Continental Navy after authorizing the construction of two warships on October 13 to defend against the British fleet. The approved rules regulating the new military service allowed both free and enslaved blacks to enlist.

1776 Prince Whipple and Oliver Cromwell crossed Delaware River with George Washington. Although slavery was one of the earliest grievances against the king, Declaration of Independence signed *without* denouncing it. Mason-Dixon Line surveyed to separate Maryland from Pennsylvania, later separated *free slave* states. Virginia opened its militia to all free males regardless of race. Blacks were initially used as pioneers (i.e., members of military construction crews), drummers, and fifers. Early in the Revolutionary War, South Carolina passed a law declaring the death penalty for any bondsman who joined the British Army or Navy. As the war progressed, all Southern states increased patrols, established local guard units, removed slaves from proximity to British forces, and imposed severe punishments on would-be defectors. But these actions could not prevent several thousand slaves from seeking service and freedom with the British.

February 21: Washington issued order 1777, reinforcing his decision to keep slaves from serving in the Continental Army.

September 26: The British in New York City executed Captain Nathan Hale of Connecticut for spying. The hangman was a loyalist slave named Bill Richmond, who later gained fame as a boxing champion in Europe.

1777    Abolition of slavery began in Vermont; in Pennsylvania and Massachusetts in 1780; in Connecticut and Rhode Island in 1784.

After it was discovered that slaves claiming to be free men had enlisted in the militia, the Virginia Assembly passed a law prohibiting blacks from joining without a certificate of freedom.

As the war with England dragged on, Congress began to assign troop quotas for each state. Consequently, the need for manpower became so great that the states began recruiting more blacks. Additional black enlistments resulted from the use of a substitution system in which those men wishing to avoid service found it easier and less expensive to provide a black substitute. Most Northern states and Maryland allowed slaves to serve.

The Rhode Island Assembly passed a resolution allowing "every able-bodied negro, mulatto or Indian man slave" to enlist in two segregated battalions led by white officers. Among the incentives offered to recruits were equal pay and freedom.

September 11: After the Battle of Brandywine fought on this date, Edward Hector, a black soldier who served in the Third Pennsylvania Artillery, was awarded a cash bonus for bravery.

October: The General Assembly of Connecticut authorized the selectmen of any town to free any suitable slaves or indentured servants who enlisted in the state militia.

1778     Four hundred blacks held off 1,500 British in Battle of Rhode Island.

April: Thomas Kench, an artillery regiment soldier, wrote to the Massachusetts Assembly to urge the enlistment of blacks in segregated units. He believed that the "ambition [of the all-black units] would entirely be to outdo the white men in every measure that the fortunes of war calls upon a soldier to endure." However, Massachusetts authorities voted to continue the state's practice of "taking Negroes in our service intermixed with the white men."

June 28: During the Battle of Monmouth fought in New Jersey on this date, Continental troops, including seven hundred black soldiers, proved to be the military equals of British regulars.

August: A black battalion of over three hundred slaves, promised their freedom after the war and given equal pay, fought during the unsuccessful Franco-American assault of Newport, Rhode Island. Continental Army officers dispatched by Washington to fill depleted ranks in that area had recruited them.

August 24: Adjutant General Alexander Scammell reported that 755 black soldiers, scattered over 14 brigades, were enlisted in the Continental Army. The majority of black soldiers came from the New England states. Of the states outside this region, Virginia sent the largest number of black troops.

December 29: During the British capture of Savannah, Georgia, 3,500 regular troops under the leadership of Lieutenant Colonel Archibald Campbell overwhelmed the patriot militia of 1,000 men. Quamino Dolly, an elderly black slave, aided the British by guiding them to the town.

1779    "Pompey" helped Anthony Wayne at Stony Point in his capacity as a spy.

Twenty slaves petitioned New Hampshire legislature to end slavery. Delegates from South Carolina objected to a proposal approved by Congress authorizing the use of slaves as soldiers during the American Revolution.

February 14: Slave patriot Austin Dabney won fame for his participation in the Battle of Kettle Creek, Georgia. During this clash, American militia successfully defeated a Tory brigade. Dabney was the only black who fought in this military action. The Georgia legislature freed Dabney in 1786 to prevent his master from exploiting his military fame. In 1821, legislators granted him a 112-acre farm in honor of his heroism during the Revolutionary War.

March: Congress urged South Carolina and Georgia to raise three thousand black troops to be segregated into all-black units. Owners would be indemnified, and though slaves would receive no payer bounties, they would be rewarded for their faithful service at the war's end with freedom and $50. However, both states rejected their recommendations, despite their desperate need for soldiers.

May 31: American troops commanded by General Anthony Wayne captured the British fort at Stony Point, New York. The success of this expedition was attributable to a slave named Pompey, who obtained a British password and helped capture one of the fort's guards. He was only one of several black spies and undercover agents aiding the patriots' cause during the American Revolution.

June: British General Sir Henry Clinton officially promised to emancipate any male slaves who escaped to join the British militia. As the war progressed, both sides increased their recruitment of black troops.

June 21: Spain declared war on England, joining France in the war raging in North America and Europe. The Spanish, however, refused to recognize American independence. Troops dispatched from Spanish Louisiana on expeditions against the British in the South and West included companies of free blacks and slaves commanded by black officers. During the successful campaign to capture Pensacola and Mobile from the British, six black officers were cited for bravery. King Carlos III later awarded medals of valor to them.

September 3: A French fleet under the command of Admiral Jean Baptiste d'Estaing in conjunction with American forces unsuccessfully laid siege to Savannah, Georgia. More than five hundred free blacks from Haiti were part of d'Estaing's troops.

1780    First preaching license issued to a black preacher.

Maryland was the only Southern state that allowed slaves to enlist in the militia.

June: An all-black unit known as the Connection Colonials served for over two years. Disbanded in November 1782, the company's fifty-two free blacks and slaves were integrated with the state's white units in the final months of the war.

September 23: Two blacks aided in the capture of British spy Major John Andre, who served as adjutant general to British General Sir Henry Clinton. Three American militiamen caught him after his meeting with American turncoat General Benedict Arnold. Andre was hanged at Tappan, New York, in October.

1781    British General Charles Cornwallis, who was forced to surrender at Yorktown, Virginia, on October 19, 1781, hired slave James Armistead to spy on the Americans. Armistead, however, was actually an undercover agent for the patriots. In recognition of his services, the Virginia legislature emancipated Armistead in 1786.

June: Maryland passed legislation subjecting all free men to a military draft. A total of 750 black troops were inducted and incorporated with other troops. The New York General Assembly authorized slaves to join the military. After three years of service until regularly discharged, those slaves who joined would become free citizens of New York.

1782    The British in New York freed those blacks who joined British ranks before November 30.

1783    Famous "Black Regiment" disbanded at Saratoga. Treaty of Paris, ending war, promised return of slaves to their owners. Many slaves freed as a *reward* for their military service.

Because the re-enslaving of black veterans became so widespread throughout the South, Virginia passed legislation that freed all those slaves who had served in the Revolutionary War.

September 3: American and British representatives signed the Treaty of Paris, recognizing American independence and ending the American Revolution. Almost ten thousand black served during the war, five thousand of whom were regular soldiers in the Continental Army. North Carolina legislators recognized Edward Griffin's meritorious service during the revolution by freeing him.

1784    Edward Griffin, hero of the revolution, given his *freedom* in North Carolina.

1785    Constitutional Convention upheld slavery in three sections of its writings. David Walker born, first black writer to openly attack slavery.

1787    Slavery outlawed in all territories included in Northwest Ordinance.

The African Free School, first free school, operated in New York City.

1789    Josiah Henson, abolitionist, born in Maryland (a model for "Uncle Tom").

1790    Out of a total population of 4 million, 757,181 were black. Only 59,557 were free.

Pennsylvania abolitionists petitioned Congress to end slavery.

Samuel Cornish, publisher, born in Delaware, approached problems of blacks with political action.

1791    Benjamin Banneker appointed by Jefferson as consultant on design for Washington, DC.

Successful revolt against French in Haiti. The US Congress passed legislation excluding blacks and Native Americans from the peacetime militia.

1792    Antoine Blanc founded first American black order of Catholic nuns.

May: Additional legislation adopted by Congress restricted enlistment in the militia to white male citizens. All of the state militia laws also reflected the same restriction. Among the reasons cited by later scholars for this decision were white fears about slave rebellions, the misguided belief that African Americans either could not or would not fight, concern that black military service would cause unwanted social changes, and the notion that the arming of blacks indicated the failure of white troops.

1793    Benjamin Lundy, colonizationist, born.

Fugitive Slave Law passed by Congress, made it a criminal offense to assist an escaping slave.

Blacks helped Dr. Benjamin Rush give medicine to yellow fever victims in Philadelphia.

1794    St. Thomas Negro Episcopal Church founded in Philadelphia.

1796    Zion Methodist Church founded in New York City.

1797    North Carolina asked for return of African Americans freed by Quakers. Congress said no.

Sojourner Truth—lecturer, abolitionist, heroine—born.

1798    Secretary of War James McHenry and Secretary of the Navy Benjamin Stoddert issued separate directives prohibiting the enlistment of blacks for use on warships of the newly established US Navy or in the nonracial enlistment policy that had been in effect since the Revolutionary War.

Despite earlier efforts to exclude them from the military, blacks served during the undeclared naval war with France. The earlier restriction was never enacted because of the navy's continual need for personnel. The hard lot of sailors in this period and the difficulty of enlisting experienced seamen left recruiters little choice but to open the service to anyone, regardless of race.

1800    There were over one million blacks, 20 percent of the population.

Gabriel Prosser led a thousand in an unsuccessful revolt; he was hanged. Others were imprisoned or hanged.

John Brown born; fought for abolition in 1856–1859.

Nat Turner born, led a revolt in 1831; ninety-nine blacks and sixty-six whites killed. Turner was hanged.

1803    Lunsford Land, antislavery lecturer, born.

1804    Ohio passed law prohibiting the restricting of movements of blacks.

1807    Ira F. Aldridge, one of the greatest Shakespearean actors of his time, born.

Three of the four sailors forcibly removed by the British after the *H. M. S. Leopard* fired on the U. S. S. *Chesapeake* were black. They were identified as William Ware, Daniel Martin, and John Strachan. The volatile incident began when the British frigate halted the US ship just outside the three-mile limit of the coast of Virginia to demand the return of the alleged deserters. The British killed three Americans and wounded eighteen, but only one of the sailors removed from the Chesapeake, a white man named John Wilson, was later proven to be a deserter. Britain returned two of the black sailors to the United States, but the third died in England.

1808    Congress prohibited further importing of slaves.

1810    Cassius M. Clay, emancipationist, born.

1812    Martin Delany—army major, newspaper editor, author, physician—born.

John Johnson, navy hero in War of 1812, died. Louisiana permitted free blacks to serve in the state militia.

1812–1815: Free blacks and slaves served during the War of 1812. The British once again recruited slaves for their navy, as well as armed escaped slaves in Florida and various Indian tribes.

1813    Henry W. Beecher, promoter of equal rights, born.

March 3: US Navy officially authorized the enlistment of free blacks because of continuing manpower shortages.

September 10: African Americans fought during the Battle of Lake Erie, a significant US victory during the War of 1812. About 10 to 25 percent of Admiral Oliver H. Perry's men were black.

1814    August 2: Almost one thousand blacks in New York City helped to fortify the Brooklyn Heights approach, guarding the town from British attack.

September 11: Black soldiers participated in the American victory in Plattsburg, New York, where US troops and militia manned field fortifications, protecting the road to the Hudson Valley and New York City.

September 21: General Andrew Jackson issued a proclamation urging the "Free Colored Inhabitants of Louisiana" to volunteer for service in his army. Black recruits were offered equal pay and the same bounty in money and lands as white volunteers. Those blacks who joined were organized into segregated units with white officers and black noncommissioned officers.

October: New York legislature authorized the formation of two black militia regiments headed by white officers. Those free blacks who enlisted received equal pay, while slaves who joined with their masters' permission were freed at the war's end.

1815    January 8: Two battalions of 430 black soldiers fought with General Andrew Jackson at the Battle of New Orleans, two weeks after the Treaty of Ghent had been signed, ending the War of 1812. Black troops from the West Indies also fought for the British.

March 3: Congress passed legislation creating a postwar army of ten thousand men, but no blacks were recruited. Later that year, the War Department issued a memorandum that included disparaging remarks about African Americans.

1816    Andrew Jackson attacked a Florida fort held by a thousand slaves and sent them back to slavery. The US Navy officially excluded slaves from serving on board ships or in shipyards.

1817    November–December: US troops destroyed the Negro fort on the Apalachicola River in Spanish Florida. Manned primarily by escaped slaves, the fortification had been used to continue attacks on the Americans after the War of 1812.

1818    Blacks fought with the Seminoles against the US Army during both the First and Second Seminole Wars. In the latter conflict, the Seminoles and their black allies held off their white adversaries from 1835 to 1843. Although ultimately defeated, it cost the US government $40 million and 1,800 lives to finally subdue this group of intrepid fighters.

1820    Harriett Tubman born. An ex-slave, she became "conductor" on Underground Railroad.

In the Missouri Compromise blacks living north of Missouri were free, while those living south of Missouri remained in slavery. Congress prohibited the enlistment of blacks or mulattos in the US Army. This was reinforced by a subsequent regulation issued by the army in 1821, limiting service to free white males. The state militias instituted similar restrictions.

1827    Slavery abolished in New York state.

First black newspaper, *Freedom's Journal*.

1830     Census showed 3,777 blacks owned slaves. Ohio passed a law excluding African Americans from serving in the state militia.

1831     Greenbury Logan, one of the first blacks to settle in Texas, was one of the few African Americans who fought for the Lone Star Republic's independence from Mexico.

1834     Slavery abolished in British Empire. In Cincinnati, blacks set up school for themselves.

1835     Elijah Lovejoy killed by mob for publishing antislavery material.

1836     Over three hundred men defending Goliad, Texas, were slaughtered by Mexican troops after laying down their arms. Included among the dead was fifer Peter Allen, a black musician who served with Captain Wyatt's company.

1839     John Quincy Adams defended successfully before US Supreme Court slave revolt on slave ship *Armistead*. In response to white complaints about the use of black sailors, the US Navy imposed a quota limiting African Americans to 5 percent of the service's total personnel.

1841     Blanche K. Bruce, first black elected to a full term in US Senate, born. James Townsend, legislator, born.

1842     Hiram R. Revels, senator, born. South Carolina Senator John C. Calhoun introduced a bill to prohibit blacks from serving in the navy, except as menial labor. Although passed by the Senate, the House never brought the bill to a vote.

1845     Scientific attack on racism by Frederick Douglass, publisher, abolitionist. Norbert Rillieux's vacuum pan revolutionized sugar refining.

1846     April 24: The excuse for war needed by President James K. Polk after Mexico refused to negotiate with John Slidell came with a minor skirmish on this date. Mexican Calvary clashed with US troops, blockading a Mexican town. Only a few African Americans served during the Mexican-American War because of the increasing racial prejudice and growing North-South split over the slavery issue. They were present unofficially with the army as personal servants of white officers and in other support roles. Officially, at least a thousand black sailors served on board US ships blockading Mexican harbors during the conflict.

1848    William Leidesdorff, originally from Saint Croix, was of mixed-race and died on May 18, 1848. He was a successful businessman and hotel builder in San Francisco.

1848    Lewis Temple invented the harpoon.

1849    "Separate but equal" doctrine established when suit for school integration is rejected in Boston.

1850    Fugitive Slave Law established bounty on returned slaves.

1852    *Uncle Tom's Cabin* published by Harriett B. Stowe.

1853    First African American YMCA in Washington, DC.

First novel by US black: *Clotel* by William Wells Brown.

1854    Republican Party formed by Whigs, ex-Democrats, and free soldiers who opposed slavery.

Kansas-Nebraska Act repealed the Missouri Compromise. If new states wanted slavery, they could have it.

Augustus Tolon, first black American Catholic priest, born.

1856    Wilberforce University found by Methodist Episcopal Church.

Booker T. Washington—moderate leader, founder of Tuskegee Institute—born.

Granville T. Woods, inventor, born.

1857    Dred Scott Decision opened new territory to slavery and denied citizenship to blacks.

1858    Charles W. Chestnutt, novelist, born.

1859    Last slave ship *Clothilde* to Alabama.

Henry Tanner, artist, born in Pennsylvania.

1860    Lincoln elected president.

1861    Hampton Institute opened.

Fort Sumter attacked. Five black girls helped Clara Barton tend wounded in Baltimore. During war, fifty thousand blacks, men and women, volunteered as nurses.

Lincoln issued proclamation, calling for seventy-five thousand volunteer troops. Blacks were not accepted in the first call.

1862    United States recognized Liberia as free nation.

Lincoln recommended to Congress a gradual compensated emancipation. Senate abolished slavery in Washington, DC. Lincoln asked for aid to states abolishing slavery.

Charlotte Forten, poetess, began teaching blacks in South Carolina.

Robert Smalls, pilot, sailed armed Confederate steamer out of Charleston and gave it to Union.

First regular black troops enlisted at Leavenworth.

1863    New York City draft riots were the bloodiest in US history.

54th Massachusetts Volunteers, first northern black regiment. Two black regiments capture Jacksonville, Florida, causing panic along Southern seaboard. Eight black regiments help control Mississippi River. Confederacy cut in two parts as a result. Medal of honor for black soldier at Fort Wagner.

Lincoln signed Emancipation Proclamation. Confederate Congress said black troops were criminals and could be executed or returned to slavery.

Kelly Miller, author and educator, born.

Dr. Mary Church Terrell, first president of the National Association of Colored Women, born.

1864  George W. Carver born.

Massacre of five hundred black troops at Fort Pillow by General N. B. Forrest.

Colonel Charles Young, highest-ranking West Point graduate of his time, born.

First daily US black newspaper, the *New Orleans Tribune*, in both French and English.

Fugitive slave laws repealed.

Black troops received equal pay.

"Blind Boone," musical genius, born.

1865  John S. Rock, first black to practice before Supreme Court.

Freedom granted to wives and children of black soldiers. Freedman's Bureau established to aid emancipated slaves. Thirteenth Amendment passed, abolishing slavery. General Lee said slaves were to be used in Confederate Army. Black regiment involved in last battle of war. Sergeant Crocket believed to be last man to shed blood. Black cavalry unit captured Geronimo.

Black troops taken into Confederate Army.

President Abraham Lincoln assassinated.

Tim T. Fortune born, founder of the *New York Age*.

Patrick Henry Healy, first black to earn doctor of philosophy degree.

Matthew Henson, explorer, born. Accompanied Peary to North Pole.

General Nathan B. Forrest began Ku Klux Klan to oppose Reconstruction.

Shaw and Howard Universities founded.

1866 Fourteenth amendment passed, making citizens of American-born blacks.

1867 Talladega and Morehouse Colleges opened.

Maggie Lena Walker, first female bank president in United States, born.

William Still successful in integrating streetcars in Philadelphia.

1868 W. E. B. DuBois—journalist, civil rights fighter, called the "voice of the Negro"—born.

Oscar J. Dunn, ex-slave, elected lieutenant governor of Louisiana.

1869 U. S. Grant became president.

Jefferson P. Long first African American in US House of Representatives.

Ebenezer Don Carlos Bennett first appointment in diplomatic service—minister to Haiti.

1870    Civil rights bill by Congress called for equal accommodations (but they could be separate).

Robert S. Abbott, founder of the *Chicago Defender*, born.

Thomas Peterson first black to vote in the United States.

1871    James Weldon Johnson—poet, educator, civil rights leader, consul to Nicaragua—born.

Oscar De Priest, first Northern black Congressman, born.

1872    John H. Conyers, first black to be admitted to US Naval Academy.

P. B. S. Pinchback became acting governor of Louisiana.

First black police officer appointed in Chicago.

Charlotte E. Ray, first woman to graduate from a university law school, first black female lawyer.

William Still published *Underground Railroad*.

1873    W. C. Handy, called "Father of the Blues," born. Richard T. Greener, first black Harvard graduate.

1874    Patrick Healy became president of Georgetown University.

1875    Blacks massacred at Hamburg, N. C. Blanche K. Bruce became first black to serve full term in Senate.

1876    Edward Bounchet, first black to earn PhD from a US university (Yale).

Black cowboy Nat Love earned title of "Deadwood Dick."

1877    "Belt" Williams, great comedian of early 1900s, born.

Henry O. Flipper, first black West Point graduate.

Frederick Douglass appointed marshal of Washington, DC, by President Hayes.

1879 William Lloyd Garrison, abolitionist, died.

Blanche Bruce presided over US Senate

1881 William Pickens, author and civil rights fighter, born.

Booker T. Washington began work at Tuskegee Institute.

1882 Violette Johnson first black woman to practice before Supreme Court.

Benjamin Brawley, social historian, born.

Tennessee passed first Jim Crow law, beginning of modern segregation movement.

John F. Slater, white manufacturer, created $1 million fund for education of Southern blacks.

1883 Jan Matzeliger, inventor, patented shoe lasting machine.

Ernest Just, marine biologist, born.

George Washington Williams wrote *History of the Negro Race in America*.

More than five thousand blacks working as cowboys in the West.

Ben Hodges and Cherokee Bill elude the law.

1884 Medico-Chirurgical Society, first American Negro medical society, founded.

John Roy Lynch presided over Republican Convention.

1886 L. Clark Broods ran first electric trolley in United States.

1889    Provident Hospital school for black nurses founded in Chicago.

A. Philip Randolph, labor leader, born.

Frederick Douglass became minister to Haiti.

1891    Peter Jackson boxed sixty-one–round draw with Jim Corbett.

1892    Luther P. Jackson, historian, born.

Lynchings in the United States reach their peak: four per week.

Unrealistic literacy and other such qualifications hindered right to vote.

1893    Walter Francis White, executive secretary of NAACP, born.

Dr. Daniel Hale Williams performed world's first successful open-heart operation.

1895    Frederick Douglass died. His home in Washington, DC, is now a national shrine.

Booker T. Washington delivered famous "Atlanta Compromise" speech at Cotton Exposition. Whites liked it because it was moderate and they considered him the "voice of the Negro." To the blacks he was an "Uncle Tom."

1986    Supreme Court upheld "separate but equal" doctrine.

Dr. Mary Church Terrell founded National Association of Colored Women.

W. E. B. DuBois published *Suppression of African Slave*.

1898    John Merrick and Dr. A. M. Moore founded N.C. Mutual Life Insurance Co.

1899    Duke Ellington born.

1900    Louis "Stachmo" Armstrong born on July 4.

Nearly all Southern states openly practiced segregation.

1901    William Trotter founded *Boston Guardian*, militant newspaper.

1903    W. E. B. DuBois published *Souls of Black Folk*.

Dr. Ralph Bunch, U.N. representative and leader, born.

1905    Black intellectuals formed Niagara Movement.

Robert S. Abbott began publication of *Chicago Defender*.

1906    Twelve died in Atlanta race riot.

Alpha Phi Alpha first black Greek-letter fraternity.

Poet Paul L. Dunbar died.

1907    Alaine Locke first African American Rhodes Scholar.

Jack Johnson defeated Tommy Burns for heavyweight championship.

1908    Thurgood Marshall born.

1909    NAACP founded after lynching In Springfield, Illinois.

Nannie Burroughs founded National Training School for Women at DC.

1910    National Urban League organized in New York City.

1914    Marcus Garvey, a black nationalist who claimed millions of followers, organized a back-to-Africa movement. He founded Universal Negro Improvement Association. In 1920, a convention was held. In 1921, he was president of Republic of Africa. He collected $10 million to build ships. In 1923, he was arrested for fraud.

1915    Professor Ernest E. Just received the NAACP Spingarn award for research in biology.

Dr. Carter G. Woodson founded Association for the Study of Negro Life and History. Supreme Court ruled it unconstitutional to have registration only for voters whose ancestors could vote.

1916    Major Charles Young received the NAACP Spingarn award for services in Liberia.

October: After joining the French Foreign Legion before the war, then serving with the French Infantry in 1915, African American Eugene Jacques Bullard transferred into the French Air Service, where he became a highly decorated combat pilot. Known as the "Black Swallow of Death," Bullard flew over twenty combat missions. Despite his outstanding record, Bullard was never allowed to fly for the United States, even after it entered the war.

1916–1917: Because of the growing bias against the use of black soldiers, African Americans serving in the regular army and National Guard numbered about twenty thousand (approximately 2 percent of all servicemen). There were only three black commissioned officers. Despite the army's need for men when war was declared, it initially continued to reject most African American volunteers.

1917    Julius Rosenwald Fund for Educational, Scientific, and Religious Purposes is founded.

Harry T. Burleigh received the NAACP Spingarn award for excellence in the field of creative music.

Dr. Louis T. Wright, the first black physician appointed to the staff of a white hospital in New York City (1919), served during World War I as a first lieutenant in the Medical Corps. He introduced the injection method of smallpox vaccination eventually adopted by the US Army.

Noted architect Vertner W. Tandy was the first black officer in the New York National Guard. Commissioned as a first lieutenant, he was later promoted to captain, then major.

Lloyd A. Hal was appointed assistant chief inspector of powder and explosives in the US Ordnance Department. He held the position for two years.

Alton Augustus Adams became the first black band leader in the US Navy.

The army forced its highest-ranking African American officer to retire, supposedly because he was unfit for duty. Although Colonel Charles R. Young suffered from high blood pressure and Bright's disease, white leaders' rejection of black proposals that Young command an all-black division may actually have been the motive behind the army's decision. Determined to continue his army career, Young rode his horse from Ohio to Washington, DC, to demonstrate his fitness for duty. However, he was not reinstated until November 1918, at which time the army assigned him to Fort Grant, Illinois, where he trained black troops.

The American Red Cross rejected the applications of qualified African American nurses on the grounds that the US Army did not accept black women.

March 25: The District of Columbia National Guard, under command of African American officer Major James E. Walker, was assigned to protect the national capital.

April 6: The United States entered World War I after President Woodrow Wilson asked Congress to declare war on Germany. The Senate concurred on April 4, while the House agreed on April 6. Over 367,000 African American soldiers served in this conflict, 1,400 of whom were commissioned officers. Most blacks were placed in noncombat Services of Supply (SOS) units (i.e., labor battalions); for example, 33 percent of the stevedore force in Europe was black. At least one hundred thousand African Americans were sent to France during World War I. Despite the American restriction on the use of blacks in combat units, about forty thousand African Americans fought in the war.

May 18: Congress passed the Selective Service Act, authorizing the registration and draft of all men between twenty-one and thirty, including African Americans. About seven hundred thousand black men volunteered for the draft on the first day, while over 2 million ultimately registered. Previously, in April 1917, the American Negro Loyal Legion advised the federal government that it could quickly raise about ten thousand African American volunteers. Shortly after the draft was instituted, the Central Committee of Negro College Men organized at Howard University furnished over 1,500 names in response to an army requirement for 200 college-educated blacks to be trained at a promised officers' school. Despite African American support for the war effort, some army leaders had doubts about enlisting large numbers of blacks, because senior officers feared the negative response of Southern politicians. They believed blacks could not fight, or were concerned about possible subversion by an "oppressed minority." Because of the large number of blacks seeking to enlist, the War Department ordered that African Americans not be recruited.

May 19: After Congress authorized fourteen training camps for white officer candidates but none for African Americans, black protests and pressure on army officials and Congress forced the War Department to correct this discriminatory situation. On this date, the US Army established the first all-black officer training school at Fort Des Moines, Iowa. About half of the black officers during World War I were commissioned in the first four months after classes began on June 15, 1917. Of these officer candidates, 250 were drawn from the noncommissioned officers of the four black regular army units.

May 21: Leo Pinckney was the first African American drafted in World War I.

June: The first American troop ship dispatched to France included over four hundred black stevedores and longshoremen. By November 1918, about fifty thousand African Americans in the US Army were employed as laborers in French ports. The SOS units handled a variety of duties: loading and unloading cargo, constructing roads and camps, transporting materials, laying railroad tracks, digging graves and ditches, serving as motorcycle couriers and military train porters, etc. Their physical accomplishments often impressed the French. In September 1918, for example, black servicemen unloaded twenty-five thousand tons of cargo per day for several weeks, well over the amount French officials estimated could be moved in one month.

August 23: Increasing racial tension involving US servicemen eventually flared into a major riot in Texas, where black troops were assigned to Camp Logan to guard the construction of a training facility. Members of the 1st and 3rd Battalions, and 24th Infantry Regiment endured weeks of racial harassment which culminated in the arrest of Corporal Charles W. Baltimore. These racial problems were compounded by the absence of the stabilizing influence of experienced black NCOs and the presence of inexperienced and insensitive white officers. At least one hundred unit members responded to the tense, rumor-charged situation by marching on the town, where they opened fire on the police station, killing sixteen whites (including five policemen) and wounding twelve others. In the next 14 months, the Army quickly court-martial six men from the 151st Battalion and 149 from the 3rd in four separate trials. Army investigators identified individual soldiers involved, and brought charges against each of them. Only one individual had charges dropped. Four were convicted of lesser charges, forty-two were given life sentences, and thirteen were condemned to die. Another sixteen men were condemned to hang in two later trials.

September: Emmett J. Scott was appointed special assistant to the US secretary of war. A former secretary to Booker T. Washington, Scott worked to assure the nondiscriminatory application of the Selective Service Act.

October 17: The Army commissioned 639 black officers who had been trained at the new all-black facility established at Fort Des Moines. By war's end, the school had produced 1,400 commissioned officers, many of whom commanded labor battalions. Others, however, served in combat with distinction.

December 11: The Army carried out the executions of the first thirteen men (one of whom was Corporal Charles W. Baltimore) condemned to die for their role in the Houston riot. To lessen public reaction, there was no prior public announcement of the executions, nor did the army allow any appeals. Because of black Americans' very negative response to these actions, President Woodrow Wilson was forced to modify existing War Department policy. From then on, the president would examine the death penalty verdicts in all military law cases. Of the sixteen men condemned in two subsequent trials, ten had their sentences commuted, while the death sentences were upheld for six soldiers found guilty of killing specific individuals.

December 27: The 369th Infantry Regiment (or Harlem Hellfighters) was the first all-black US combat unit to be shipped overseas during World War I. Unfortunately, this distinction was the result of a violent racial incident in Spartanburg, South Carolina. The unit's unquenchable desire to win justice and avenge a physical attack on their drum major, Noble Sissle, ultimately forced the War Department to send them to Europe. Because there was no official combat role at this time for America's black soldiers, General John J. Pershing responded to France's request for troops by assigning the 369th (and the 93rd Division's other regiments) to the French Army. The Germans dubbed the unit the "Hellfighters," because in 191 days of duty at the front they never had any men captured or ground taken. Almost one-third of the unit died in combat. The French government awarded the entire regiment the Croix de Guerre. Sergeant Henry Johnson was the first African American to win this prestigious award when he single-handedly saved Private Needham Roberts and fought off a German raiding party.

1917–1918: African American women supported the WWI effort by organizing and serving as hostesses at YMCA centers for black soldiers ready to depart for France. They also served as nurses with the integrated Field Medical Supply Depot in Washington, DC.

1917–1918: After the racial clashes in Texas and other parts of the United States, army leaders became increasingly distrustful of the army's long-standing black units. The 24th and 25th infantry Regiments never went to France. Instead, the 24th Infantry spent the entire conflict guarding far-flung outposts on the Mexican border, while the 25th Infantry was sent to the Philippines and Hawaii. The army also abandoned its plans to raise sixteen regiments to accommodate the numerous black draftees, because it feared the likelihood of other violent racial incidents. It eventually activated the all-black 92nd and 93rd Infantry. These units experienced incomplete training, severe prejudice from white officers, inadequately prepared replacements, and the lack of Army enthusiasm and support. Compounding these handicaps was the fact that all too often during combat in World War I, black troops were also blamed unfairly for problems caused by inadequate white leadership, as well as ineffectual combat planning and coordination.

1917–1918: Although it was never formally organized as a division (it had only four infantry regiments and no service or support units), the 93rd Infantry Division actually achieved a better combat record than the 92nd Infantry Division. Much of the division's success in battle was the result of unit cohesion among the former National Guard unit members who made up the bulk of the 93rd Division's troops. Another important factor was the assignment of the division to the French, who trained, equipped, and fielded these men without regard for race. Strangely enough, white US Army officers thought they were disparaging the combat effectiveness of the 93rd by attributing it to the integration of the French forces. It took the US military three more decades and two more overseas wars to realize the inefficiency of its shortsighted and discriminatory policy of racial segregation.

1918    William S. Braithwaite received the NAACP Spingarn award for distinguished achievement in literature. National Liberty Congress of Colored Americans petitioned Congress for anti-lynching bill; succeeded in 1922.

The 369th Infantry's regimental band, conducted by noted black musician and composer James Reese. Europe was credited with introducing American jazz to France and the rest of Europe. The band traveled throughout France in the early months of this year, giving concerts that featured this uniquely African American music. Black musicians in other regiments also helped to spread an appreciation for jazz to Europe's civilian population.

Ralph Waldo Tyler, a reporter and government official, was the first and only official African American war correspondent in World War I. The Committee on Public Information accredited Tyler to report on war news of interest to black Americans.

A racial incident in Manhattansville, Kansas, was sparked by a local theater's refusal to admit a black sergeant, a type of discrimination prohibited by state law. The theater owner was fined after other African American soldiers and the black press openly protested the event. To avoid similar problems in the future, however, the local army commander ordered black servicemen "to refrain from behavior that would provoke a racial response."

June: The all-black 92nd (Buffalo) Division, which had been activated in October 1917, arrived in France and then moved to the front in August 1918. Formed entirely of African Americans draftees, many of the division's men (mainly those from the 365th and 366th Regiments) were assigned to road-building details. However, members of the 367th and 368th regiments remained under fire almost constantly until the armistice of November 1918. Despite individual acts of heroism, army leaders maintained that the division did not perform well under combat conditions. Much of their criticism was based on the 368th Infantry Regiment's inability to withstand the German assault in the Argonne forest in September 1918, although white units in the area suffered the same failure. After its transfer to another command, the 92nd Division's performance improved with better training and increased morale. For its combat success and bravery at Metz in November 1918, the French awarded the Croix de Guerre to the 1st Battalion, 367th Infantry Regiment. Unfortunately, the division's accomplishments could not overcome the racism of its white leadership. The latter's poor opinion of the unit, which they attributed to undesirable racial characteristics, had a significant impact on the US armed forces' subsequent policies on the use of African American servicemen. The unit was disbanded after World War I but was reactivated in October 1942 for duty during World War II.

July: In an editorial written for the NAACP publication, *Crisis,*

W. E. B. DuBois urged black Americans to put the war effort before their own needs by "closing ranks" with white Americans in support of the fighting in France. His sentiments were based partly on the continuing belief that African American military participation might help win greater acceptance and freedom for all blacks in the United States. They were also based partly on DuBois's own desire to win a commission with army intelligence, which he later declined.

August: Senior US Army officers had the 369th Infantry's musicians ordered back from the front to support troop morale by entertaining Allied soldiers in camps and hospitals.

August 7: At the urging of US Army officers, the French liaison to the American Expeditionary Force (AEF) Headquarters issued a "secret" memorandum instructing his fellow officers and civilian authorities on how to "handle" African American troops during World War I. To avoid any unpleasantness with the Americans, he advised other French officers to keep their distance from any black officers, to give only moderate praise to black troops, and to keep black troops and white French women apart.

September: The all-black 809th Pioneer Infantry arrived in France. During the fourteen-day voyage aboard the troop ship *President Grant*, about half of the five thousand men on board fell ill with Spanish flu (a global influenza epidemic that killed millions of people in 1918–1919). So many men died en route that their bodies had to be buried at sea. The first task allotted seventy-five of the unit's men upon the ship's arrival in France to unload the bodies of additional flu victims. Called "Black Yankees" by the French (an ironic nickname since many of the 809th men were from the South), this pioneer infantry unit (i.e., a construction crew) built hospitals and completed extensive repairs and new construction at the French port of St. Nazaire, where many American soldiers disembarked in World

War I. Although trained to fight, the 809th worked mainly in construction until the armistice.

September 3: German propaganda leaflets dropped on African American troops attempted to exploit the contradictory attitudes reflected in American society. The Germans touched on a sensitive area by noting that black troops were sent to fight for democracy in Europe, while being denied this same personal freedom at home. The leaflets unsuccessfully urged black soldiers to defect. "To carry a gun in this service is not an honor but a shame. Throw it away and come over to the German lines. You will find friends who will help you."

September 16: The US Army executed the last six soldiers sentenced to die for their involvement in the Houston riot. For the next two decades, the NAACP campaigned to win the release of the remaining imprisoned rioters. This effort eventually resulted in the freeing by 1938 the last men involved in the deadly incident.

November: The 3691st (or Harlem Hellfighters) was the first Allied regiment to reach the Rhine River during the final offensive against Germany.

Members of the 3701st Infantry Regiment won twenty-one American Service Crosses and sixty-eight French Croix de Guerre during World War I. This all-black unit from Illinois fought in the last battle of World War I and captured a German train a few minutes after the armistice was declared.

November 13: The Army Nurses Corps accepted eighteen black nurses on an "experimental" basis following the influenza epidemic. The army sent half of them to Camp Grant, Illinois, and the other half to Camp Sherman, Ohio. Although their living quarters were segregated, they were assigned to duties in an integrated hospital. Because of the postwar reduction in force, the army released all eighteen women in August 1919.

1919    W. E. B. DuBois organized first Pan-African Congress in Paris.

KKK sponsored twenty-five race riots.

Archibald K. Grimke received the NAACP Spingarn award for distinguished service to race and country.

Despite the valor and efficiency with which most black Americans discharged their duty to the United States during World War I, they received little recognition for their efforts once they returned home. Although the 369th Infantry Regiment was honored with white soldiers in a grand parade down New York City's Fifth Avenue, other areas either ignored or downplayed the African American contribution to Allied victory. However, many blacks refused to quietly accept such slights. In St. Joseph, Missouri, for example, black veterans would not march at the back of a victory parade because it was incompatible with the democratic principles for which they had fought. The US government also did not award any of the 127 medals of honor earned in World War I to an African American serviceman. This error was corrected on April 24, 1991, when President George Bush posthumously awarded the 128th WWI medal of honor to Corporal Freddie Stowers, a black soldier killed on September 28, 1918, while leading an assault on a German-held hill in France.

During the summer following the armistice of November 1918, racial violence spawned serious riots in Texas; Nebraska; Illinois; Washington, DC; and other parts of the United States. This same year, ten veterans were among the seventy-five African Americans lynched by white mobs. Unlike most confrontations before and during World War I, however, African Americans fought back in these postwar flare-ups. Some scholars attribute this new spirit of resistance to the changed attitudes of black veterans. Their experiences in the war, as well as the lack of

French racial prejudice toward them, made many African American veterans unwilling to passively endure continued discrimination and ill treatment once they returned to the United States.

March 15: Delegates representing AEF units met in Paris, France, to form the American Legion, a veteran's organization. Black veterans were allowed to join, but only in segregated posts.

May 9: The 369th Infantry Regiment's former band leader, James Reese Europe, was stabbed to death by Herbert Wright, an unstable, disgruntled musician. In the few short months between the end of World War I and his death, Europe composed and recorded music based on his experiences during the Great War. Sung by Noble Sissle, who had been the drum major for the 369th, songs such as "On Patrol in No Man's Land" and "All of No Man's Land Is Ours" described the harsh combat conditions of the Western front.

July 14: The US Army prohibited African American soldiers from participating in the Bastille Day victory parade held in Paris.

June 1920: Congress passed the National Defense Act, which downsized the army to thirty thousand officers and enlisted men. All four of the army's long-standing black units survived the cutbacks, primarily because white leaders feared the legal and social ramifications of eliminating them. Necessity also dictated the retention of both infantry and cavalry units to prevent the possibility of integrating brigades, as well as to provide troops for duty in the Philippines.

1920    W. E. B. DuBois received the NAACP Spingarn award for scholarship, for founding *Crisis*, and for creating Pan-African Conference.

1921    Charles S. Gilpin received the NAACP Spingarn award for acting role in O'Neill's *Emperor Jones*. The army disbanded the 3rd Battalion, 24th Infantry Regiment, which had been relegated to duty at various isolated posts in New Mexico in the aftermath of the deadly Houston riot of 1917.

1922    Mary B. Talbert received the NAACP Spingarn award for service to women of her race and for restoration of Fredrick Douglass's home. Joseph H. Ward was named medical officer chief of the Veterans Administration (VA) hospital in Tuskegee, Alabama. He was the first African American appointed to head a VA hospital. As a result of severe cutbacks in military spending after World War I, the 24th Infantry Regiment was reduced to 828 men. The unit was stationed at Fort Benning, Georgia, where it helped transform the previously temporary home of the Army Infantry School into a permanent facility. Kept segregated from the rest of the post, unit members were classified as riflemen and machine gunners, but they actually performed mostly manual labor: maintenance, construction, logging, deliveries, gardening, and cleanup details. Except for some instruction in marksmanship, close-order drill, and military courtesy, black troops received little combat training between the wars. By 1934, the army had made some attempts to improve the 24th Infantry Regiment's ability to perform its military mission, but few real changes were implemented.

James 8: The army's highest-ranking black officer, Colonel Charles R. Young, died while serving as the US military liaison in Nigeria.

1923    George Washington Carver received the NAACP Spingarn award for research in agricultural chemistry. First Catholic Seminary for black priest in Mississippi.

1924    Roland Hayes received the NAACP Spingarn award for artistry in singing black folk music. Fletcher Henderson's jazz band opened Roseland Ballroom.

1925   James Weldon Johnson received the NAACP Spingarn award for distinguished achievements as author, diplomat, and public servant.

In Greenwood, Mississippi, KKK ministers and businessman led lynch mobs. At Oscella, Louisiana, mobs flogged and shot ministers for preaching equality.

Four hundred thousand KKK marched in front of white House.

A. Phillip Randolph organized Brotherhood of Sleeping Car Porters.

Countee Cullen, poet, awarded Phi Beta Kappa key.

An Army War College study reported that African Americans would never be fit to serve as military pilots because of their supposed lack of intelligence and cowardice in combat. The famed Tuskegee Airmen, however, would later completely disprove these questionable conclusions during combat in Europe. Between 1943 and 1945, the group earned 150 Distinguished Flying Crosses, 14 Bronze Stars, 8 Purple Hearts, 3 Distinctive Unit Citations, as well as several other awards.

1926   Carter G. Woodson received the NAACP Spingarn award for services as historian, recorder of black life in America.

1927   Anthony Overton received the NAACP Spingarn award for successful business career. Supreme Court rejected Texas law barring blacks from voting in "White Primaries."

1928   Charles W. Chesnutt received the NAACP Spingarn award for his literary work depicting black life.

1929   Mordecai Wyatt Johnson, born January 4, 1890, served as the first black president at Howard University from 1926-1960. He died September 10, 1976.

KKK sponsored ten known lynching of blacks.

Alonzo Parham entered the US Military Academy at West Point, the first black cadet to be accepted since the graduation of Charles R. Young in 1889. He left after only one year. The next African American cadet was not admitted until 1932.

1930    *New York Times* began capitalizing "N" in Negro. R. B. Harrison opened on Broadway in *Green Pastures*.

Jack Thompson became welterweight champion of the world.

Henry A. Hunt received the Spingarn award for educational progress in rural Georgia.

1931    Richard B. Harrison received the Spingarn award for his role as "De Lawd" in *Green Pastures* and for a long life of dramatic performances.

1932    Robert Russa Moton, principal of Tuskegee institution, received the Spingarn award for long conservative service to the African American.

The US Navy again allowed African Americans to enlist, lifting the restriction in place since the end of World War I that excluded blacks from serving in this branch of the US armed forces. However, they were only admitted into the predominantly Filipino Steward's Branch.

1933    NAACP's first legal attack on discrimination in education lost on a technicality. Max Yergan received the Spingarn award for service as missionary, bringing American culture to the motherland (Africa).

1934    William Taylor Bowell Williams, dean of Tuskegee, received the Spingarn award for efforts in the field of education.

1935    National Council of Negro Women founded by Mary M. Bethune.

Joe Louis defeated Primo Carnera.

Mary McLeod Bethune received the Spingarn award for work in establishing Bethune-Cookman College.

1936    NAACP filed first suits in campaign to equalize teachers' salaries and educational facilities.

Jesse Owens won four medals in Berlin Olympics.

John Hope, president of Atlanta University, received the Spingarn award for efforts on behalf of his race.

Benjamin O. Davis Jr. graduated from West Point, after enduring four years of "silencing." The academy's fourth African American graduate, Davis was the first to be commissioned in the twentieth century. Second Lieutenant Davis reported to Fort Benning to join the 24th Infantry Regiment, which continued to function primarily as a labor pool.

James Johnson received an appointment to the US Naval Academy, but he was forced to resign after only eight months because of ill health. George Trivers followed in 1937 but left one month later for academic reasons. Both cadets suffered severe hazing by white midshipmen and discrimination by instructors.

1937    Joe Louis defeated Braddock, gained heavyweight boxing title.

Walter White, executive secretary of NAACP, received the Spingarn award for investigation of forty-one lynchings and lobbying for anti-lynching bill.

Willa Beatrice Brown, the first African American woman to get a commercial pilot's license, and her flight instructor, Cornelius

R. Coffey, cofounded the National Airmen's Association of America to promote African American aviation. The following year, they established the Coffey School of Aeronautics, where Willa Brown served as director. The army and Civil Aeronautics Authority (CAA) selected the Coffey School "to conduct the 'experiments' that resulted in the admission of African Americans into the Army Air Forces." The school trained about two hundred pilots between 1938 and 1945, some of whom later served as part of the famed Tuskegee Airmen, when Coffey became a feeder school for the official flight program at Tuskegee Institute.

1938　US Supreme Court said all states must provide equal educational facilities. NAACP did not award the Spingarn award this year.

1939　J. Matilda Bolin, first black female judge in New York City, appointed by Mayor LaGuardia.

Mrs. F. D. Roosevelt resigned from DAR in protest. Marian Anderson barred from Constitution Hall in Washington, DC.

Ethel Waters starred in *Mamba's Daughters*.

Senator Bilbo from Mississippi introduced "Back to Africa" bill.

NAACP established Legal Defense and Educational Fund as separate organization.

Marian Anderson received the Spingarn award for her performances in the field of music for dignity and for unassuming posture in the face of success. After the number of African American soldiers had dropped to less than four thousand, and in response to growing black demands, the US Army began accepting black volunteers in proportion to their demographic presence (about 9 to 10 percent of the US population). The only black regiments in the National Guard were the 369th New

York, 8th Illinois, and the 372nd Regiment, which included men from Maryland, Massachusetts, New Jersey, Ohio, and the District of Columbia. African American servicemen represented only 2 percent of the nation's fighting force before World War II.

The Committee for the Participation of Negroes in National Defense was formed. Headed by noted black historian Rayford W. Logan, who served as acting chair, the committee successfully helped to get nondiscrimination clauses inserted into the Selective Service Act passed in September 1940.

May: Sponsored by the National Association and aided by the *Chicago Defender*, a black newspaper, African American aviators Chauncey Spencer and Dale White lobbied for the inclusion of blacks as pilots in the Civilian Pilot Training Program then being debated in Congress. They won the support of several congressmen while in Washington, DC, including that of Missouri Senator Harry S. Truman.

June 27: Congress passed the Civilian Pilot Training Act to create a pool of trained aviators in the event of war. Civilian schools, at least one of which was supposed to accept black pilots, provided the required flight training. Willa B. Brown lobbied for the inclusion of African Americans in both the training program and the Army Air Corps. At least seven different institutions enrolled blacks for flight training, but the Army Air Corps continued to exclude African American pilots.

September 3: Britain and France declared war after Germany invaded Poland, while President Franklin D. Roosevelt announced American neutrality in a fireside chat. During the years between World War I and World War II, the US armed forces had continued to underuse and segregate African American servicemen. The army restricted its African American soldiers to all-black units, while the navy relegated black sailors to menial labor and service tasks, primarily in the nonwhite Steward's Branch. The US Marine Corps (USMC), like the Army Air Corps, continued its traditional exclusion of African Americans.

1939–1940: To absorb the larger numbers of African Americans being admitted, the army formed several new all-black units, primarily in the service and technical forces. The 47th and 48th Quartermaster Regiments formed in 1939 were followed in 1940 by the 1st Chemical Decontamination Company (August 1), the 41st General Service Engineer Regiment (August 15), as well as artillery, coastal artillery, and transportation units.

1940    Benjamin O. Davis Sr. made brigadier general in US Army.

Louis T. Wright, surgeon, received the Spingarn award for his work on behalf of black doctors and nurses.

President Franklin D. Roosevelt signed the Selective Training and Service Act, the first peacetime draft in US history. The act contained an antidiscrimination clause and established a 10 percent quota system to ensure integration. Shortly thereafter, Assistant Secretary of War Robert Patterson issued a memo on segregation that seemingly contradicted the new legislation's racial policy. Segregated troops remained official US Army policy throughout World War I, because it did not consider racial separation to be discriminatory. The Army did attempt to dispel racist beliefs among its white officers by issuing a book titled *Army Service Forces Manual, Leadership and the Negro Soldier*. Classified "restricted," this publication tried to avoid condescension and stereotyping, while insisting on identical treatment for all soldiers, regardless of race. It also provided some sociological and historical information meant to eliminate erroneous beliefs concerning the use of African American combat troops.

September 17: Black leaders met with the secretary of the navy and the assistant secretary of war to present a seven-point program for the mobilization of African Americans. Included were demands for flight training, the admission of black women into Red Cross and military nursing units, and desegregation of the armed forces.

President Roosevelt issued a statement on October 9, 1940, that argued against the latter demand on the basis that it would adversely impact national defense. Although he promised to ensure that the services enlisted blacks in proportion to their demographic presence, Roosevelt basically continued policies dating back to World War I. Many African Americans were angered by the White House's erroneous claim that the black leaders had approved the statement. However, additional political pressure by African Americans and some Republicans convinced Roosevelt to do more. Consequently, Benjamin O. Davis Sr. was promoted to brigadier general, flight training for blacks was planned, more blacks were drafted, Judge William H. Hastie was made a special aide to the secretary of war, and a black adviser was appointed for the Selective Service Board.

October: African American servicemen in the US armed forces prior to the nation's entry into World War II in December 1941 totaled only 13,200 in the army and 4,000 in the navy. During this month, the War Department established its basic racial policy by continuing segregation and by establishing a quota for enlisting blacks based on a percentage of their general population.

October 1: African American physician Dr. Charles Richard Drew—who pioneered a system for storing blood plasma, thereby originating the "blood bank"—served as director of the First Plasma Division Blood Transfusion Association. This British organization supplied plasma for British troops during World War II. In 1941, Drew was appointed to be the first director of the American Red Cross Blood Bank, which supplied blood to US forces. He resigned from this position, however, to protest the organization's November 1941 decision to exclude black blood donors. Dr. Drew's research was responsible for saving countless lives during World War II.

November 1: Judge William H. Hastie, dean of Howard University Law School, assumed the position of civilian aide to the secretary of war in matters of black rights. The position was similar to that held by Emmett J. Schott during World War I.

December 18: The US Army Air Corps sent plans to Tuskegee Institute in Alabama concerning the training of African American pilots. On January 6, 1941, General Henry H. (Hap) Arnold informed the assistant secretary of war about his decision to restrict the training of black flyers to Tuskegee, where the necessary facilities to more quickly implement the program were available. In addition, the school was close enough to Montgomery to be supervised by the Maxwell Field commander. Despite this decision, Arnold remained opposed to allowing African American pilots into the air corps, and he made several attempts to disband the program. By 1943, however, political considerations and increasing reports of the combat successes achieved by black aviators forced Arnold to stop tampering with the Tuskegee Airmen.

1941    US Supreme Court ruled separate facilities on railroads must be substantially equal.

Doris Miller, who downed four planes at Pearl Harbor, awarded the Navy Cross.

Richard Wright, author, received the Spingarn award for making Americans aware of the effect of segregation and denial of opportunities on blacks. Willa B. Brown became a training coordinator for the Civil Aeronautics Administration and a teacher in the Civilian Pilot Training Program.

January: Black labor organizer and civil rights leader (and later politician, writer, and professor) Ernest Calloway was the first black to refuse to be inducted, because he objected to the army's racist segregation policy. He was a member of the Conscientious Objectors against Jim Crow, a group that claimed African Americans should be exempt from military service because of discrimination. Calloway's protest and subsequent imprisonment generated a lot of national publicity. Although this particular group disbanded after Calloway was incarcerated, over four hundred other black men also became Conscientious Objectors during World War II. Some were members of the Nation of Islam who refused induction on religious grounds, while others, like William Lynn, refused to serve because the quota system established by the armed forces contradicted the antidiscrimination clauses of the September 1940 Selective Service and Training Act.

Labor and civil rights leader A. Philip Randolph, president of the Brotherhood of Sleeping Car Porters, proposed a massive march on Washington in July 1941 to protest unfair labor practices in the defense industry and the military's discrimination against African Americans. During World War I, Randolph had not endorsed other black leaders' calls to put aside their own grievances and unite behind the war effort, stating "that rather than volunteer to make the world safe for democracy, he would fight to make Georgia safe for the Negro." His demands for full black participation continued in World War II.

January 9: Secretary of War Henry L. Stimson formally approved the establishment of the flight training program at Tuskegee Institute.

January 13: The US Army established the 78th Tank Battalion, the first black armor unit. The first African American tankers reported to Fort Knox, Kentucky, to begin armored warfare training in March 1941. The 78th was re-designated on May

8, 1941, as the 758th Tank Battalion (Light). It was the first of three tank battalions comprising the 51st Tank Group, which was made up of black enlisted men and white officers. The other two tank battalions were the 761st and 784th. Initially inactivated on September 22, 1945, at Viareggio, Italy, the 758th was reactivated in 1946 and later fought in the Korean War as the 64th Tank Battalion.

February: The 1st Battalion, 351st Field Artillery Regiment was activated at Camp Livingston, Louisiana, as part of the 461th Field Artillery Brigade. Redesignated the 351st Field Artillery Battalion in 1943, the unit arrived in Europe in December 1944. The African American enlisted personnel were officered by sixteen blacks and fifteen whites. While stationed in England from December 1944 to February 1945, the 351st Field Artillery Group-Colored's 50-man Caisson Choir sang for the British public in such notable places as Westminster Abbey and St. Paul's Cathedral. After being transferred to France in March 1945, the unit was attached to the 9th U.S. Army. While engaged in fighting with the Germans, the 361st fired over 6,200 rounds of 155-mm Howitzer artillery ammunition into enemy territory.

June 25: President Franklin D. Roosevelt issued Executive Order 8802, which reiterated the federal government's previously stated policy of nondiscrimination in war industry employment. It also created a committee on fair employment practice to oversee the application of the president's directive and to expand new job opportunities for black workers. This action was in keeping with a promise made to A. Philip Randolph if he would call off his planned "March on Washington" to protest discrimination and segregation.

June 29, 1941, to November 16, 1944: While on assignment with the army's inspector general, Brigadier General Benjamin O. Davis Sr. completed several notable inspections involving black troops stationed at Northern and Southern posts. In a memorandum on November 9, 1943, Davis pointed out the nearly impossible task of African American soldiers in developing "a high morale in a community that offers him nothing but humiliation and mistreatment." He reported that instead of working to eliminate Jim Crow laws in the military, "the Army, by its directives and by actions of commanding officers, has introduced the attitudes of the 'Governors of the six Southern states,' in many of the other 42 states of the continental United States." He also conducted several important inquiries into racial clashes between white soldiers or civilians and black soldiers stationed at Fort Bragg, North Carolina; Alexandria, Louisiana; Fort Dix, New Jersey; Selfridge Field (now Air Force Base), Michigan; and Camp Stewart, Georgia. In his reports, Davis recommended that African American soldiers gradually be removed from Southern posts and that black officers be assigned to command black troops. General Davis also represented the War Department at numerous functions involving black civilians, such as war bond rallies or speeches given to war industry workers.

July: The Army opened its integrated officers' candidate schools. For the first six months, however, only twenty-one of the more than two thousand men admitted were black. Whites protested the policy, and some black leaders demanded a quota be established to ensure parity, but the Army justified its policy of ignoring race in regard to officer training on the grounds of efficiency and economy. Unfortunately, race still continued to determine assignments after newly commissioned officers graduated. Too often more qualified African American officers were put in charge of service units, while less qualified white officers continued to be assigned to black combat units. The degree of authority and respect given to black officers also remained a serious problem, since African American officers were unable to command even the lowest-ranking white soldiers.

July 19: The US Army Air Corps began training African American pilots at the Tuskegee Institute in Alabama. Actual flight instruction began on August 25. The Tuskegee Institute, which prepared the 926 members of the famed Tuskegee Airmen for combat in World War II, remained the only official military flight training school for black pilots until its program closed with the graduation of the last class on June 26, 1946.

August 4: The first commanding officer of Huntsville Arsenal (Alabama), Colonel Rollo C. Ditto, arrived and broke ground for the initial construction of the installation. Huntsville Arsenal, which was part of the Chemical Warfare Service, was the sole manufacturer of colored smoke munitions. It also produced gel-type incendiaries and toxic agents, such as mustard gas, phosgene, lewisite, and tear gas. The Army broke ground on neighboring Redstone Arsenal on October 25, 1941. This Ordnance Corps installation manufactured chemical artillery ammunition, burster charges, rifle grenades, and various types of bombs. African American men and women worked at both arsenals during World War II. By May 1944, when civilian employment reached its wartime peak of 6,707 men and women, blacks represented 22 percent of the workforce at Huntsville Arsenal.

1942    Blacks and whites formed Congress of Racial Equality.

A. Philip Randolph received the Spingarn award for leadership in labor and for organizing the march on Washington in 1941.

1943    William H. Hastie, jurist, received the Spingarn award for his uncompromising fight against racial injustice.

1944    US Supreme Court outlawed "White Primaries," which had made voting for blacks almost impossible.

Black women admitted to WAVES.

Dr. Charles R. Drew, scientist, received the Spingarn award for his work in blood plasma and for the blood bank.

1945    One thousand white students walked out of Gary, Indiana, school in protest over integration.

Paul Roberson, baritone, received the Spingarn award for distinguished service in the theater.

October 1: Secretary of War Robert P. Patterson ordered the US Army to review its racial policies. Consequently, Lieutenant General George C. Marshall established a board headed by Lieutenant General Alvan C. Gillem Jr. to study the situation and prepare a directive on the use of African Americans in the postwar army.

November 17: The Gillem Board finished its study of the army's racial policies and sent its report to the chief of staff. Although it came close to recommending that the army integrate its forces, the Gillem Board members ultimately decided not to do so because integration *"would have been a radical step, out of keeping with the climate of opinion in the country and in the Army itself."* Instead the board provided eighteen specific recommendations based on the principles that African Americans had "a constitutional right to fight" and the Army had to *"make the most effective use of every soldier".* Although the Gillem Board advised army leaders to provide more opportunities for qualified blacks based on individual merit, it sidestepped the fundamental problem of segregation and only committed the army to limited reforms.

1946    US Supreme Court ruled no more segregation on interstate buses.

Thurgood Marshall, special NAACP counsel, received the Spingarn award for his work before Supreme Court to end disenfranchisement.

February 27: The US Navy published Circular Letter 48–46,

making black sailors "eligible for all types of assignments in all ratings in all activities and all ships of Naval service." It also directed that "housing, messing, and other facilities" no longer be segregated. Although this new policy was a step forward, there were still no high-ranking black officers, no whites in the Steward's Branch, and no African Americans in any specialized assignments.

February 28: Secretary of War Patterson approved the army's new racial policy. The ambiguous recommendations of the Gillem Board had been "blessed" by Army Chief of Staff Dwight D. Eisenhower before they were submitted to the Office of the Secretary of Defense (OSD).

March 4: The army released the Gillem Board Report to the press. Many black members took a cautious approach to accepting the new policy as a significant change in traditional army attitudes and procedures.

April 10: War Department Circular 105, which provided the assignment of men to critically needed specialties, "explicitly excluded Negroes." It was later revised to include all enlisted men, regardless of race.

April 27: The secretary of war directed the rapid distribution of War Department Circular 124, as the army's new racial policy and the full Gillem Board Report were now known. However, the lack of specific guidance on how to implement the Gillem Board's "recommendations on how best to employ blacks within the traditional segregated framework" made the new policy almost useless. Despite its shortcomings, the Gillem Board's comments were a step forward, because the board rejected the racist attitudes limiting the military role of African Americans and made integration the army's ultimate goal.

July 1: The US Army Air Force (AAF) argued for the exclusion of African Americans in its branch, as well as a halt to the enlistment of blacks in the regular army. Although the AAF later backed off these demands, it continued to press for a significantly lower quota of black soldiers, along with restrictions on the areas where they could be used.

July 17: The secretary of war suspended black enlistments in the regular army.

August 10: The army began using Army Regulation (AR) 615-369 to eliminate the least qualified men (most of whom were black) after a reasonable attempt was made to use them.

September 19: After meeting with a delegation from the National Emergency Committee Against Mob Violence, President Harry S. Truman established the President's Committee on Civil Rights to investigate racial violence. The committee would also study ways to strengthen and improve the federal, state, and local governments' ability to protect the civil rights of all Americans.

October: The Army again began accepting qualified African American recruits. The Adjutant General announced on October 2 that the Army would accept limitations of all former officers and noncommissioned officers who volunteered for service. On October 31, however, the army established a score of one hundred on the Army General Classification Test (AGCT) for all African American enlistees (as opposed to seventy for whites), while at the same time rescinding the choice-of-assignment provision for them. The army argued that its policies "regarding the quality of [its black] recruits" were justified because they "followed the spirit if not the letter" of the Gillem Board Report. These obviously discriminatory guidelines generated a lot of opposition and criticism, particularly in regard to the quota. Considered a temporary provision by the Gillem Board members, army traditionalists used the quota as a way to restrict the number of African American soldiers.

1946–1948: The US Navy was unable to attract many African Americans in the postwar period. "The Navy was beginning to welcome the Negro, but the Negro no longer seemed interested in joining" primarily because of the nonwhite Steward's Branch. By 1948, the navy's main racial problem was a serious lack of black sailors.

1946–1949: The army practice of attaching rather than assigning black combat units to white "parent units" weakened the morale of African American troops and hampered their training because of the men's sense of impermanence and alienation. By 1950, however, the army changed this policy by assigning "black units as organic parts of combat divisions." It also started assigning African American personnel "to fill the spaces of white units," although army leaders still "opposed ... the combination of small black with small white units" into a single battalion. Such practices continued to elicit harsh criticism from black leaders throughout the United States.

1947    Dr. Percy L. Julian, research chemist, received the Spingarn award for his many technical discoveries.

Army leaders in the United States began accelerating efforts to discharge soldiers who had scored less than seventy on the AGCT, supposedly in an attempt to close the education/training gap between black and white servicemen. At the same time, however, Lieutenant General Clarence R. Huebner initiated a major project to educate and train thousands of African American soldiers in Europe. By 1950, this program was not only "producing some of the finest trained black troops in the Army," but provoking charges of discrimination from white soldiers excluded from the project. The program's success could also be seen in the improved morale and conduct of black troops in Europe, along with a corresponding decline in racial incidents, crime, and venereal disease rates. Despite the clear connection between education and better performance, the army never implemented this program in all of its commands.

The Marine Corps modified its segregated racial policy because of the inefficiency of assigning surplus combat-trained African Americans to service and supply units when the Fleet Marine Force (FMF) units were seriously under strength. During this year, the corps began attaching black units to the undermanned FMF, creating composite units similar to those in the postwar army.

During the summer of this year, the AAF closed the flight training program at Tuskegee Airfield, Alabama, ending the last segregated officer training in the armed forces. Integrated aviation classes were established at Randolph Field, Texas.

A. Philip Randolph and other black leaders formed a committee against Jim Crow in military service. The group planned another march on Washington, DC, to reinforce African American demands that the federal government draft a nondiscrimination measure for the military. Randolph and his committee later focused on defeating any selective service bill containing provisions for segregated troops.

February: Less than a year after the publication of the Gillem Board Report, army leaders still considered segregation to be a policy worth retaining indefinitely. From their viewpoint, integration would only become feasible once the army "completed the long, complex task of raising the quality and lowering the quantity of black soldiers."

May: The secretary of war adopted a National Guard Policy Committee resolution, allowing individual states to determine the issue of "integration above the company level," although the army continued to prohibit "integration at the company level." That same year, New Jersey became the first state to specifically end segregation in its militia. This action created new problems for army leaders, who now had to deal with "an incompatible situation between the segregated active forces and the incompletely integrated reserve organization."

June 30: By this time, African American soldiers represented 7.91 percent of the army's total manpower. Instead of being based on their demographic presence in the US population, however, black enlistments were "geared to a percentage of the total Army strength." By adjusting the enlistment quota, the army could easily increase or decrease the percentage of blacks within its ranks.

July 25: Congress passed the National Security Act, reorganizing the US military establishment. The new legislation created the Office of the Secretary of Defense (OSD), a separate air force, the Central Intelligence Agency, and the National Security Council. It also reorganized the War Department as the Department of the Army and made the Joint Chiefs of Staff a permanent agency.

October: To avoid the political backlash if he failed to act on discrimination in the federal government, President Truman's political advisers decided that his best move was to issue an executive order "securing the civil rights of both civilian government employees and members of the armed forces."

October 29: The President's Committee on Civil Rights presented President Truman with a comprehensive survey on civil rights conditions in the United States, and made several sweeping recommendations to correct the situation. In addition to such remedies as permanent civil rights and fair employment practices, and commissions and legislation to eliminate discrimination in the nation's legal and electoral systems, the committee called for laws and policies to end discrimination and segregation in the armed forces. The committee even went so far as to urge the President to use the military "as an instrument of social change."

December: Although the army had been reporting that it provided its African American troops equal access to all army schools, in reality over half were closed to black soldiers, "regardless of qualifications." During this month, however, the army began a special effort "to broaden the employment of Negroes under the terms of the Gillem Board policy." It converted 19 general reserve units to black, recruited six thousand African Americans, increased the quotas for specialist schools, raised the number of courses with black quotas, and opened new courses to African Americans. By March 1949 though the number of training spaces for black soldiers had declined again.

1948 Supreme Court ruled that agreements to restrict housing were unenforceable.

Lieutenant General Idwal H. Edwards, Deputy Chief of Staff for Personnel; Lieutenant Colonel Jack F. Marr, a member of General Edward's staff; and Major General Richard E. Nugent, then-Director of Civilian Personnel, were the principal developers of the now-separate US Air Force's racial policy. After abandoning full integration to pursue a plan of limited integration based on "the Navy's program, the group's proposals provoked widespread opposition from many Air Force officers. But if integration, even in a small dose, was unpalatable, widespread inefficiency was intolerable." For that practical reason, therefore, the air force was poised to take further action.

Black leaders and the press became increasingly disillusioned with the disparity between the army's supposed goal of complete integration and the reality of continued segregation in the service.

February 2: Because of his concern about the passage of a new draft law containing a provision for universal military training,

President Truman removed the parts relating to the military when he transmitted to Congress on this date the recommendations of the President's Committee on Civil Rights.

April: There were still only forty-one black officers in the regular army, up from eight in June 1945. At this time, the army began a major effort to recruit more African American officers. In compliance with Circular 124, the army was able to significantly improve these figures by June 3, 1948, when it reported a total "of 1000 black commissioned officers, 5 warrant officers, and 67 nurses serving with 65,000 black enlisted men and women."

April 26: African American leaders met with Secretary of Defense James V. Forrestal at a National Defense Conference held at the Pentagon. Instead of uniting behind Forrestal's gradual plan to integrate the armed forces, the group supported A. Phillip Randolph's argument that "segregation itself was discrimination."

Although the secretary of defense agreed with the group's goals, he remained convinced that his gradual approach was best. A few months later, however, President Truman rejected this method by issuing his own directive on the matter.

May 28: The first real breakthrough in the USMC's policy of rigid racial segregation came with the commissioning of Lieutenant John E. Rudder, the first black to receive a regular commission in the Marine Corps. Rudder's brief active career, which ended for personal reasons in 1949, was nonetheless important "because it affirmed the practice of integrated officers training and established the right of Negroes to command." However, the Marine Corps was still committed to segregated units.

June 19: Georgia Senator Richard B. Russell introduced an amendment to the Selective Service Bill being debated by Congress. Russell's amendment "would guarantee segregated units for those draftees who wished to serve only with members of their own race." Senator William Langer of North Dakota countered with an amendment to prohibit all segregation. The draft bill passed by Congress contained no special provisions on race.

June 24: President Truman signed the Selective Service Act reinstituting the military draft. This action caused an inter-service squabble over how the increased number of African Americans inductees would be distributed among the different services.

July 15: The Democratic National Convention renominated Harry Truman for president, despite growing Southern opposition to the strong civil rights platform accepted by Truman. The president's political advisers viewed black votes as "an essential ingredient in a Truman victory."

July 17: The "Dixiecrats," who bolted the Democratic Party after it passed a campaign platform with a strong civil rights plan, met as the state rights Democrats to nominate South Carolina Senator Strom Thurmond for president.

July 26: President Truman signed Executive Order 9981, providing for equal treatment and opportunity for African American servicemen. Because of Cold War concerns in European and the mostly nonwhite "Third World," as well as growing black demands, integration had become a major defense issue. Political considerations in a presidential election year and the appointment of James V. Forrestal as secretary of defense were two other significant factors influencing Truman's decision to issue his order.

July–December: Executive Order 9981 actually had little immediate impact on the armed forces. Neither the army nor the navy planned to alter their existing racial policies. Their decisions were partly based on the mistaken assumption that Circular

124 and Circular Letter 48–46 were already in compliance with the president's order for equal treatment and opportunity. Despite evidence to the contrary, the US Armed Forces in this period did not consider segregation to be discriminatory. The fact that Truman was not favored for reelection also influenced the initially low-key reaction to Executive Order 9981. Even Congress responded with a wait-and-see attitude.

September: Although the army staff objected, Secretary of the Army Kenneth C. Royall began developing a plan to experiment with integrated units in order to prove that integration on a large scale would not work. The army presented its formal proposal on December 2, 1948, but nothing came of the plan because the navy and air force strenuously objected to being included in it. As a result, Secretary of Defense Forrestal decided "that inter-service integration was unworkable."

September 16–18: The White House released the names of the men selected to service on the presidential committee established "to oversee the manpower polices of all the services … The success of the new policy (Executive Order 9981) would depend to a great extent, as friends and foes of integration alike recognized, on the ability and inclination of this committee." President Truman selected Charles Fahy, an attorney and former solicitor general, to chair the new group. Officially known as the Committee on Equality of Treatment and Opportunity in the Armed Services, it was more commonly referred to as the Fahy Committee.

December: Despite the availability of statistics supporting the navy's claim for having a progressive racial policy, 62 percent of all African American sailors still served in the nonwhite Steward's Branch. In addition, the navy's statistics showed a significant increase in the percentage of blacks assigned to the integrated general service branch (up from 6 percent in 1945 to 38 percent in 1947). However, the number of black sailors in the navy overall dropped from 9,900 in 1946 to 6,000 by 1948. Almost all of these men were also in the enlisted ranks; there were only four African American naval officers by this month and only six black WAVES.

The navy rationalized its inability to attract African American recruits by claiming that "Negroes favored the Army because they were not seafaring people." This claim not only blatantly ignored the navy's own history, but greatly minimized the adverse impact on black perceptions arising from the navy's unwillingness to provide greater opportunities for African Americans or to integrate the Steward's Branch.

Channing H. Tobias, defender of civil liberties as member of the President's Committee on Civil Rights, received the Spingarn award.

## 1948–1950

The service that complied most easily and quickly with Executive Order 9981 was the air force, which had already begun to review and revise its racial policy before the president took action. Air force manpower experts, however, based their criticism of segregation on issues of efficiency rather than compliance with Truman's new policy influenced by political interests, manpower concerns, and black aspirations of his manpower experts to substantially change his service's racial policy.

1949    Dr. Ralph J. Bunche received the Spingarn award for his part in the settlement of the Middle East conflict.

The War Department was experiencing growing problems with its racial policies, most of which were under increasing attack by black leaders and civil rights groups. The army's continued insistence on racial quotas was particularly troublesome. Despite the army's argument supporting quotas "as a guarantee of black participation," it actually limited the number of African

Americans admitted into the service, as well as the variety of training and jobs available to them. Traditionalists seeking to maintain a segregated army could not prevent all racial progress, but the use of quotas and the remaining restrictions on how black soldiers were employed slowed reform efforts.

Despite a lot of "foot-dragging," the army confronted and overcame to some extent such obstacles to reform entrenched racial prejudice, institutional inertia, and the poor education system of many black enlistees. Consequently, "the Army's postwar racial policy must be judged successful, and considered in the context of the times, progressive." Yet, the continuation of racial disturbances and "disproportionate black crime and [venereal] disease rates" were significant indicators that the army's policy of segregation remained a serious problem in the postwar period.

The postwar practice of excluding African American servicemen from some Allied nations became a problem once some of the services began to integrate. Although it became Department of Defense (DOD) policy to freely assign black troops any place US forces were sent, the individual services continued to limit foreign assignments for African Americans, although not always at the Allied nation's request.

The Marine Corps commandant defended the USMC's segregated racial policy by arguing that the armed forces should follow society's lead in this area, not vice versa.

January: Congress began to debate more frequently the integration of the armed forces.

Renewal of the Selective Service Act in 1950 focused the racial debate on an amendment resubmitted by Georgia Senator Richard B. Russell. This modification allowed servicemen to serve in segregated units if they so desired. Considered to be "the high point of the congressional fight against armed forces integration," the Russell amendment was eventually defeated, as was a similar House amendment submitted in 1951.

January 6: The air force proposed to open "all jobs in all fields" to African Americans, limited only by individual qualifications and "the needs to service." The new plan retained some black service units but eliminated all of the air force's other all-black organizations. However, some serious problems arose during the four-month delay between the proposal's submission and its approval on May 11, 1949. Black morale problems surfaced, and congressional debate was sparked after part of the plan was leaked to the press. Despite African Americans' fears that they would not fare well under the proposed policy, "the Air Force's senior officials were determined to enforce the new program both fairly and expeditiously."

February 28: DOD's newly created Personal Policy Board drafted a common racial policy that abolished all racial quotas and established uniform draft standards with provisions to divide enlistees qualitatively and quantitatively in times of national emergency. The proposed directive also provided African Americans the opportunity to serve as individuals in integrated units. All of the services were to be fully integrated by July 1, 1950. During the interim, however, the number of blacks in integrated units would still be limited, while enlisted men could choose to serve under officers of their own race. Secretary of Defense Forrestal's resignation, opposition from the various service secretaries, and serious defects in the proposed policy eventually killed this first attempt to establish a DOD-wide racial policy.

March: The Fahy Committee initiated its efforts "not to impose integration on the services, but to convince them of the merits of the President's order and to agree with them on a plan to make it effective." The committee's first goal was to overcome the army's determination to retain segregation because of senior leaders' twin beliefs that blacks were unreliable and ineffective in combat and that white soldiers would not serve with African Americans. The committee's investigations established that "an indivisible link existed between military efficiency and equal opportunity." It used the "efficiency argument" to undermine the army's rationale for determining military occupational specialties (MOS), limiting the number of black specialists, and maintaining its racial quota.

March 28: Louis Johnson became secretary of defense.

April 5–6: DOD's Personal Policy Board approved, and Secretary of Defense Johnson signed, a general racial policy statement that "reiterated the President's executive order." Not meant to be an endorsement of current service policies, the DOD directive sought to make individual merit and ability the basis for the military's personnel decision. "All persons would be accorded equal opportunity for appointment, advancement, professional improvement, and retention." However, the policy stopped short of full integration, its authors satisfied that "although some segregated units would be retained 'qualified' Negroes would be assigned without regard to race."

May: The army and navy failed to significantly change their racial policies in keeping with the secretary of defense's new racial policy statement. Unsatisfied with their initial response, Secretary of Defense Johnson ordered both services to revise their policies by May 25. However, the Personnel Policy Board and the secretary of defense approved "the Air Force's proposal for the integration of a large group of its black personnel."

May 11: Air Force Letter 35–3, published the same day that the secretary of defense approved it, "spelled out a new bill of rights for Negroes in the Air Force." Living quarters, as well as workplaces, were no longer separated for most units.

May 23: The navy committed itself "to a program that

incorporated to a great extent the recommendations of the Fahy Committee." Among the reforms suggested were a "vigorous recruiting program" to dispel black suspicions about the navy and its nonwhite Steward's Branch; making chief stewards similar in rank to chief petty officers and establishing "the same entry standards as the Army."

May 26: Despite pressure from the secretary of defense and the Fahy Committee, the army continued to defend Circular 124. Although the army was ordered to prepare another response, OSD and the Fahy Committee drew further apart on what this response should be. The two fundamental points on which the army and the committee disagreed dealt with the free assignment of school-trained blacks and abolition of the army's racial quota.

June 1949–May 1950: The Air Force's 106 black units and 167 integrated units dropped one month later to 89 black units (with 14,609 men) and 350 integrated units (which included 7,369 African Americans). Less than a year later there were only 24 black units (with 4,675 men) and 1,506 integrated units (with 21,033 blacks). Although the program was initially conceived as limited integration, it quickly achieved universal application, which "progressed rapidly, smoothly, and virtually without incident."

June 7: The military branch least affected by Executive Order 9981 (theoretically, at least) was the US Navy, although it had an established racial policy of equal treatment and opportunity. It was applied poorly. The navy's new racial plan, submitted on this date, provided specific actions to bring its policy and practices "into line." Despite this effort, the Navy still did not attract many African American recruits. Between 1952 and 1959, the increased numbers of blacks in the navy came "from the men forced upon it by the Defense Department's distribution program."

July 1: The postwar downsizing of the USMC greatly affected its ability to maintain its original racial policy. On this date, the Marine Corps commandant ordered that African American recruits be trained in separate platoons at Parris Island, South Carolina. By September 22, 1949, the corps had eliminated even the segregated training platoons. This led to the integration of black NCO platoon leaders and various on-post NCO clubs and other facilities. The last two segregated groups at Montford Point, the USMC's all-black training facility near Camp Lejeune, North Carolina, had previously been inactivated on July 31 and September 9, 1949. Though these policy changes appeared to be in keeping with Executive Order 9981, they were actually driven by defense budget cuts. The Marine Corps still remained committed to segregation, which it instituted through the use of "colored" jobs designed to keep black and white marines separate from each other.

September 18: A panel of senior army officers, chaired by Lieutenant General Stephen J. Chamberlin, produced a report that was "perhaps the most careful and certainly the last apologia for a segregated Army." It reiterated the traditional arguments for resisting integration and called for the retention of the 10 percent quota. "The board called on Army Secretary Gray to repudiate the findings of the Fahy Committee and the stipulations of Executive Order 9981 and to maintain a rigidly segregated service with a carefully regulated percentage of black members."

September 30: Secretary of Defense Johnson approved Army Secretary Gordon Gray's new racial policy and then announced it to the press, all without consulting the Fahy Committee. The army's new policy opened all occupational specialties to those qualified, abolished racial quotas for army schools, and ended its racially separate promotion systems and standards. But it did not address the two main areas of contention: the racial quota and the free assignment of blacks. Unsuccessful in breaking the stalemate between the army and the committee, Johnson had also hoped this action would dispel continuing public criticism and mitigate the personal political liability of the still-unsettled question of race in the armed forces.

October 1: The adjutant general of the army dispatched "additional policies" based on the army's new racial plan, which had been proposed as a revision of Circular 124. Some commanders began integrating African American specialists into white units in what they thought was accordance with these "additional policies." Consequently, officials in the army's personnel and training divisions sent a second message on October 27, essentially "ordering commanders to interpret the Secretary's plan in its narrowest sense, blocking any possibility of broadening the range of black assignments." Secretary of the Army Gray rescinded the latter message after learning about it from unfavorable press reports.

October 6: In a news conference, President Truman supported the Fahy Committee's position on the army's proposed racial policy by referring to Johnson's earlier announcement as a "progress report." Acknowledging that it would be a gradual process, the president "declared that his aim was the racial integration of the Army."

November 25: The Fahy Committee received the army's revision of Circular 124. Despite several weeks of review by various army staff agencies, the proposed plan was basically the same one originally submitted to DOD by Army Secretary Gray on September 30, 1949. It "still contained none of the committee's key recommendations ... The quota and assignment issues remained the center of controversy between the Army and the committee."

December 14 and 27: In meetings held with President Truman

and the army on December 14, and Secretary of the Army Gray and the army chief of staff on December 27, the Fahy Committee made considerable progress in reconciling the stalemate over assignments and the quota. "Gray began with a limited view of the executive order." The army must eliminate racial discrimination, not promote racial integration. In their meeting on December 27, Fahy was able to convince Gray that the former was impossible without the latter.

1949–1954: Both the navy and the air force made significant changes in their racial policies, primarily to make more efficient and effective use of available manpower. "In a period of reduced manpower allocations and increased demand for technically trained men, these services came to realize that racial distinctions were imposing unacceptable administrative burden and reducing fighting efficiency."

1950     Charles H. Houston received the Spingarn award as a phenomenal teacher, civil rights leader, and as the NAACP Legal Committee.

January 16: After compromises on both sides, the army published Special Regulation 600-629-1, Utilization of Negro Manpower in the Army, which the Fahy Committee accepted. One significant aspect of the new policy was in accord with the published first list of vacancies in critical specialties that were to be filled without regard to race.

March 27: Secretary of the Army Gray ordered the service to open its recruiting without regard to race. He did so after winning President Truman's agreement to a proviso that the army could reinstitute a racial quota if the new policy resulted in "a disproportionate balance of racial strengths."

April: Despite the Marine Corps' determination "to retain its system of racially segregated units indefinitely," several factors forced the service to change its "exclusionist policy." The airpower demands that would arise from the Korean War, the imposition on this date of the secretary of defense's "qualitative distribution of manpower," and the draft opened the corps to a large influx of African American recruits.

The army integrated basic training at the Women's Army Corps (WAC) Training Center at Fort Lee, Virginia.

May 22: The Fahy Committee presented its final report, "Freedom to Serve: Equality of Treatment and Opportunity in the Armed Services," to President Truman. Although the committee recommended that it be retained on standby or that a watchdog group be established, the president decided against this course and publicly dissolved the committee several months later.

June 25: North Korean troops armed with Soviet-made weapons crossed the 38th parallel, invading South Korea and sparking the outbreak of the Korean War. Within five months of this action, the US Army had doubled in size. "This vast expansion of manpower and combat commitment severely tested the Army's racial policy and immediately affected the racial balance of the quota-free Army."

July 6: As part of the Army Organization Act of 1950, Congress repealed the statutory requirement for the service's four all-black regiments.

August: The army assumed the former Selective Service "task of deciding the race of all draftees." A lot of effort between 1949 and 1951 was devoted to establishing acceptable racial categories and definitions. Although not used for assignment, "racial statistics had to be kept," hence the need for "racial tags."

August: The 1st Provisional Marine Brigade was assigned several African Americans during the fighting on the Pusan Perimeter, which was "the first time black servicemen were integrated as individuals in significant numbers under combat conditions."

August–December: Eight army commanders in Korea began filling losses in their white units with individuals from "a growing surplus of black replacements arriving in Japan." By early 1951, "9.4 percent of all Negroes in the theater were serving in some forty-one newly and unofficially integrated units. Another 9.3 percent were in integrated but predominantly black units. The other 81 percent continued to serve in segregated units." This limited conversion to integrated units became permanent because "it worked … The performance of integrated troops during this period was remarkable with little racial conflicts.

September: Beginning this month, the 1st Marine Division was assigned numerous African American marines, "the clearest instance of a service abandoning a social policy in response to the demands of the battlefield."

September 20: Retired General George C. Marshall became secretary of defense.

1951 PFC W. H. Thompson, Korean War hero, won Congressional Medal of Honor.

Race riots in Cicero, Illinois, worst since 1919.

Mabel K. Staupers received the Spingarn award for leadership in integrating nursing.

The Marine Corps' segregated racial policy "ended with the cancellation of the last all-black designation."

February: The Chamberlin Board reconvened "to reexamine the Army's racial policy in light of the Korean experience." Despite the widespread support for further integration in the Far East, continuing support for segregation was still the norm throughout the rest of the army. "This attitude was clearly reflected again by the Chamberlin Board," which still unsuccessfully called for segregated units and a racial quota.

March: At least half of the African Americans serving in the Marine Corps under combat conditions were assigned to integrated units. They "performed in a way that not only won many individuals decorations for valor but also won the respect of commanders for Negroes as fighting men."

The Army's nine training divisions were integrated by this time, after a "trouble-free and permanent" conversion period, which began late in 1950. Fort Ord was the first training division "to adopt the expedient of mixing black and white inductees in the same units for messing, housing, and training." It was quickly followed by the other army training divisions and replacement centers, "with Fort Dix, New Jersey, and Fort Knox, Kentucky, the last to complete the process."

April: By this time, "black units throughout the Army were reporting over strengths, some as much as 60 percent over their authorized organization tables." Unlike World War II, however, when only about 22 percent of all African Americans in the army served in combat units, black soldiers during the Korean War were "assigned to the combat branches in approximately the same percentage as white soldiers, 41 percent."

The secretary of defense alleviated army fears of becoming "a dumping ground for the ignorant and un-trainable" by ordering the qualitative distribution of troops among all the services.

April 10: Secretary of Defense Marshall approved the Qualitative Distribution of Military Manpower Program. It required "the Navy and Air Force to share responsibility with the Army for the training and employment of less gifted inductees." The new program upgraded the army, placed more African Americans in the other services, and ultimately "destroyed the Army's best argument for the reimposition of the racial quota."

May: The army still had not carried out the policy to which it had agreed with the Fahy Committee. "Much of the army clung to old sentiments and practices for the same old reasons, "but the Korean War ultimately changed these outmoded attitudes and practices forever."

May 14: Lieutenant General Matthew B. Ridgeway, who replaced General Douglass MacArthur in Korea, formally requested authority to abolish segregation in the Eighth Army.

July: By the third anniversary of Executive Order 9981, OSD had dealt with some race issues but had really done little to push the armed forces closer to full integration. "The integration process that began in those years [1948–1951] was initiated … by the services themselves."

July 26: On the third anniversary of President Truman's order, the army announced the integration of its Far East command. "The 77th Engineer Combat Company was the last combat unit to lose the asterisk, the Army's was of designating a unit black." About 75 percent of Eighth Army infantry units were integrated before November 1951. "It was not until May 1952 that the last divisional and non-divisional organizations were integrated." The integration of the US Army in Korea led to greater racial harmony and military efficiency.

September: Senior army leaders moved closer to accepting full integration. Their attitude was affected partly by the percentage of blacks in the army by this date, and partly by the successful integration of the Eighth Army in Korea and training camps at home.

November: A contract study "on the Army's experiences with black troops in Korea," known as Project CLEAR, confirmed earlier findings that African American soldiers in integrated units fought as well as whites. It also reported that integration improved black morale and did not lower that of whites. "In sum, the Project CLEAR group concluded that segregation hampered the Army's effectiveness while integration increased it."

December: By the end of this year, about 7 percent of black enlisted men, 17 percent of black officers, and all black WACs were serving in integrated units in Europe, even though initially there was little support for full integration in this area.

December 13: The USMC commandant announced a general policy of racial integration. Six months later, he advised the chief of naval personnel that there were no more segregated units in the Marine Corps and that integration "was believed to be an accomplished fact." However, restrictions on how African Americans were employed continued into the 1960s. Another problem area was the corps' continued use of all-black stewards. The corps did not begin signing up white stewards again until 1956.

December 29: The army chief of staff ordered all of the service's "major commanders to prepare integration programs for their commands. Integration was the Army's immediate goal, and … it was to be progressive, in orderly stages, and without publicity."

1952    Tuskegee Institute reported that 1952 was the first in seventy-one years with no reported lynching.

Harry T. Moore, NAACP leader, received the Spingarn award. He was assassinated while crusading for freedom.

Despite some changes, the navy's nonwhite Steward's Branch was still 65 percent black (the rest were Filipino). In February 1954, the navy ended the separate recruitment of stewards, except for Filipinos under contract. As a result, by 1961, blacks were a minority in the Steward's Branch for the first time in thirty years.

April: The Army European Command's integration program began "quietly and routinely, with no publicity and without incident." The army completed this program in November 1954, when it inactivated "the last black unit in the command, the 94th Engineer Battalion."

September: The Air Force had "only one segregated unit … left, a 98-man outfit, itself more than 26 percent white [about 25 men]. Negroes were then serving in 3,466 integrated units."

December: The army chief of staff ordered worldwide integration of this service. All of the earlier fears cited to support the continuation of a segregated army proved to be groundless. There was no increase in racial incidents, no breakdown of discipline, no uprising against integration by white soldiers or surrounding white communities, no backlash from segregationists in Congress, and no major public denouncements of the new policy.

1953     October: Because of the Korean War, the number of African American marines rapidly grew from 1,525 (half of whom were stewards) in May 1949 to 17,000 (with only 500 stewards) by this time. "As the need for more units and replacements grew during the war, newly enlisted black marines were more and more often pressed into integrated service in the Far East and at home … The competence of these Negroes and the general absence of racial tension during their integration destroyed long accepted beliefs to the contrary and opened the way for general integration [of the Marine Corps]."

NAACP set integration as a goal, dropped old "separate but equal" theory.

Paul R. Williams received the Spingarn award for his contribution to architectural beauty and design.

1954    US Supreme Court ruled segregation in public schools unconstitutional.

October 30: The secretary of defense announced that the last racially segregated unit in the armed forces of the United States had been abolished. All armed forces integrated.

Theodore K. Lawless—physician, educator, and philanthropist— received the Spingarn award for his work in the field of dermatology.

1955    Segregated waiting room and buses banned in interstate travel.

Carl Murphy, editor and publisher, received the Spingarn award for his fight against barriers in education, employment, and recreation.

1956    US Supreme Court ruled no segregation of public facilities, rejected "separate but equal" doctrine.

One hundred Southern congressmen denounced Supreme Court's decision on school desegregation.

"Jackie" Robinson received the Spingarn award for superb sportsmanship and for his civic consciousness.

1957    Martin Luther King Jr. received the Spingarn award for his contribution to the fight for freedom and his leadership in the Montgomery bus boycott.

1958    First sit-in at lunch counters by NAACP Youth Council in Oklahoma City.

Mrs. Daisy Bates and the Little Rock Nine received the Spingarn award for courage in the face of harassment and threat of bodily injury.

1959 Lorraine Hansberry's play *Raisin in the Sun* opened on Broadway.

Duke Ellington received the Spingarn award for universal acclaim in the field of music.

1960 Elijah Muhammad, black internationalist leader, called for creation of black state; ninety-four percent of blacks still in segregated schools.

Langston Hughes, poet, received NAACP Spingarn award for his universal acclaim; considered by many to be the poet laureate of the African Americans.

1961 Black and white "Freedom Riders" protested discrimination on Southern buses.

Interstate Commerce Commission ordered interstate passengers seated without regard to race.

New Rochelle, NY, Board of Education convicted of gerrymandering to promote segregation.

W. E. B. DuBois gave up his US citizenship and moved to Ghana.

Kenneth B. Clark, psychologist, received the NAACP Spingarn award for research contributing to banning of segregation.

1962 James Meredith was the first African American to be admitted to the University of Mississippi. Meredith's goals was to exercise his constitutional rights by applying, getting admitted, and putting pressure on the Kennedy administration to enforce equal rights for blacks.

Integration in public schools began in all but three states.

Robert C. Weaver received the NAACP Spingarn award for long years of dedicated public service.

1963    Over two hundred thousand blacks and whites marched on Washington to dramatize desegregation.

Vivian Malone and James Hood entered the University of Alabama without violence.

President Kennedy assassinated in Dallas, Texas.

Four black girls killed in a Birmingham, Alabama, church bombing; Addie Mae Collins, Cynthia Wesley, Carole Roberson, and Denise McNair.

Medgar Evers, NAACP field secretary and Spingarn award recipient, assassinated.

1964    Civil Rights Act passed, outlawing discrimination in public places.

Martin Luther King Jr., age thirty-five, became youngest winner of the Nobel Peace Prize.

One black, and two white civil rights workers murdered in Mississippi.

Freedom Democratic Party organized in Mississippi, nominated three blacks for Congress the first since Reconstruction.

Roy Wilkins received the NAACP Spingarn award for his contribution to the advancement of the American people.

1965    Selma-to- Montgomery marchers, led by Dr. King, protested the denial of registration of black voters. Voting Rights Act became law, suspending literacy tests and using federal registration of voters.

Reverend Harold Perry appointed Bishop—first twentieth-century black bishop.

Malcolm X, black nationalist, assassinated in New York City.

Leontyne Price received the NAACP Spingarn award as an outstanding soprano.

1966    US Supreme Court outlawed poll tax for all elections.

Constance B. Motley became first black woman named to federal judgeship.

Edward Brooke, Republican, elected the first black senator in one hundred years.

A ten-point black Panther Manifesto demanded freedom, employment, fair trials, and the end of police brutality.

John H. Johnson received the NAACP Spingarn award for his enhancement of the black's self-image through his publications.

1967    Thurgood Marshall became the first black Supreme Court justice.

NAACP created division of legal information and community services to inform blacks of their rights in housing, health, employment, etc.

Race riots in over one hundred cities resulted in an estimated one hundred deaths, five thousand injuries, and twelve thousand arrests.

Stokely Carmichael, SNCC chairman, convicted of inciting riots in Atlanta, Georgia.

Edward W. Brooke III received the NAACP Spingarn award for his career as a public servant; elected to US Senate.

June 10: Major Robert H. Lawrence Jr., USAF, became the first African American astronaut.

1968    Dr. Martin Luther King Jr. assassinated by sniper in Memphis, Tennessee.

Civil Rights Act of 1968 prohibited racial discrimination in sale or rental of 80 percent of US housing. "Poor People's Campaign" brought fifty thousand to Washington in protest over poverty in the United States. Twenty-eight percent of all black households earned $7,000 or more per year, but 40 percent earned less than $3,300.

Sammy Davis Jr. received the NAACP Spingarn award for achievement in the arts and work in civil rights movement.

1969　US Department of Labor initiated "Philadelphia Plan" to promote black employment in federally funded construction.

Justice Department filed desegregation suit against Georgia—first such suit against an entire state.

Dr. Clifton Wharton Jr. elected president of Michigan State University—first black to head a major, predominantly white university.

Health Education and Welfare (HEW) authorized Antioch College to operate all-black studies program.

Clarence Mitchell received the NAACP Spingarn award for his role in the enactment of civil rights legislation.

1970　Wilson Riles became the first black elected to statewide office in California, defeating the incumbent superintendent of schools.

Two black students killed after a night of violence at Jackson State College in Mississippi.

President Nixon established a cabinet-level task force to assist local schools ordered to segregate immediately.

Leaders at the sixty-first annual NAACP convention called the Nixon administration anti-black, listed supportive grievances.

Jacob Lawrence received the NAACP Spingarn award for his portrayal of black life in America.

1971 Reverend Leon Sullivan received the Spingarn award for contributing to the economic progress of blacks.

1972 Gordon Alexander Buchanan Parks received the Spingarn award for his unique achievement as a photographer, writer, filmmaker, and composer.

1973 Wilson C. Riles received the Spingarn award for the stature he attained as a national leader in the field of education.

1974 Damon J. Keith, distinguished jurist, received the Spingarn award for being a compassionate interpreter of the law and dedicated public servant.

1975 Henry "Hank" Aaron received the Spingarn award for his contributions to baseball and to the community in which he lives.

1976 Alvin Ailey received the Spingarn award for his accomplishments as a choreographer.

1977 Alexander P. Halley received the Spingarn award for the research and literary skill combined in his book, *Roots: the Saga of an American Family.*

1978 Andrew Young received the Spingarn award for his distinguished service as US United Nation ambassador.

1979 Rosa L. Parks received the Spingarn award for her quiet courage when she refused to surrender her seat to a white man on an Alabama bus.

September, Hazel Winifred Johnson became the first black woman to attain the rank of General Officer in the Army Nurse Corps.

1980    Rayford W. Logan received the Spingarn award for his lifetime of service as an educator, historian, and author.

Vincent K. Brooks, first African American cadet in the history of West Point to serve as the Cadet Brigade Commander (the senior ranking cadet).

1981    Coleman Young received the Spingarn award for his lifetime of service as first black mayor of a major US city; he became the voice of black political leaders during the 1970s.

1982    Benjamin E. Mays received the Spingarn award for his lifetime of service as an educator, author, and spiritual mentor of Martin Luther King Jr. and Julian Bond.

1983    Lena Horn received the Spingarn award for her achievements as a jazz and pop singer, dancer, and actress.

1984    Tom Bradley received the Spingarn award for his lifetime of service as a politician, and Los Angeles first black mayor.

1985    Bill Cosby received the Spingarn award for his lifetime achievements as an educator, actor, comedian, and human rights activist.

U.S. Army Major General Leo A. Brooks, Sr., retires from the Army after 30 years. Both of his sons Leo Jr. and Vincent would go on to be promoted to General Officers, becoming the only African American family in the nation's history to produce three general officers.

1986    Benjamin L. Hooks received the Spingarn award for his lifetime dedication as a lawyer, Baptist minister, and civil rights activist.

1987    Percy Ellis Sutton received the Spingarn award for his service as a US legislator, public official, community activist, and educator.

1988    Frederick Douglass Patterson received the Spingarn award for his service as educator and founder of the United Negro College Fund.

1989    October 3: Secretary of Defense Dick Cheney swore in General Colin Powell as the twelfth chairman of the Joint Chiefs of Staff.

Jesse Jackson received the Spingarn award for his service and dedication as political leader, clergyman, Baptist minister, and civil rights activist.

1990    L. Douglas Wilder received the Spingarn award for his service as American political leader by becoming the first US senator since Reconstruction.

1991    Colin T. Powell received the Spingarn award for his achievements as the first African American and the youngest person to chair the Joint Chiefs of Staff and the first African American to serve as secretary of state.

1992    Barbara Charline Jordan received the Spingarn award for her amazing contributions as a lawyer, public official, and educator. In 1966, she became the first African American to be elevated to the Texas Senate and, six years later, the first to be elected to the US House of Representatives from the South since Reconstruction.

1993    Dorothy Irene Height received the Spingarn award for her service as an African American administrator, educator, and social and civil rights activist. She served as the president of the National Council of Negro Women from 1957 to 1997.

1994    Maya Angelou received the Spingarn award for her literary contributions as a writer and performer. She read her poem "On the Pulse of Morning" at the inauguration of President Clinton in 1993.

1995 John Hope Franklin received the Spingarn award for his role as an educator, author, and historian. He was awarded the Presidential Medal of Freedom in 1995 and appointed President Clinton's adviser on race for two years.

1996 A. Leon Higginbotham Jr. received the Spingarn award for his contributions as a lawyer and district court judge. He received the Presidential Medal of Freedom in 1995.

1997 Carl Rowan received the Spingarn award for his lifetime service and commitment as a columnist and best-selling author who specialized in race relations. He served as deputy assistant secretary of state and ambassador to Finland under President John F. Kennedy.

1998 Myrlie Evers-Williams received the Spingarn award for her consistent dedication to civil rights and literary contributions as an author. She was married to civil rights leader Medgar Evers in 1951.

1999 Earl Gilbert Graves Sr. received the Spingarn award for his accomplishments as a distinguished author, publisher, entrepreneur, and philanthropist. He is the founder of *Black Enterprise* magazine.

2000 Oprah Winfrey received the Spingarn award for her success as an Emmy Award–winning television talk-show host, actress, and producer. Her *Oprah Winfrey Show* is the highest-rated show in syndication history.

2001 Vernon E. Jordan Jr. received the Spingarn award for his accomplishments as an African American civil rights leader and lawyer. He was executive director of the United Negro College Fund and president of the National Urban League.

   Leo A. Brooks, Jr., promoted to Brigadier General, U.S. Army. He would later retire in the rank of Major General.

2002    John Lewis received the Spingarn award for his lifetime commitment to civil rights. He was also a politician, minister, and US congressman.

2003    Constance Baker Motley received the Spingarn award for her work as prominent civil rights attorney. In 1966, she became the first black woman to become a federal judge.

2004    Robert L. Carter received the Spingarn award for his contributions as a civil rights activist, author, and judge. He was the cofounder of the National Conference of Black Lawyers.

2005    Oliver W. Hill received the Spingarn award for his life and achievement as a civil rights attorney.

2006    Benjamin S. Carson Sr. received the Spingarn award for his amazing success as a noted neurosurgeon. He became the director of pediatric neurosurgery at Johns Hopkins Hospital when he was only thirty-three years old.

2007    John Conyers Jr. received the Spingarn award for his lifetime contributions of growth and singular achievement. He went from the bottom of his fifth grade class to become the youngest-ever chief of pediatric neurosurgery in the United States.

        General William "Kip" Ward selected to command U.S. Africa Command.

2008    Ruby Dee received the Spingarn award for her accomplishments as an actress, poet, playwright, and civil rights activist.

        November 4: Senator Barack Hussein Obama elected as the forty-fourth president of the United States of America, and first African American to be elected to the highest position in the nation.

2009    Julian Bond received the Spingarn award for his legendary contributions as a civil rights activist, and former chairman of the NAACP board of directors.

2010    Cicely Tyson received the Spingarn award for her contributions as a civil rights activist and actress.

2011    Frankie Muse Freeman received the Spingarn award for her contributions as an attorney and civil rights activist.

2012    General Larry O. Spencer becomes first black general officer to serve as the U.S. Air Force Vice Chief of Staff. He presides over the Air Staff and serves as a member of the Joint Chiefs of Staff Requirements Oversight Council and Deputy Advisory Working Group.

General William "Kip" Ward, U.S. Army, demoted and allowed to retire as a lieutenant general for allegations of lavish spending.

2013    Harry Belafonte received the Spingarn award for his contributions as a singer, songwriter, actor and social activist.

U. S. Army General Vincent K. Brooks, become first African American selected to command Third Army at Shaw Air Force Base.

# REFERENCES

Personal interviews/surveys were submitted in support of *Striving for Perfection: Developing Professional Black Officers*.

**Staff Sergeant George Jones, USAF (Ret.),** was born in New Orleans, Louisiana, and graduated from James Walden Johnson Grammar School and Booker T. Washington High School in New Orleans. He joined the air force in 1951 and served twenty years and one day on active duty. He is a member of the Buffalo Soldiers and Leathernecks Association. After his military career he worked in construction and for the National Park Service. He is a historian and loves both military and African American history. (Chapter 10)

**Chief Master Sergeant Willie Upshaw, USAF (Ret.),** served in the air force for over twenty-eight years. He graduated from South Girard High School in Phenix, Alabama, in 1968, enlisted in the air force in August 1969, and was assigned duties as a security police specialist. During his tenure he served at Ellsworth AFB in South Dakota, Kimpo and Osan Air Base Korea, Vandenberg AFB, California, Robins AFB Georgia, Yokota Air Base, Japan, and Wright Patterson AFB, Ohio. He currently resides in Dayton, Ohio. (Chapter 10)

**Chief Master Sergeant Vernon F. Boardley** is from Baltimore, Maryland, and graduated from Calvet1 High School in Baltimore in 1981. Chief Boardley has completed all phases of professional military education and has a bachelor's degree in liberal arts from Excelsior College in New York, and a master of science degree in administration from Central Michigan University in Michigan. He is currently responsible for Air Combat Command's largest Services Squadron at Nellis AFB. (Chapter 10)

**Chief Master Sergeant Raymond R. Campbell, USAF,** graduated from Forest Park High School in Cincinnati, Ohio, in 1981. He entered the air force on June 29, 1983, and started out as a fuels specialist. He has held numerous fuels positions throughout the world. He has a bachelor's degree in occupational education, and a master's degree in management, both from Wayland Baptist University. (Chapter 10)

**Chief Master Sergeant Fermon S. Reid, USAF,** was born in Belle Glade, Florida, and graduated from Clewiston High School in 1981. Currently he is the 99th Mission Support Group superintendent at Nellis AFB, Nevada, where he provides leadership and management in organizing, equipping, and training 2,400, and services for a community population of over 40,000 people. He is a graduate of the Senior Noncommissioned Officer Academy and holds two associate degrees in applied science and management studies. (Chapter 10)

**Chief Master Sergeant (Ret.) Aeron P. Curtis, USAF**, is originally from Columbus, Mississippi, and graduated from Stephen D. Lee High School in June 1981. The chief graduated from the Morse Systems Operator course in Keesler AFB, MS, as the top student in his class—a Samuel F. B. Morse honor graduate. He retired after being the superintendent of the 543rd Intelligence Group and senior enlisted adviser for the Medina Regional Security Operations Center at Lackland AFB, Texas. He is currently the youth director at Macedonia Baptist Church in San Antonio, Texas. He has a bachelor's degree in management studies from the University of Maryland, and a master's degree from Webster University. (Chapter 9)

**2LT Ayana N. Floyd-James, USAF**, entered the air force as an enlisted member for a few years and decided she wanted more out of life and applied and was accepted to the United States Air Force Academy, where she was commissioned and graduated with a degree in political science in June 2007. She is a logistics readiness officer stationed at Minot AFB, North Dakota. (Introduction)

**ILT Corey L. Trusty, USAF**, is the deputy chief of contingency operations, 45th Operations Support Squadron, at Cape Canaveral Air Force Station, Florida. He graduated with a bachelor's degree in biology from Tuskegee University, and a master's degree in bioethics. He began his military career as a recruiting officer for Detachment 015, where he provided critical information to youth and parents making life-changing decisions. (Chapter 9)

**LT Joseph D. Lett Jr., USAF,** originally served almost fifteen years as an enlisted member and the last five as a commissioned officer. He received his commission from the Air Force Officer Training School, and his bachelor's degree from the University of Nebraska at Omaha. He most admires Dr. William Cosby, Oprah Winfrey, General (Ret.) Newton, and President Barack Obama. (Chapter 8)

**1LT Rakanem Milligan, USAF**, is from Santurce, Puerto Rico, and while still a young child his family moved to Hollywood, Florida, where he completed high school. He has a bachelor of science in electrical engineering from Tuskegee University, Alabama. The best advice that he received was that not all black faces are your friend (officer or enlisted). The advice he wants to pass on is that you should control your destiny, meaning you need to develop a plan for where you see yourself in ten years and you should write it down. (Chapter 4)

**ILT Frankie A. Locus, USAF,** enlisted in the US Air Force and served for six years before separating and enrolling in the University of Central Florida, in Orlando, where he received his commission via Air Force ROTC. He states that serving in the military was the vehicle that God has used to draw him closer and show him who he is and how the Lord works. His experiences allowed him to serve as a deployed communications squadron commander at the tender rank of lieutenant. (Chapter 5)

**1LT Isaac A. Wright, USAF**, received his commission via Air Force ROTC while a member of the SOAR (Exceptional Airman to Officer Program). He started his career as an enlisted member and decided that he desired a career in the military as an officer. He is originally from Memphis, Tennessee, and most admires his parents. (Chapter 4)

**1LT Perry L. Russell, USAF**, is the section commander for the service squadron at Luke Air Force Base, Arizona. He entered the air force in October 2001 and was commissioned through the Air Force Officer Trainee School two years after graduating from Brigham Young University. He has a master's degree in human resources from Webster University. (Chapter 5)

**Captain Angela C. Holmes Kinsey, USAF**, graduated from Tennessee State University in Nashville, Tennessee, and was commissioned via Air Force ROTC. She considers her father her role model and the person she most admires. She states that her work ethic is becoming stronger because of her service in the military. (Chapter 9)

**Captain Hilary R. Johnson-Lutz, USAF**, enlisted in the air force and has served an impressive nineteen years, while only six of those years have been as an officer. She received her commission from the Air Force Officer Training School and her undergraduate degree from National Louis University while serving on active duty as an enlisted member. She thanks Colonel (retired) Michelle Gardner-Ince for her success because of her infectious positive attitude and her willingness to give you time she doesn't have. She states that serving in the Air Force has greatly enhanced her life, and "wearing the uniform is a huge source of pride for me and will always be." (Chapter 1)

**Captain Cedric E. Way, USAF**, is a Medical Service Corps officer in the 622nd Aeromedical Evacuation Squadron (McDill AFB, FL),

United States Air Force Reserve. He has been deployed to Bagram AB, Afghanistan, (October 2004–January 2005) in support of Operation Enduring Freedom, and he was also deployed to New Orleans (September 2005) in support of Hurricane Katrina relief. He is a deacon at 34th Street Church of God (Tampa, FL), employed with Verizon as a systems engineer (twenty-seven years), and has obtained certifications with Cisco Systems and Network General. Lastly he is also employed with St. Pete College (Largo, FL) as an adjunct professor teaching the Cisco System Networking Academy. (Chapter 4)

**Captain Derrick D. Modest, USAF**, was born and raised in Ruston, LA, and is the oldest of thirteen siblings. He joined the Marine Corps at seventeen, because he needed direction in his life. After a brief stay in the USMC, he separated and joined the Army National Guard. While in the Army Guard, he joined USAF ROTC and later received a commission in the air force. He is currently serving at Maxwell AFB and assigned at the prestigious air force's School of Advanced Air and Space Studies (SAASS). (Chapter 5)

**Captain Avonne D. Rosario, USAF**, is currently assigned at the 96th Security Forces Squadron, Eglin AFB, Florida. She is a graduate of the US Air Force Officer Training School, where she received her commission. She has a bachelor's degree in criminal justice and plans on making a career in the air force. She had a tough start in life and is a living example of commitment and dedication. (Chapter 3)

**Captain LaMont A. Coleman, USAF**, has been on active duty for over ten years and received his commission from Air Force ROTC at the University of Michigan, and graduated from Wayne State University in Detroit, MI. He most admires Michael Jordan, Tiger Woods, and the Honorable Condeleezza Rice. He states the best advice was to learn how to write and speak the military way. (Chapter 7)

**Captain Brendan Epps, USAF**, earned his commission from the Air Force Academy and entered the air force as an ICBM maintenance officer. Since that time, he's held several ICBM maintenance positions. When his career field merged with ammunitions maintenance, he later became the munitions accountable systems officer for Vandenberg Air Force Base. Following that assignment, Captain Epps attended the Naval Postgraduate School, where he earned an MBA in logistics management. He currently works as an integrated logistics support manager, acting as a liaison for maintainers working on the C-17 A Globemaster III aircraft. (Chapter 7)

**Captain Braden E. Friday, USAF**, has served over twenty years in the air force, most of which has been as an enlisted member. He received his commission via Air Force Officer Training School and attended and graduated from Newman University in Wichita, KS. He states that he most admires his father, retired Chief Master Sergeant Ceaser. He advises new officers not to act hastily, sleep on it, and if it is still bothering you, you have tomorrow to deal with it. (Chapter 7)

**Major Elaine R. Washington, USAF**, is a health-care integrator at Randolph AFB in San Antonio, Texas. She was born in Columbia, South Carolina, graduated from the University of South Carolina, and received a direct commission in the Air Force Nurse Corps as a Second Lieutenant in 1988. She has a master's degree in human resource management from Troy State University, and nursing from University of Phoenix. (Chapter 2)

**Major Jacqueline Randolph, USAF**, is a pilot, author, business owner, and veteran of community theater, community service (group homes, hospice, and domestic violence), and missionary trips (Africa, Alaska, and Mexico). She has traveled throughout the world as a C-130 aircrew member, performing military special operations (famed 101st and 82nd Airborne) and NASA shuttle support missions, and delivering United Nations aid to countries ravaged by war and natural disasters. She has served as a college professor in the Mississippi Delta and commanded the Global Positioning System (GPS) satellite constellation and ballistic missiles. She is an adventurer who enjoys ballroom dancing, rafting, skiing, trips to the arctic/Antarctic circles, and skydiving, ballooning, and gliders. An inductee in Marquis's 2003–2005 Who's Who in America, she aspires to be an Alaskan bush pilot, Peace Corp volunteer, and third world missionary pilot. (Chapter 2)

**Major (Dr.) Kimberly Finney, USAF**, entered the Air Force in 1989 as a laboratory officer, with a specialty in immunohematology. In 1994, she left active duty, joined the Air Force Reserve Corps, and completed a doctoral degree in clinical psychology. She reentered the air force in 1998 and now serves as a clinical psychologist, working with service members who suffer with posttraumatic stress disorders. Most recently she completed a postdoctoral master's degree in psychopharmacology, and she is one of a few in the field who is trained to prescribe medication. She is currently stationed at Hickam AFB, Hawaii. (Chapter 5)

**LT Colonel William Simmons, USAF,** has been in the Air Force for over thirty years and has amassed a tremendous amount of experience during his journey. From 1996 to 1999, he served as the chief of the Traffic Management Division at Wright Patterson AFB, and later as the chief of Reserve Force Readiness for United States Central Air Force at Shaw AFB in South Carolina. (Chapter 1)

**LT Colonel Christopher C. Herring, USAF,** is on the fast track by being promoted two years below the zone to Lieutenant Colonel. He was commissioned and received his degree from the Air Force ROTC from Boston University. He most admires General Benjamin O. Davis Jr. He states that you should never place limits on yourself, and know the rules of engagement. We are keeping a close eye on this officer and expecting only the best! (Chapter 8)

**LT Colonel Alvis W. Headen III, USAF**, is a graduate of South High School in Denver, Colorado. He has an industrial engineering bachelor of science degree from the University of Southern Maine, and a master of arts degree in environmental policy and management from the

University of Denver, Colorado. Currently, he is the 436th aeromedical dental squadron commander at Dover AFB, Delaware. (Chapter 3)

**LT Colonel Baron D. Canty Sr., USAF,** is director, International Armaments Cooperation's, Joint US Military Affairs Group Korea, Seoul, Korea. He was born in Charleston, South Carolina, and received his commission from the ROTC program at the University of South Carolina, along with a BS in applied mathematics. He received a masters of arts degree in curriculum and instructions with an emphasis in educational leadership from the University of Colorado. (Chapter 6)

**LT Colonel Joseph C. Richardson, USAF,** was born in Chicago, Illinois, and enlisted in the US Air Force in 1983. Shortly after completing technical school and serving as a personnel specialist, he submitted documents to attend the USAF Academy Preparatory School and Academy, where he received a bachelor of science in history. He has a master of science in aeronautical science technology from Embry Riddle Aeronautical University, and a master of arts in counseling and leadership from University of Colorado at Colorado Springs, CO. Colonel Richardson has completed all phases of professional military education, including Air War College. He is a command pilot with over 3,400 flying hours, including 153 combat hours. (Chapter 6)

**Major General Charles "CQ" Brown, USAF**, graduated from Texas Tech University as a distinguished graduate of Air Force ROTC. He has held various squadron and wing-level positions during operational assignment, including wing and group commander. He has over 2,500 combat flying hours in T-37, T-38, and F-16. He holds a master of science from Embry Riddle Aeronautical University, and a national defense fellow from Institute for Defense Analyses in Alexandria, VA. (Chapter 6)

## Chapter One

Abdul-Jabbar, K. (2004) *Brothers in Arms: The Epic Story of the 761st Tank Battalion, WWII's Forgotten Heroes*. New York: Broadway Books. Accessed 2006.

Adde, N. and Coates, L. (1984) "From the 'Buffalo Soldier' to the Astronaut." *Air Force Times*. 44, 35–36.

Asante, M. K. and Mattson, M.T., (1992) *Historical and Cultural Atlas of African Americans*. New York: Macmillan.

Baker, Ray Stannard. (1908) "Following the Color Line." *American Magazine*. http://www.digitalhistory.uh.edu/learning_history/lynching/baker2.cfm, Accessed 2006.

Braziel, J.E. (1992) *History of Lynching in the United States*. Urbana and Chicago: University of Illinois Press.

Christian, C.M. (1995) *Black Saga*. New York: Houghton Mifflin Company.

Cowan, T. and Maguire, J. (1994) *Timelines of African American History—500Years of Black Achievement*. New York: A Roundtable Press/Perigee Book.

Daniels, C. (2005) "Pioneers." *Fortune Magazine*. 152, no.4 (August 29, 2005).

MacGregor, M. J. Jr. (1981) *Integration of the Armed Forces, 1940–1965*. Washington, DC: Center of Military History, United States Army.

Moore, C. P. (2005) *Fighting For America: Black Soldiers—The Unsung Heroes of World War II*. New York: One World Ballantine Book.

Nalty, B. (1986) *Strength for the Fight: A History of Black Americans in the Military*. New York: The Free Press.

Remington, Frederic. (1889) "A Scout With the Buffalo Soldiers." *The Century illustrated Monthly Magazine.* (April 1889). http://www.pchswi.org/oldestlbuffalosoldiers.html. Accessed 2006.

Schubert, F.N. (1997) *Black Valor: Buffalo Soldiers and the Medal of Honor 1870–1898.* Scholarly Resources.

Turnage, Sheila. (2000) "Claiming the Sky." *American Legacy* 6, no. 1.

## Chapter Two

Betances, S. (2006) "The Challenge of Becoming an Effective Diversity Practitioner Training Session." Souder, Betances and Associates.

Brandt, N. (1996) *Harlem at War: The Black Experience in WWII.* New York: Syracuse University Press.

Hughes, L., et al. (1995) *A Pictorial History of African Americans— From 1619 to the Present.* New York: Crown Publishers.

## Chapter Three

Adams, D. E., Major. (1997) "Mentoring Women and Minority Officers in the US Military." Air Command and Staff College, AU/ACSC/97-0607B/97-03.

Butler, Remo. (1999) "Why Black Officers Fail." *Parameters,* Autumn, 54–69. http://carlislewww.army.millusawc/parameters/99autumnlbutler.htm, Accessed 2007.

Covey, S. R. (1991) *Principle-Centered Leadership.* New York: Free Press.

Murphy, J. D., Major. (1997) "The Freeman Field Mutiny: A Study in Leadership." Air Command and Staff College, AU/ACSC/0429/97-03.

Yale, C. (2004) *Writing Center Guidelines.* US Air Force Academy.

## Chapter Four

McKinnon, J. (2002) *The Black Population in the United States: March 2002*. US Census Bureau, US Department of Commerce.

Richardson, J. C. (2005) "Inputs for Lt Colonel Curry." Personal Interview, USAFA.

Zimmermann, R. W.. (1999) *Why Are the Best and Brightest Leaving the Military?* Memorandum for Commanding General, Ft. Carson, Co, http://www.d-ni.netJfcs/comments/c302.htm, Accessed 2007.

## Chapter Five

Tidwell, B. J. (1991)"More Than a Moral Issue: The Costs of American Racism in the 1990s." *Urban League Review* 14, no. 2: 9–28.

Trader, H. P. (1977) "Survival Strategies for Oppressed Minorities." *Social Work* 22: 10–13.

## Chapter Six

Fowles, D. (2006) "Emergency Funds." *Your Guide to Financial Planning*. http://financialplan.about.com/cs/personalfinancial/a/EmergencyFunds.htm, Accessed 2006 .

Fowles, D. (1999) "The Net Worth Statement: Your Financial Snapshot." *Your Guide to Financial Planning*. http://financialplan.about.com/cs/personalfinance/alNetWorthStmt.htm, Accessed 2006

Rand, D. (2002) "Types of Life Insurance, Assortment, Information and Advice You Want to Know." http://coco.essOltment.comllifeinsurancecep_nnee.htm, Accessed 2006.

Williams, K. R. (1984) "Economic Sources of Homicide: Reestimating the Effects of Poverty and Inequality." *American Sociological Review* 49: 283–289.

Woodard, D. (1999) "Before You Buy Mutual Funds." *Your Guide to Mutual Funds.* http://mutualfunds.about.com.cs.beforeinvestinglbblbefore. htm, Accessed 2006.


## Chapter Seven

Hansen, R. S., (2004) "Quintessential Careers: Dealing With a Bad Boss: Strategies for Coping." http://www.quintcareers.com/printablelbad_bosses.html, Accessed 2006.

Loo, T., (2000) "How To Deal With a Difficult Boss." http://conflicI911.com/giestconflictldifficultboss.htm, Accessed 2006).

Pavlina, S. (2004) "Dealing with Difficult People." November 20, 2004. http://www.stevepavlina.comlblogl2004/ll/dealing-withdifficult-people/htm, Accessed 2006.

Puder-York, M., (2002) "Anxiety at Work: Managing Your Boss." http://www.healthyplace.comlcommunities/Anxiety/work_5. asp/htm, Accessed 2006.

Schurr, A., (2002). "Dealing with Difficult Bosses." MSN Careers. 2002. http://vsbabu.org/mtlarchievesl2002/08/19/dealing_with_a_ difficulty_boss.htlm, Accessed 2006


## Chapter Eight

Betances, S. (2006) "The Challenge of Becoming an Effective Diversity Practitioner Training Session." Souder, Betances and Associates.

## Chapter Nine

100 Black Men of America, Inc. (2007)
    http://www.l00blackmen.org/, Accessed 2006.

African Methodist Episcopal. (2007)
    http://www.ame-church.com, Accessed 2006).

Alpha Kappa Alpha Sorority, Inc. (2007)
    http://www.akaI908.com/, Accessed 2007.

Alpha Phi Alpha Fraternity, Inc. 2007.
    http://www.alphaphjalpha.net/, Accessed 2006.

Blacks In Government, Inc., (2007).
    www.bignet.org, Accessed 2006.

Christian Methodist Episcopal. (2007).
    http://www.c-m-e.org, Accessed 2006.

Church of God in Christ. (2007). http://www.cogic.org,
    Accessed 2006.

Delta Sigma Theta Sorority, Inc. (2007).
    http://deltasigmatheta.xohost.comindex.htrnl, Accessed 2007.

Iota Phi Theta Fraternity, Inc. (2007).
    http://www.iotaphitheta.org, Accessed 2007.

Kappa Alpha Psi Fraternity, Inc. (2007).
    http://www.kappaalphapsi1911.com, Accessed 2007.

National Association of Black Accountants, Inc. (2007).
    http://www.nabainc.org, Accessed 2007.

National Association of Black Journalists. (2007).
    http://www.nabj.org, Accessed 2007.

National Association of Colored People. (2007).
    http://www.naacp.org/home/index.htm, Accessed 2007.

National Association of Colored Women's Clubs, Inc. (2007).
http://www.nacwc.org/intro.htm, Accessed 2007.

National Association of Negro Business and Professional Women's
Club. (2007). www.nanbpwc.org, Accessed 2007.

National Baptist Convention of America, Inc. (2007).
http://www.nbcamerica.net, Accessed 2007.

National Baptist Convention, USA, Inc. (2007).
http://www.blackandchristian.comlblackchurch/nbcllsa.shtml,
Accessed 2007.

National Black MBA Association. (2007).
http://www.nbmbaa.org/, Accessed 2007.

National Black Nurses Association, Inc. (2007).
http://www.nbna.org/, Accessed, 2007.

National Coalition of 100 Black Women. (2007).
http://www.ncbw.org/, Accessed 2007.

National Organization of Black Law Enforcement Executives. (2007).
http://www.noblenational.org, Accessed 2007.

National Society of Black Engineers. (2007).
http://national.nsbe.org/, Accessed 2007.

Omega Psi Phi Fraternity, Inc. (2007).
http://www.omegapsiphifratemity.org/, Accessed 2007.

Phi Beta Sigma Fraternity, Inc. (2007).
http://www.pbs1914.org/, Accessed 2007.

Prince Hall Freemasonry. (2007).
http://www.princehall.org/, Accessed 2007.

Progressive National Baptist Convention, Inc. (2007).
http://www.pnbc.org, Accessed 2007.

Sigma Gamma Rho. (2007).
http://www.sgrho1922.org/, Accessed 2007.

Southern Christian Leadership Conference. (2007).
http://sclcnational.org/content/sclc/splash.htm Accessed 2007.

The Links, Inc. (2007). http://www.linksinc.org/, Accessed 2007.

The National Congress of Black Women, Inc. (2007).
http://www.npcbw.org/newweb/aboul.htm, Accessed 2007.

The National Urban League. (2007).
http://www.nul.org/, Accessed 2007.

TransAfrica Forum. (2007).
http://www.tunsafricaforum.org/, Accessed 2007.

United Negro College Fund. (2007).
http://www.uncf.org, Accessed 2007.

Zeta Phi Beta Sorority. (2007).
http://www.zphib1920.org/, Accessed 2007.

## Appendix

Bennett, L. Jr. (1982) *Before the Mayflower: A History of Black America.*
New York: Penguin Books.

Bowers, W.T. et al., (1996) *Black Soldier White Army.* Washington, DC:
United States Army Center of Military History.

Carruth, G. (1993) *The Encyclopedia of American Facts and Dates.* New
York: Harper Collins.

Circle Association. (2005) "African American History of Western New
York State, 1770 to 1830." http://www.math.buffalo.edu/~sww/
Ohistory/1770-1830.html, Accessed 2005.

Dupuy, R. E. and Dupuy, T. N. (1986) *The Encyclopedia Of Military
History.* New York: Harper & Row.

Foner, E. and Garraty, J.A. (1991) eds. *The Reader's Companion to American History.* Boston: Houghton Mifflin Company.

Gladstone, W. (1990) *United States Colored Troops: 1863–1867.* Gettysburg, PA: Thomas Publications.

Harley, S. (1995) *The Timetables of African American History: A Chronology of the Most Important People and Events in African American History.* New York: Simon & Schuster.

Horton, J. O. and Horton, J.E. (1995) eds. *A History of the African American People.* London: Salamander Books Limited.

Kinsey, D. (2001) "African-American History." Florence Darlington Technical College. http://kinsey.schema.calAAH/AAH-Intro.htm, Accessed 2006.

Lanning, M.L. (LTC, ret.) (1997) *The African American Soldier: From Crispus Attucks to Colin Powell.* Secaucus, NJ: Birch Lane Press.

Low, W.A. and Cliff, V.A. (1981) *Encyclopedia of Black America.* New York: McGraw-Hill.

MacGregor, M.J. Jr. (1981) *Integration of the Armed Forces, 1940–1965.* Washington, DC: Center of Military History, United State Army.

Quarles, B. (1983) *The Negro in the Making of America.* New York: Perigee Books.

Wilson, J.T. (1994) *The Black Phalanx: African American Soldiers in the War of Independence, the War of 1812, and the Civil War.* New York: Da Capo Press.

# ABOUT THE AUTHOR

Colonel (Ret.) Gerald D. Curry, USAF, served on active duty for twenty-seven years and has dedicated his life to educating and mentoring today's most valuable assets, our youth. *Striving for Perfection: Developing Professional Black Officers,* is his first attempt at documenting the valuable lessons that were essential to his success. Curry serves as the Chief of Staff for Defense Security Service (DSS) Industrial Security Field Office Directorate, located at Quantico, Virginia. Colonel Curry commanded an impressive six times during his career. He retired from the Air Force in September 2010, and resides in the suburbs of Washington DC.

Originally from Nashville, Tennessee, Colonel Curry was raised with both parents who valued education and raised their family with a strong belief in God. The family moved to Rivera Beach, Florida, and where he graduated from Palm Beach Gardens High School. He completed his undergraduate degree at Tennessee State University. He earned a masters degree from Troy State University while serving in Europe, and recently (2013) a doctorate degree in management with a focus in global leadership from Colorado Technical University.

Curry is a proud member of Omega Psi Phi Fraternity, Inc., ASIS International, and Toastmasters International and is available for talks on the subjects of global leadership, officer development, diversity, and workplace civility. Don't hesitate to e-mail him at GeraldDCurry@yahoo.com.